250 FAVOURITE
· HOT & SPICY DISHES ·

250 Favourite
HOT & SPICY
· D I S H E S ·

PAT CHAPMAN

BCA

LONDON   NEW YORK   SYDNEY   TORONTO

ACKNOWLEDGEMENTS

The author and publisher would like to thank **Global Village, The Pier** and **David Mellor** for their very generous loan of items for use in the photographs.

This edition published 1994
by BCA by arrangement with
Judy Piatkus (Publishers) Ltd

CN 8049

Design/artwork by Paul Saunders
Photography by James Murphy
Printed in Great Britain

CONTENTS

INTRODUCTION *page 6*

JOURNEY INTO SPICE *page 8*

CHILLIES *page 27*

SPICY WORKSHOP *page 41*

APPETISERS *page 50*

SOUPS *page 78*

MEAT DISHES *page 94*

POULTRY DISHES *page 130*

FISH AND SEAFOOD DISHES *page 154*

VEGETABLE AND PULSE DISHES *page 178*

DAIRY AND EGG DISHES *page 214*

RICE DISHES *page 230*

BREADS *page 254*

SWEET THINGS *page 270*

CHUTNEYS, SAUCES AND CONDIMENTS *page 286*

GLOSSARY *page 297*

USEFUL ADDRESSES *page 300*

INDEX *page 301*

INTRODUCTION

For some years I have been watching food trends on both sides of the Atlantic. We Brits have always said that what happens in the States happens in Britain some while afterwards. Nylons, supermarkets, mass-produced cars, discos and burger bars are just a few examples. We are slower, perhaps, to remember what has gone the other way – such as our language, jet engines, the Jaguar car, the mini skirt and the music of the Beatles. In any event, a trend that is dear to my heart is in the process of being transported in two directions, so to speak, from the United Kingdom to the United States, and vice versa. I confidently predict that after two or three decades spent establishing a presence in the USA, curry is about to boom there in exactly the same way as it has in Britain over the last 20 years. Meanwhile, Britain and the rest of the developed world is about to be bowled over by America's great new love – the chilli. And that's what this book is all about – the enjoyment of hot and spicy food the world over.

Those readers who are kind enough to write and tell me how much they like my books will know that I am an avid collector of recipes, particularly from the curry lands. They will also know that my collection extends to places beyond.

For this book I decided it was necessary to undertake a research trip to the New World and the birthplace of the chilli.

The trip was a huge success, and I not only met the chillies I'd read and written about for years, but also some wonderful people in both Mexico and south-west USA.

In Mexico there were huge black dried chillies tasting of liquorice and others smelling like tobacco; there were bright orange manzana chillies with the fragrance of apples and there were the flat stubby savoury jalapeños (pronounced hala-paynee-yows). Then there were the celebrated red and yellow habaneros – supposedly the hottest chillies on earth – and many more.

In the USA itself were the unique and very strange Peter peppers (see page 37) and the massive 10-inch-long 'Big Jim's', bred for their size and flavour. Conversely there were tiny bright red round seeds, about the size of peppercorns, and easily mistaken for them. These are the original chilli, called the *chiltecpin*, from which, it is said, all today's diverse chillies developed.

As for the people, you'll find no kinder or more helpful friends anywhere. There was Jesus ('call me Jesse') Larazua in Mexico City, who drove us here, there and everywhere in search of chillies and spicy food, and his friend Raymundo Espinosa who runs the best taco bar in the world. There was Mike Morris, sales manager at Tabasco, and there were Dave DeWitt, Mary Jane Wilan and Nancy Gerlach, themselves authors and self-confessed chilli addicts, who laughingly taught us, in their gorgeous Albuquerque drawl, that the word in America is 'chilie' and that they regard themselves as 'chilie-heads'. They were keen to impress upon us that, whilst curry may not yet have caught on in the States, the chilli has, and there are millions of 'chilie-heads' like them. In fact the chilli is so popular there that it is creating a whole new subculture. And as this is America, the land which produced Hollywood and Disneyland, they've managed to give the humble chilli plenty of charisma and status.

As far as I know, there is no Chilli Club (I thought of it first, folks) like my own Curry Club, but there is a magazine which parallels my *Curry Club Magazine*, called *Chilie Pepper*. It is published every two months and sells 80,000 copies per issue. Albuquerque's Dave DeWitt is behind it, as well as numerous books on the chilli. And there are many good restaurants offering superb chilli dishes. Mark Miller combines the best of both worlds with his astoundingly popular Coyote Café in Santa Fe, and his equally successful cookbooks.

But one of the most exciting developments is a succession of chilli shops. At the Tabasco factory, for example, there is a supremely well stocked shop, primarily aimed at the 2000 tourists who tour the Tabasco factory and estate every day. The famous chilli sauce is on sale, of course, in bottles ranging from an eighth of a fluid ounce to a gallon. Other chilli products include the Tabasco Bloody Mary mix, Tabasco chilli powders and blends, Tabasco spicy olive oil, Tabasco spiced snacks, chilli jam, chilli mayonnaise and chilli pickles. There are cookbooks, posters and recipe cards, mugs, plates, glasses, coasters, playing cards, wall clocks, earrings, T-shirts, silk ties, shopping bags, belts, hats, towels and even night dresses. Well over 200 products are on offer, all branded with the Tabasco label. But that's not all, Tabasco franchise shops are sprouting up all over the USA in shopping malls.

And it's not just Tabasco. In many a shopping mall there are specialist cookery schools. These too have shops at which chilli products feature prominently. In Santa Fe there are three or four such shops selling dried chillies (dozens of types), chilli mixes and complete ranges of chilli products rivalling even the aforementioned variety of Tabasco items. For a start, there are literally hundreds of rival bottled chilli sauces. The picture on page 291 shows but a few. And there are chilli popcorn, chilli honey, even chilli underpants. And yes, I've got two pairs of boxer shorts, one with red chillies on black and the other – oh well never mind!

There is simply no end to the range of chilli-related products available. And if there ain't a store near you, then git-a-writin to one of the many mail order suppliers I've listed on page 300.

And then there are those amazing food festivals to be found only in the USA. There are garlic festivals, strawberry festivals, crawfish festivals, citrus festivals and – of course – chilli festivals. These take various forms. At one type they have chilli (con carne) cooking contests; at others the highlight is a competition to find out who can eat the most chillies at one sitting (the record is 146, according to the *Guinness Book of Records*).

Not surprisingly chillies feature largely in this book – and so they should, being the world's most popular spice – but they are not used in quantities which will blow your head off. If you like your food very hot, however, I have indicated how you can alter the recipes accordingly. Most people, I suspect, will be content with a modest level of chilli in their cooking, and that's what I've used unless otherwise stated. Not every recipe includes chilli, of course, though there are, I hope, some revelations – like the chilli ice cream on page 278. Try it! You'll be surprised. And there are 249 other remarkably spicy finds in this book.

I'm sure that existing chilie-heads and curryholics need no more encouragement to get stuck in, and I'm equally sure that each will enjoy the other's food styles, finding them assuredly addictive, certainly spicy, positively sophisticated, definitely 'red hot' and let's hope conclusively attracting more and more converts. And if the following armchair 'journey into spice' leads you to decidedly daring dishes and magnificently modish menus, then I'll be pleased as punch. I hope you enjoy reading and cooking from the book as much as I enjoyed writing it.

Pat Chapman
Haslemere

If you would like more information about The Curry Club, write (enclosing S.A.E.) to: **The Curry Club, PO Box 7, Haslemere, Surrey GU27 1EP**

JOURNEY INTO SPICE

When I was a young lad living in Ealing in West London I sometimes used to walk to Haven Green and stand at the railings overlooking the railway cutting. Four gleaming tracks took trains to and from Paddington and the West Country. Screeching puffing steam trains roared past with resplendent olive green locomotives and chocolate and cream coaches bearing names like 'The Cornish Riviera Express' and 'The South Wales Pullman'. For one whose horizons had not previously extended beyond Chessington Zoo on the number 65 London bus, Cornwall and South Wales seemed unimaginably glamorous. I longed to be on those trains, journeying to exotic places never before visited by mankind; at least never before visited by this small boy of seven or eight. I imagined arriving and planting my flag and claiming the territory for king and country.

I would run home and open my Philips school atlas and stare at the pages, dreaming about all these wondrous places. Like Hugh Lofting's Doctor Dolittle I would shut my eyes and stick a pin in the map on whatever page the book fell open to and I would voyage there at once.

In those days it never occurred to me that the food in those exotic lands was any different from my own. That discovery came years later when I began to travel to some of those wonderful places. The expectation of travel is exciting, though the reality is often less glamorous than the dreams. But one thing which never lets me down is the local cuisine waiting to be explored at my destination.

But why is the food of one country different from the one next to it? How did all these wonderful tastes and culinary styles develop? Where did the ingredients originate? Why did they successfully migrate around the world to some countries, and not to others? The answers to these questions will help you to understand and enjoy 'the world on your plate', and to cook hot and spicy dishes which are authentic and delicious.

Come with me on an exciting culinary journey, which will take us back in time, then on to our contemporary world, to find out what is eaten where. Let's journey into spice.

A BRIEF HISTORY OF SPICES

Five hundred years ago, the known world was a small place consisting of a single connected landmass containing civilisations at various stages of development. There was the Chinese dynasty, then controlled by the Ming emperors. There was India, which was in the hands of the Moghuls, and Persia with its shahs. The Turkish Ottoman emperors had taken control of the Muslim Mediterranean, while outer Europe was in the hands of numerous kings. Spain was at war with Portugal. England, with its newly established Tudors, was at the end of a century of war with France, and Italy was in the hands of wealthy rival dukes from Genoa and Venice.

It was a world which had built up ancient trading patterns and routes over many centuries, to exchange, for example, wool and tin from England for silk and spices from China and India. Venice and Genoa traditionally controlled the Mediterranean with their gun boats. They were thus able to operate a duopolistic trade arrangement with Arab merchants whose territory started and ended at the eastern Mediterranean but took them, overland, thousands of miles eastwards into the fabled lands of the Orient. Few non-Arabs were ever permitted to travel these routes, so the sources of the traded goods were kept secret and the prices were inflated.

Pepper, for example, began its journey from southern India at relatively low prices. It would travel by land through several hands, and therefore several price mark-ups to the north-west Indian coast, where it would be purchased by Arab mariners. They would sail with it to the Red Sea, where it would pass through several more Arab hands until it reached the Mediterranean. There it would be purchased by mariners from Venice. On arrival there it had yet to disperse across Europe, again via many hands, with the inevitable marking-up in price. It had been traded like that for over 1500 years.

England, France, Holland, Spain and Portugal were on the edge of the known world. For centuries they had been of little consequence as traders. At the end of this long chain, it is easy to see how pepper, to give just one example, could command extraordinary prices in the northern European markets. It was very much in demand – so much so that it was used to pay taxes and debts. Today 'a peppercorn rent' means a minimal sum of money. In those days it meant rent at the market price, payable in expensive pepper, a commodity which was valued as highly as gold or silver. Other spices were equally popular and equally expensive.

The northern European countries were far from content with this situation. A significant number of European explorers had by then travelled to China and India and discovered where most spices originated. Marco Polo was one. The realisation that spices were simply crops available at source for next to no money simply added to European outrage and the determination to do something about it. Despite the fact that they shared the Atlantic seaboard, the outer European countries had little maritime experience. Spain, Portugal and even England had occasionally ventured into the Mediterranean with disastrous consequences. Their inadequate ships were inevitably sunk by the heavily armed, more manoeuvrable Genoese or Venetian warships.

In any case their top priority was internecine wars. But the price of spices rankled.

They were so expensive that only the nobility could afford to use them. Ironically these were the very people who could well afford to buy luxuries – they simply put taxes up. On the other hand they resented being overcharged, and creating profits for their enemies. They wanted those profits for themselves. To make matters worse, in 1453 the loss of Constantinople to the Ottoman Turks was followed by a virtual cessation of trade with Europe. Pepper became even more expensive. It became abundantly clear that the only way to change the situation was to find an alternative route to the spice lands.

Two possibilities were suggested. However both options required enormous funding and success was by no means certain. It was literally a journey into the unknown. Portugal opted to explore Africa, and spent nearly a century tentatively probing further and further south down the African coastline to find out whether there was a sea route eastwards to the Orient. When they eventually did round the Cape of Good Hope it took just one more voyage to make landfall in India.

The other option was to head westwards, across the Atlantic. Christopher Columbus had been touting his Atlantic crossing plan for 20 years, during which time he had been refused finance by several countries, including his native Genoa, Portugal, Spain and even England (under King Henry VII), despite promises of gold, spices, power and glory for all concerned. Such talk was enticing, but it met with much incredulity. The fact was that no one had ever sailed further than a few score miles from land. Here was a proposal to sail for thousands of miles, out of sight of land, and thousands of miles back again. It would take months, if not years, and above all it would take a lot of funding. Everyone by now knew that the world was round and that India and China must be attainable in a westerly direction, but no one knew just how far they lay from Spain.

Portugal's impending rounding of southern Africa injected a new sense of urgency into the Atlantic plan. Spain was left with no alternative but to finance Columbus. If they did not,

England might even be persuaded. The year was 1492. So Spain gave Columbus the go-ahead.

No one, not Columbus nor anyone else, could know that it was not the Orient, but another landmass and another ocean – America and the Pacific – which lay between him and his objective. And that landmass was much further than even the most pessimistic estimate. But reach it he did. The land that Columbus discovered in 1492 was one of the American offshore islands, probably Dominica. Almost at once he realised that the sea around him was studded with islands. Certain he was in an archipelago off India, he named the islands the West Indies – hence today's confusing name for islands some 8000 miles from India.

The natives welcomed Columbus and his crews and the cheap glass beads and trinkets they were given. They told of gold and silver and huge cities and directed the explorers to the largest island, Cuba. When he landed there Columbus found none of these but he so con-

vinced himself and his men that they had reached China that he sent a team of men to search for the Emperor. Desperate to find pepper, he showed bemused natives some dried black peppercorns. It was, no doubt, a strange request. These god-like figures from another world had descended on the helpless natives and were asking for, of all things, some useless seeds and weeds. Trying hard to please, the natives showed him the nearest thing they had to pepper. They were allspice berries – round, peppercorn-sized, black when dried, but clearly not pepper. This did not seem to bother Columbus, who in great delight, called them *pimento*, the Spanish word for pepper.

That was not the end of it. Columbus was also shown fleshy pods, known locally as *axi*, *carib* or *chili*. They were small, possibly the round wild *chiltecpins* (see page 32), and they were very hot. They were not pepper either. They were what we now call capsicum or chillies (or chilies in the USA).

Columbus confused the issue even further by calling all capsicum plants *pimento* or pepper as well. These mighty misnomers have persisted to this day. Columbus died later convinced that he had reached India and its pepper, unaware that his confusion would remain indelibly preserved in our language.

He never realised that he had 'discovered' a New World with its own civilisations. The Peruvian Incas and the Mexican Aztecs had developed over many centuries into independent empires ruled by god emperors. The two civilisations were literate and linked by trade. Each was highly developed, having vast cities, stone buildings, and a culinary tradition as advanced as anything in the contemporary old world. Yet there had been no contact with the old world from the moment the land bridge that linked America and Russia, the Bering Strait, disappeared 8000 years earlier. The tribes who passed into the Americas then spawned the many 'Indian' races that still live there today – Red Indians, Eskimos and Latin American Indians. The development of the Incas and Aztecs had taken place in isolation, yet was no less remarkable than that of the empires in the old world.

This was of no consequence to the post-Columbus Spanish conquistadors, who murdered the Inca and Aztec emperors and virtually wiped out their populations in a genocide so rapid that their religion, culture and cuisine was all but extinguished. Fortunately for the world, a Spanish scholar rescued some young upper-class Aztecs and wrote down all they knew. Many aspects of their culture were recorded, including ancient Aztec recipes. These formed the basis of today's Mexican and Latin American cuisines.

Columbus did not discover pepper. What he and his successors found was a wealth of produce totally unknown to the peoples of the old world. And it took them some time to realise its value. Imagine a world without tomatoes and potatoes, chocolate and sweetcorn, avocado and vanilla, kidney beans and peanuts, string beans and tobacco. But above all, imagine it without chillies. It was the humble capsicum which figuratively and literally fired the European palate quicker than any other New World discovery!

But it was not the Spanish who were responsible for spreading the chilli worldwide. It was the Portuguese. Still content with their African route, they agreed to leave the Americas to the Spanish, with the exception, that is, of Brazil. They had found a quicker route to the Cape of Africa by following the south-western tides in a wide arc across the Atlantic and on to southern Africa. On one such voyage they went wider than usual and stumbled on Brazil and its chillies.

It was only a matter of time before chillies appeared in Africa and the Gulf, India and the Orient. No written record of the use of chilli appears in any of these countries before 1500. Today, it would be inconceivable to contemplate the cooking of these nations without the chilli. In fact the chilli was received in the Portuguese colonies (though not back home in Portugal) with great delight and it fitted as easily into their spicy culinary repertoires as if it had been the missing piece in a jigsaw.

Meanwhile, chocolate passed into the world's culinary repertoire, first as an alternative beverage in smart Georgian coffee houses and later as the main ingredient in confectionery. The tomato, however, remained the subject of deep suspicion, despite being related to the chilli family (both are descended from the deadly nightshade family). It was not until well into the nineteenth century that tomatoes became accepted in Europe.

The greatest irony of all was that there turned out to be very few unique and indigenous spices in the New World. Allspice (pimento) was really the only find, and despite the fact that it had a wonderful aromatic flavour – a sort of combination of cloves, cinnamon and pepper – little effort was made to export it until quite recently.

Portugal had indeed found everything it wanted, and it built a great empire around the world. Spain continued exploring westwards until she too eventually discovered the Orient. Venice, Genoa, the Arabs, and the old silk and spice routes were finished. Still the quest for spices and wealth, in a world as yet largely undiscovered, went on. Others learned to master the seas, none more effectively than

Britain, on whose mighty empire at one time it seemed the sun would never set. It made Britain very wealthy.

Despite five centuries of empire-building, it is only in the last few decades that different countries around the world have become aware of each other's food styles. Consequently, and fortunately, national culinary identities have been strictly preserved in the form of traditional methods and traditional ingredients. For example, to this day the dishes of India are unlikely to contain items such as sweetcorn or brussels sprouts, avocado or leeks, cheese or chocolate, turkey or paprika. Even the tomato is a relative newcomer to India. Its cooking styles and implements are unique to India. It is the same in China, where the food is unlikely to contain milk or cream, okra or oranges, millet or mutton, potatoes or grapes. Again the tomato is a newcomer to this cuisine. The traditional dishes of Mexico and Latin America did not, until the Spanish conquest, include lamb or wheat products, strawberries or cabbages, peas or garlic, onions or chicken, and this is still reflected in their daily fare.

It is the same story with traditional Middle Eastern, African, Thai, Singaporean and Indo-Chinese cuisines. Only in recent years have 'unfamiliar' ingredients been introduced to these countries. Old habits die hard. Now such places have realised that their climates enable them to grow most crops, and that it is remunerative for them to do so. Air-freighting has made it possible for fresh produce to be available halfway across the world next day.

Air travel has also been responsible, along with television and a vastly greater disposable income, for the inquisitive populations of the developed world demanding access to what were, until recently, obscure, romantic, impossible, impassable places. Before that, such places were the preserve of a few foolhardy eccentrics, and the food of such places was considered 'exotic' and 'dangerous'. Sadly, tourism itself, and a natural Third World desire to emulate the affluence it sees on television and in Western tourists, is changing the world we all so desperately wish to conserve.

Whilst we are never happier than trampling around over someone else's native territory, seeking out their cottage industries and their hand-made artefacts, their straw skirt dancers and relishing their ethnic food, after the performance is over, those same people pocket our dollars, don their blue jeans, hop on their mopeds, shriek back to their overpopulated city and into the local disco to enjoy a hamburger. Such is progress!

But we are fortunate that the world still does maintain a rich and exciting variety of culinary traditions. We are also lucky that just about any ingredient is now available just about anywhere in the world. This makes it possible for us to recreate very accurately specific tastes from specific regions wherever we may be living. And before the developing world does lose track of its long-established culinary traditions in favour of the hamburger, it is my privilege and duty as a food writer to preserve some of these wonderful dishes in the pages of this book.

So come with me now for a flying visit to the main culinary areas of the world to examine their particular tastes.

THE OLD WORLD

EUROPE

I am starting here, partly because England is my home, but also because it is only quite recently that northern Europeans have rediscovered spices, garlic and chilli. And rediscovery it is because, apart from chilli, the English acquired the taste for spices during Roman times. It was the same all over the empire. The Romans controlled the Mediterranean, and even traded by sea directly with India, travelling across the Red Sea and overland to the Indian Ocean. There is ample evidence to prove that they traded in Cochin and Madras, as did the Chinese as early as the first century AD. Because they traded directly at source, spices were relatively inexpensive in all parts of the empire. When, in the fourth century AD, the Roman Empire withdrew from outer

Europe, so too did the availability of spices. The Normans reintroduced them into England following the 1066 conquest but, by then, as already mentioned, prices were so high that only the nobility could afford them. It was hardly surprising that by Stuart times Britain's taste for spicy food had waned almost to extinction, and the vacuum was filled by sugar. We developed a sweet tooth instead.

Ironically, it was precisely during this period that the British East India Company was taking control of India and its spicy wealth. Pepper, mustard and cloves had remained in the British repertoire but turmeric, cummin, coriander, garlic and ginger had slipped from memory. Despite enthusiastic reports from expatriate Britons returning home after a lifetime of service and spicy cuisine, backed up by a few recipes from the cookbooks of the day, the British did not revert back to their spicy ancestry. In fact the British gained a reputation for being the world's worst cooks, and least reliable gourmets. As anyone who knows regional British food will testify, this is somewhat unfair. It was probably disseminated by the French who loved garlic which was intransigently hated by the British.

Against all the odds, therefore, since the Second World War Britain has rocked the world by its increasing adoration not only of garlic, but all 'ethnic' foods, especially curry. It is now regarded almost as a national dish by its supporters and, with today's Britons willing to try anything, there are more 'ethnic' and Italian restaurants in Britain per head of population than in any other developed country. Meanwhile, the new wave of British chefs is elevating the nation to new culinary heights.

The strenuous efforts of the expats of the eighteenth century were by no means wasted however. What they did achieve was the invention of a range of hot and spicy sauces and condiments which were immediate successes. These products enlivened otherwise bland spiceless food and are now major exports worldwide. Our Worcestershire sauce was launched as a bottled product in 1837 by Lea and Perrins of Worcester. Containing, amongst other ingredients, molasses, tama-

rind, garlic, coriander and chilli, it predates Tabasco by 31 years and is as widely used.

As for English mustard, there is nothing like it on earth. Unlike French mustard, which is ochre in colour, made from black or brown seeds, and contains a lot of vinegar, English mustard is bright yellow in colour, made from white mustard seeds and is sold as a powder or a paste. Both are pungent, although the paste contains citric acid, salt and sugar to help preserve it. The powder contains none of these (although it does contain turmeric to strengthen the colour, and flour to stabilise it). Mixed with water, it is hotter than a good many chillies, with the 'afterburn' affecting the nose rather than the throat. Horseradish is a root indigenous to northern Europe and Britain. Some varieties are hotter than many chillies, and can have equally violent effects on the unsuspecting diner. It is available fresh, or as a thick coarse ready-to-use purée.

For more than two centuries these condiments have accompanied our roasts and hotpots, our fries and stews. British use of spices was traditionally minimal but none the less important. Consider our hams studded with cloves or coated in mustard before being roasted, or our pork pies with ground mace, the bay leaves which enhance our stews, and the blue poppy seeds or sesame which adorn our loaves, the caraway seeds in our cakes, and the nutmeg grated and sprinkled over our desserts. Pepper became increasingly widely used as it became cheaper, though always the ground white variety. Whole black peppercorns in twist mills are a relatively new phenomenon in Britain. Onions go back for centuries, but garlic fell out of the British diet once direct links with France were severed.

To wave the Union Jack I've included a wonderful Beef Casserole Spiced with Horseradish and Mustard and a chilli version of Toad in the Hole.

Across the English Channel the French have scarcely noticed the massive growth in demand for ethnic food in Britain. You'll find a handful of Indian restaurants in Paris, and just one or two in French cities elsewhere. Chinese and North African restaurants have had more success but, with a rather blinkered self-satisfied attitude towards their own *haute cuisine*, change is unlikely to take place rapidly.

The Germanic countries are larger importers of pepper, cinnamon and other spices, but many of these are used in their *wurst* products rather than in their cooking. I have tracked down three rather tasty spicy recipes, one for Spiced *Red Cabbage*, one for *Sauerkraut Chilli* and one for *Burgenlander Chicken* from Austria. Eastern Europe has little time for chilli and spices, though of course Hungary has become the home of the paprika pepper and this book would not be complete without *Goulash*.

You might expect that Spain and Portugal would be a haven for hot and spicy dishes, given their deep historical involvement with the spice trade. In fact, their populations never became big spice users, although garlic has always been indispensable to their cuisines. Try the delicious *Sopa de Ajo* (Garlic Soup) recipe, from Portugal, for example. Portugal and Spain have a cooking technique involving the initial stir-fry of garlic, onion and oil. In Spain it is called *sofrito* and in Portugal it is *refogago*. A similar technique is also found in Central and Latin America and in India where it is called the *bhagar*.

Chillies appear at Spanish markets and you will come across *piri-piri* (a bottled African chilli sauce) in Portugal and recipes for shrimps and chicken cooked with chilli in Portugal and Spain. *Piri-piri* is the African word for chilli, and you will find Portuguese-influenced dishes in a number of African countries. Portugal has for centuries had a tradition of marinating meat in wine, vinegar and garlic. Called *Vinho e Alhos*, it is this technique which, with chillies added, evolved into the famous Indian *Vindaloo* curry. The Portuguese sausage, *chorizo*, has found its way around the world, getting hotter (with the addition of chillies) the further from home it got.

Rice grows in Spain and Italy, having been established in both countries by the Arabic Moors 1000 years ago. The national dish of Spain is arguably *Paella*, and its ancestry is clearly traced back to the Iranian *Pollou*; the Spanish *Arroz con Azafran* (Saffron Rice) and their saffron plantations are proof of other Arab inheritances.

Italy, like the rest of Europe, is not a big spice user either, and, whilst chillies are grown in Calabria (the perochino chilli is an example) and Sicily, it is almost ignored elsewhere. However, *Sicilian Spicy Mince sauce* is delicious with pasta, and *Arabiata*, with chilli, ham and tomato, can be used as a condiment as well as a sauce.

THE MIDDLE EAST

Civilisation began in the Middle East when mankind learned to cultivate and farm 10,000 years ago. Egypt and Mesopotamia were the first civilisations to become literate and, despite their decline long before the birth of Christ, they established culinary traditions which remain with us to this day. Baking, egg and fish hatcheries, brewing, winemaking and marinating all started in those days. Trade with the only other known civilisations, those of India and China, led to an acceptance of the use of spices in cooking. This ancient connection has made the Middle East the second-greatest user of spices, after India.

My culinary version of the Middle East is based on Ottoman and Arab influences and includes Greece, Turkey, Cyprus, North Africa, Egypt, the Levant and Gulf countries right through to Iran. The food has a lot in common although there are a great many regional differences.

Moroccan food is one of the best regarded, combining a little French influence with traditional Arab styles to create a complex cuisine. Their use of dried fruit, nuts, spices and meat ingredients in certain dishes greatly resembles Iranian and Parsee Indian techniques, although the tastes are different. *Mishmisheya la Kama* (Spicy Vegetables with Apricot) is a typical example. *Chermoula Samak* is a Moroccan fish dish with a spicy chilli coating. Tunisia has similar dishes, although they enjoy their food somewhat chilli hotter. Their *Harissa* chilli sauce proves that point.

Turkey has a food style all its own, developed centuries ago for its finicky Ottoman emperors. Chilli heat is rather more controlled here, and the result is quite sophisticated dishes. As the Turks invented the *kebab* and the skewer (*shish*), I could not omit a typical recipe, and *Kilich Shish* is a skewered fish example. Turkish vegetable cooking is supreme and I've included *Sebzeler Plaki* (Baked Vegetables) and the renowned *Pitta* Bread as well as a crispy bread called *Kavgir*.

Neighbouring Greece is represented by some of its national dishes, *Moussaka*, tasty mince topped with aubergines and cheesy white sauce, and *Pilafi*, the Greek variation of the Iranian *Pollou* rice, with a chilli version, *Filfil Pilav*, from Cyprus.

True Arab dishes, such as those in Saudi or the Yemen, were created by the needs of the desert nomads. These were the characters who from centuries BC travelled with their camel caravans, linking the merchants of India and China with those of Europe. Their meat-orientated food is, by definition, easily cooked over the camp fire, and is spicy and thoroughly delicious. The use of spices varies from minimal, where the place concerned had no trading links with India, to very heavy where they did. Try, for example, the bread of the Yemen, for centuries a maritime trading base used by Arab and Indian merchants. *Saluf bi Hilbeh* is a traditional Yemeni flat bread punctuated with spicy fenugreek, or there is Oman's *Filfil Ahmar Baidh*, a chilli omelette.

Arabia's omelette *Ijjah bil Tawabel* is somewhat less spicy, as is *Blehat Samak* (Arabic Fried Fish Balls) and *Sheik-el-Ma'shi* (Stuffed Courgettes). *Shabbat Kuwaiti* is a lightly spiced fish dish, and Egypt's *Fasooli Khadra* brings that country's enjoyment of beans (second I believe only to Mexico's) into the picture.

Iran

I've placed Iran in its own category in our journey into spice because it has a special place in culinary history, being itself very ancient, and very influential on the cooking of the Indian subcontinent. There have been a number of Persian empires over the centuries. Each has sent its invading army into India, and each has left its gastronomic mark on that country. Indeed, India's greatest rulers of all time, the Moghuls, had Persian ancestry, spoke Persian and developed Iranian cooking into Moghul cooking, now the backbone of Northern Indian cuisine. Iran (Persia) has always cultivated and enjoyed aromatic spices and delicate fragrances, cooked with clarified butter (*smen* or ghee). This is nowhere better exemplified than in Iran's most popular rice dish *Pollou*, the great grand-daddy of Indian *Pullao*, Turkish *Pilav*, Greek *Pilafi* and Spanish *Paella*. To represent Iran's delightful aromatic spicy slow-cooked stews, I've chosen the outstanding *Faisinjan Koresh*. This one uses duck, and the Koresh style itself developed into India's creamy dreamy *Korma*. Herbs and vegetables also play a great part in Iranian cuisine, and I've chosen *Sabzi Koresh* to demonstrate this.

INDIA

India became the world's third literate society as early as 2500 BC, with its Indus Valley civilisation. Since then India has been dissected and divided by all sorts of invaders and conquerors. Among them have been Greeks, Persians, Romans, Chinese, Arabs, Moghuls, Portuguese, French, Dutch, Danish and Japanese. Not only has this deeply affected India's culinary repertoire, it has regularly changed India's territorial boundaries. Several times during its history India has been one enormous subcontinent under the control of king emperors such as the Mauryas, Ashokas and the Moghuls. At the same time the subcontinent was divided into numerous kingdoms. The final invader was Britain, who slipped in by the back door.

India is a land of great contrasts, of wealth and poverty, beauty and ugliness, happiness and despair, technology and primitivism, superstition and cynicism, modernity and antiquity, wealth and poverty. The sights and smells shock first-time visitors. Despite the problems that beset India, her people are the friendliest, most hospitable, most colourful and most likable I've ever met. As a food producer she is self-sufficient, with significant exports and few imports. Out in the villages hunger, in drought-free years, is not the problem; it is in the cities that the crises arise. Drawn by the lure of wealth, villagers continue to pour into the cities to find only the prospect of eking out a hand-to-mouth existence.

The food of India is as complex as her history. In the following thumbnail sketch of India and her surrounding spicy neighbours, we are only able to get a glimpse of the extraordinary wealth which is the food of the area. Readers who wish to know more are referred to my various books, all of which contain many authentic regional recipes. See page ii.

Punjab

Punjab is split by the north-west border with Pakistan. Punjabi food is very spicy and forms the basis of the menu in every curry house in the Western world. Back in the 1950s the earliest curry houses were owned and run by Punjabi Pakistanis. Their food was Punjabi- and Moghul-based and their successful formula was, quite simply, copied by most of the 7500 restaurants which followed. Wheat is the major staple and breads of many types, such as the *Puri* and the *Chupatti*, are two of the forms it takes. Meat-eating is widespread. Robust spices such as fenugreek (*methi*) and asafoetida (*hing*) are combined with green leaves (mustard, spinach, mint or coriander, for example) with meat or vegetables. *Haryali Aloo* (literally meaning Greens and Potatoes) is a typical Punjabi dish.

Gujarat

Gujarat is a state on India's north-west coastline, which contains more vegetarians (69 per cent) than anywhere else in India. It also enjoys India's least spicy food, preferring the subtleties of sour and sweet to heat. Their delight in gram flour (*besan*) is nowhere better

illustrated than by the onion version of their popular *Bhajias* (deep-fried gram flour and vegetable fritters) which have become practically a cliché in the curry houses of the Western world. Instead of this dish I've chosen the Gujarati samosa, the *Singhoda*, as well as *Falavda* (Spicy Vegetable Fritters). I've also included *Bindi Karhi* (Okra Curry)

Royal India

The seventeenth-century Moghuls did to Indian cooking what the contemporary King Louis did to French. They perfected it. Creamy sauces, steaming techniques (*dum*), lightness of touch and supreme aromas were the result. Birianis (rice dishes), scrumptious breads, like *Parathas*, and tender *Kormas*, were examples of Moghul cuisine. A great example is *Lal Qila Khurma Ki Shah Jehan*, known apocryphally as 'the Emperor's Last Stew'. The flamboyant royals of Lucknow, the Nawabs, developed their own style of cooking a century later. *Dum Ki Batar Karsha* (Duck Stuffed Quails) is my chosen representative of this cuisine. Further south lies Hyderabad. Until recently it was home to the richest royal on earth, the Nizzam. This Muslim enclave enjoys one of India's hottest cuisines, as indicated by the favourite Hyderabadi dish *Mirchi Ka Salan* (Chilli Curry). *Khara Soti Boti Kebab* shows its Muslim origins, being a meat kebab, but is given a Hyderabadi twist (literally) by twirling it in beaten egg.

Goa

Portugal has played a large part in the history of the world's food, and her influence in India is still very noticeable in Goa, her main Indian base for over 460 years. It is largely Christian but, though I've never met a Portuguese in Goa, I've met a great many Goans with Portuguese surnames like Albuquerque, De Silva and Fernandez, and Christian names like Maria, Antonio and Thomas. They are small in build but huge in personality and generosity.

The combination of Indian and Portuguese cooking makes a fascinating marriage. Goan dishes use the full range of Indian spices, and the age-old Portuguese technique of marinating is widely employed. Pork, that Portuguese favourite, is more widely eaten in Goa than elsewhere in India, and it is popular in many guises, from *chorizo* sausage enlivened with chilli to bacon. Pork is also marinated with vinegar, wine, chillies and spices to create the famous Goan *Vindaloo* (pronounced vin-dar-loo), that hot spicy curry which, in a different guise, has become such a celebrated dish at curry restaurants. A recipe for the real thing appears on page 116. As a contrast, I've included a light Goan pudding, *Moira Banana*.

South India

So different from the north, with a completely different evolution, southern Indian food is rice-based, with lentils playing a large part. Coconut, pepper and curry leaves are local crops, incorporated into southern Indian food over thousands of years. On its arrival, just over 400 years ago, a mere snip in South Indian terms, the chilli was integrated into the south's cooking as if it had always been there. Recipes calling for the use of several types of chilli are not uncommon. In my recipe for *Mirchi Rasam* (Pepper Soup), for example, ground red chillies are fried in the initial stir-fry. Fresh green chillies are incorporated into the main cooking, as are fresh green peppercorns, and chilli powder or crushed dried red chillies are sprinkled on the finished dish as a *tarka* (spicy topping). Only Mexican cooks equal such imaginative use of the chilli.

INDIA'S NEIGHBOURS

Encircling India are the following equally spicy countries: Afghanistan, Pakistan, Nepal, Bangladesh, Burma, Sri Lanka. The islands of the Maldives, Mauritius and the Seychelles are included.

Afghanistan

Afghanistan contains few original culinary masterpieces, being home to a fierce, rugged, tribal people, who throughout history have preferred war to cooking. There are a few dishes which have evolved from either Iran or India, and Afghan use of spices is quite substantial. Being Muslim, Afghanis are big meat-eaters, particularly enjoying charcoal-cooked kebabs. They also like pulses, rice and root vegetables. Dairy products are important and I've chosen just one Afghan dish *Q'root* (pronounced kroot), a tasty yoghurt cooler.

Pakistan

Pakistan was born in 1947. Until then it had, for centuries, been part of India. Whilst its population is largely Muslim, its way of life and much of its food is indistinguishable from certain parts of northern India.

Tandoori cooking originated in the North-West Frontier district of Pakistan, whilst balti cooking is from her most northerly state. To represent Pakistan, I've chosen *Tandoori Aloo Peshwari*, an unusual potato recipe cooked tandoori-style. *Naan* is the traditional tandoori bread, *Sindhi Luki Masale Dar* is pumpkin curry, and *Alu Chole Pullao* a chickpea, potato and rice combination.

Nepal

Nepal, high in the Himalayan mountains, is celebrated for its Ghurka troops and its tough Sherpas who make it possible for Western mountaineers to ascend Everest. Their food is very similar to that of northern India, and it continues to grace the tables of the troops in British barracks, with dishes like *Gurkha Dhal*, spicy lentils, and *Dhai Kaju Gosht*, a lamb and cashew curry.

Bangladesh

Bangladesh is the former largely Muslim part of Bengal which became East Pakistan, before achieving its current name and independence in 1962. Bangladeshis greatly prefer fish and prawns to meat, and lentils are very popular, as exemplified by *Dhal Nehri*. Rice is the staple, and mustard and poppy seeds are popular spices. *Phanch Phoran*, a mixture of five spices, is a typical Bengali combination, and you will not find a sweeter taste anywhere in the subcontinent. Many of India's dairy-based sweet dishes such as *Kulfi* originated in this area.

SRI LANKA AND THE INDIAN OCEAN

South of the Indian landmass lies Sri Lanka. Literally meaning 'the resplendent isle', it was called Ceylon in the time of the British Raj. This small island is indeed very beautiful, though its tranquillity is currently marred by racial tension, between the Tamils and Sinhalese. It is a major producer of cinnamon, tea, rice and coconut. Sri Lankan food resembles Indian but it has some distinctive and delicious specialities. The chilli brought to Sri Lanka by the Portuguese makes frequent appearances in Sri Lankan cuisine, as do cashew and coconut, fish and fragrant spicing. My choice of Sri Lankan dishes reflects all of this, with *Kari Patis* (Curry Patties).

The Indian Ocean is bejewelled with coral islands. They are becoming popular as tourist destinations, and I've singled out the Maldives, the Seychelles, the Andamans and Mauritius for culinary recognition in this book. They have in common their beauty, and their largely southern Indian populations. Their food is spicy and not dissimilar to that of southern India and Sri Lanka. Recipes include *Kokis* (Coconut Fritters), *Murgh Cutliss* (Chicken Rissoles) and *Parippu* (Creamy Coconut Lentils) from the Maldives; *Karamba Kulkul Issu* (spicy minced chicken with prawns spiked with coconut toddy) from the Seychelles; and *Kakuluo* (Crab Curry) from Mauritius.

INDO-CHINA

Sometimes called Farther India, Indo-china is the South-East Asian peninsula between India and China, containing Burma, Thailand, Laos, Cambodia and Vietnam.

Burma

Burma shares its borders with Bangladesh, India, China and Thailand, and all those influences are incorporated in her food. Burma became independent from Britain in 1948, but since then she has been isolated behind a screen of dictatorial Communism. The result is a virtual absence of tourism and exports, a decline into poverty and no restaurant tradition in the West. The developed world has, quite simply, passed Burma by. This is a pity, because Burma is exquisite and quite unique. Her population is Bhuddist and her food combines the spices of India with the ingredients of Thailand and the cooking techniques of China. She is a kind of bridge between these three culinary giants.

Because of her isolation, Burma has not departed greatly from traditional recipes, so the ingredients of the New World, such as potatoes, maize, tomatoes and beans, are absent. The chilli did, however, make it into Burmese cooking. They like it hot there! My two Burmese recipes are *Kaushwe-Kyaw*, a deliciously simple starter including noodles and garam masala, and *Chin-Hin*, a favourite dish, typically Burmese in taste. It is a soup or thin stew made with fish, herbs, tamarind, soy and chilli.

Thailand

Sharing her borders with Burma, Laos, Kampuchea and Malaysia, Thailand has a relatively short history, just about 1000 years. She has nevertheless developed a cuisine which is unique amongst these older countries, and is little influenced by them. Thai cooking is much admired and is rapidly becoming popular in the West. It is the refined combination of hot chilli spices with flowery fragrances and savoury tastes which makes Thai cooking so popular. The chillies are minute cayenne peppers, pretty to look at, explosive to taste. Savoury flavours come from shrimp paste (*kapi*, known as *blachan* in Malaysia) and thin clear fish sauce (*nam pla*) which never dominate, but enhance the other ingredients, and coconut milk which gives a creamy texture. Finally there is the combination of fragrances unique to Thai cooking. The three key items are lime leaves (*markrut*), lemon grass stalks (*takrai*) and holy basil leaves. All these ingredients are becoming more easily available in the specialised stores of the West, many of them air-freighted in.

Appearance matters greatly in Thai cooking, and colour combinations are given great importance. Thai curries, for example, traditionally get their names, Red Curry, Orange Curry and Green Curry, from the colour of the ingredients used. I have given recipes for one of each (see Index) and there is also a recipe for *Tom Yam Kaeng*, the popular Thai prawn soup. Finally, since Thais adore heat, I've included a recipe for *Nam Prik* (literally translated as 'sauce chilli hot'!). Thais, incidentally, do not use chopsticks, preferring spoons and forks.

Korea, Vietnam and Kampuchea

These actual or near neighbours of Thailand and China have identifiable cuisines, each slightly different, but all including chilli. They are rice cultures, and their foods are more akin to those of China than Thailand. You'll enjoy *Kochujaang* and *Nuoc Cham* (chilli sauces from Korea and Vietnam respectively) as accompaniments with any dish. *Cha Gio* are crispy crab-filled rolls from Vietnam, whilst from Kampuchea (formerly Cambodia) I've selected *Kari Nuoc*, a delicious scallop curry showing an interesting mixture of Thai and Chinese influences.

THE EAST INDIES

It did not take the Portuguese long to find the spices they so desperately sought. They reached India in 1498. By 1512 they had discovered the home of the clove, on the minute island of Ternate, and nutmeg and mace on the equally small neighbouring island of Tidore. These were the fabled spice islands, which are part of the Moluccas. First reports tell of aromatic winds leading the early navigators to these dots in the seas. More remarkable still was the discovery that, despite over 1500 years of dealing with the Chinese, the natives were still quite unaware that their indigenous spices had any value. They were happy to load Spanish ships with nutmeg, mace and cloves in return for trinkets. Back home, one full shipload yielded enough cash not only to pay for the voyage but to create a huge profit for the mariner and his financier. It earned Francis Drake his knighthood. The locals had no use for these spices in their cooking. Even to this day, Indonesians' main use of the clove is to smoke it with tobacco in a cigarette called a *kretek*.

Columbus had discovered his West Indies in 1492. Magellan's ships finished their circumnavigation in 1522, and, for the first time, scholars were able to begin the process of mapping the world. It had become certain that Columbus had in fact discovered a 'New World'. India's latitude was known by now, as were those of China and the Moluccas. For the first time the dimensions of the earth could be calculated. It was apparent that the West Indies were at the opposite end of the world to the spice islands. Someone came up with the notion of calling the entire Malay archipelago the East Indies, though this nomenclature was perhaps a little perverse for a land whose nearest point is nearly 2000 miles from India!

Nevertheless the name has stuck and today it refers to Malaysia, Singapore, Indonesia (of which the Moluccas are now a part) and the Philippines.

The food of Malaysia, Singapore and Indonesia has much in common. It is rice-based, and influenced by Indian as well as Chinese cooking techniques.

Malaysia

Malaysia's population is composed of Chinese, Indians and Malayans, and whilst it is easy to find here plenty of traditional Chinese and Indian cuisine in both homes and restaurants, there is also a combination of both of these which makes a distinctive Malaysian food style, a particular type of which is known as *Nonya* cuisine. *Inche kabin*, chicken coated in a thick curry paste and grilled, is a prime example of this. *Soto Ayam* is virtually the national dish of Malaysia. It is a chicken soup, more like a thin gravied stew, packed full of flavourings and spices. *Satay* is one of Malaysia's best known dishes, and *Teochew Satay* is grilled pork in a spicy peanut marinade.

Indonesia

Adjacent to Malaysia is Indonesia, the former Dutch East Indies. It consists of over 13,000 islands, some of which are uninhabited.

The fourth largest population in the world lives on the remaining islands which include Sumatra, Borneo, Java, New Guinea, and the celebrated spice islands – the Moluccas. Spices, ironically, earn relatively little income for Indonesia. Most Malaysian dishes will be found in Indonesia and vice versa. *Nasi Goreng* is Indonesia's celebrated fried rice dish. And it goes well with *Sajur Tempur*, a vegetable dish, and with the two Indonesian fish dishes *Malacca Ikan Manis*, and *Boembe Bali Ikan*. *Telur Goreng* is a tasty omelette using many typical local flavourings. Chilli is used in many forms, most popularly in *sambals* (chutneys), such as the sweetened *Sambal Manis* or the hot and tart *Sambal Oelek*.

Singapore

Singapore was founded in 1867 by Sir Stamford Raffles and was used by the British as their major trading post in the area, the legacy of which is today's major business centre.

Singapore's population is the most cosmopolitan of the area, with Indian, Chinese, Malay, Indonesia and European influences reflected in a culinary 'free for all'. You will find restaurants of all nationalities in Singapore, but you will not find a true Singapore cuisine.

The Philippines

One of the most northerly Philippine islands (there are some 7000 of them) was the first landfall in the East Indies made by Magellan on his world voyage in 1521. He proudly gave the islands their name in honour of his sponsor, King Philip of Spain. The Philippines remained Spanish until 1898, when they were taken by the USA. They became independent in 1946. Despite a population largely of Malay origin, the Philippines have crops, such as maize, and a culinary style which shows considerable New World Hispanic influence. I have included a recipe for marinated fish, *Kilawin*. Containing coconut, chillies, nutmeg and cloves, it makes an interesting comparison with the Latin American *Ceviche*.

CHINA

I've by no means done justice to the country with the world's largest population and most ancient cuisine, with just six recipes and four of those Hong Kong-style bottled sauces – chilli sauce plain, with garlic and with ginger, and Sichuan (the new official Chinese spelling for Szechuan) chilli sauce. Mind you, these are excellent and they go with any savoury recipe in this book. I am left with only enough space to add two more Chinese recipes, *Shark's Fin Chilli Soup* and *Sichuan Hot and Sour Soup*.

There are more Chinese restaurants in the world than any other 'ethnic' style. Indeed there is hardly a country on earth without one. We know Chinese food as bright, fresh colourful stir-fries with crispy additions and rice, but of course there is much more to China than that. I refer those who want to learn more to my book *The Curry Club, Chinese Restaurant Cookbook* (see page ii).

In three of the four Chinese culinary regions, spicing is minimal, but what is used is exquisite. Star anise, for example, or cassia bark, are divine and have become essential to cuisines other than Chinese, being major exports in the days of the ancient spice routes. *Chinese Five-Spice* and *Ten-Spice* are outstanding flavours (see Index). The only districts of China which enjoy and widely use chilli are the western provinces of Sichuan and Yunnan which share their borders with Tibet and Burma respectively.

JAPAN

Japan is an archipelago and former empire in eastern Asia. Its relative isolation meant that little was known about it until the twentieth century. Marco Polo learned of its existence but did not visit Japan when he reached Shanghai in 1280. In the absence of any other information, Polo's account of these islands was still relied upon 200 years later by Columbus, which explains why he believed some of the West Indies islands to be those of Japan. It was not until 1543 that the Portuguese landed there. Incredibly, they found a nation which had had no previous visitors, and whose total record of exploration was confined to the occasional piratical foray to nearby China.

The Portuguese established a base in Nagasaki and for a century traded Japanese silver for Chinese silk, until they were ousted. Despite a brief period of Dutch trading, Japan continued to lead an isolated life with a unique cuisine.

One Portuguese legacy was the chilli. The santaka chilli, a hot cayenne variety, and hontaka, a serano type, gradually crept into traditional Japanese food. In powdered form, chilli is currently a major crop for export to the USA. Chilli features as an option in all seven Japanese recipes in this book, and in the delicious *Japanese Seven-Spice Powder*, a tasty condiment. *Wasabi* (Japanese horseradish), the traditional hot flavour, available in powder form, is also widely used.

My recipe selection includes *Tempura* (fresh items of your choice, dipped in batter and deep-fried) and *Kuroke* (Spicy Japanese Fish Fingers), both served with a spicy dip. *Yakitori* (Skewered Grilled Chicken) whose marinade includes sake (Japanese rice wine) and chilli, and two spicy soups *Miso Shiru* (Asparagus and Red Soy) and *Gohan Zoshui*,

made with rice, seaweed, wasabi and wine. *Tamago-Yaki* is an omelette containing wine and marinated mushrooms, and *Tori-Maki* is a variant containing shredded chicken.

Modern Japanese, incidentally, have begun to develop a passion for curry, with a restaurant and product potential, say the experts, as big as Britain. It is a trend worth watching.

THE NEW WORLD

MEXICO

My look at the New World began in Mexico City where I was overwhelmingly reminded of Bombay. It began with the smell. Even at 3000 feet up, and 5 miles out in a pressurised aircraft, the stench of sewage of the world's most populated city (22 million at the time of writing) percolated into the cabin. On land there are people everywhere and shanty towns spreading out of town in concentric rings, like a fungus, covering every millimetre of land, including steep hillsides. Mexico's traffic is as intense and noisy as Bombay's, with its hooting and grating of gears. The difference is that the thousands of cabs are lime green VW Beetles rather than the yellow-roofed black-sided Ambassadors of India. As for the people, they are excitable, exuberant, noisy, fun-loving and plentiful, just as in India.

Although the objective of my trip was to explore Mexico's food, rather than to make comparisons, I could not help but compare Mexican techniques with those of the Old World, especially India. My primary purpose was to check out chillies, corn and chocolate, Mexico's main indigenous foods. I was not disappointed.

The chilli is alive and well, the people's adoration and addiction stronger than ever. I found dozens of chilli varieties, and an expertise on them unparalleled anywhere.

Corn means maize or sweetcorn. Until the arrival of the Spanish, corn was the New World staple. There was no wheat, rice or other grains, so corn was used in many forms,

The secret ingredients of Mexican chocolate molé include the holy trinity of dried pasilla, ancho and mulato chillies. Here the finished molé is poured over the huge turkey drumstick (see pages 134–135). Note the tiny pot of sauce (top centre) from Mexico City's molé fair, the bowl of cocoa beans, and the two types of Mexican chocolate

none more important than as flour (cornmeal) for bread-making in the form of Tortillas. The techniques for making Tortillas go back thousands of years and developed concurrent to, but completely in isolation from, India's wheat-based Chupattis. Both are unleavened flat, thin discs, dry-fried or fried on a slightly concave, steel pan (the Mexican *comal* is virtually indistinguishable from the Indian *tava*, see Glossary).

I did track down the famous blue tortillas, which in Mexico are bright turquoise (they are slate blue in the USA) and made from maize whose cobs are purply-indigo in colour and range in length from 1 foot (30.5cm) to 2 inches (5cm). A picture of these beautiful specimens appears on page 255, and the picture on page 262 shows a blue tortilla being prepared on a huge *comal*.

Cocoa is also indigenous to Mexico. It was

very highly regarded by the Aztecs, so much so that, as with spices in Europe, its use was confined to the Aztec nobility. The final Aztec emperor, Montezuma, was particularly partial to cocoa and water as a beverage.

The other totally unique and quite extra-ordinary Aztec use of cocoa is as a spice in a complicated mixture or *molé* (pronounced mow-lay). The Aztecs had developed dozens of molé recipes, ranging from mild to hot, and of varying colours. Some earned the name *manchamanteles* ('tablecloth stainers'), so strong and permanent was their colouring. Each contains a number of ingredients, including spices, which are finely stone-ground with water into a thick mouldable paste. This is then used as a cooking base, in exactly the same way that the Indian spice mixture, the *masala*, is used.

Of all the molés, none is more revered or

complex than the one containing chocolate. Called *Molé Poblano*, it can contain as many as 30 ingredients. In Aztec times it was considered such a luxury that only the royals were allowed it. The chief Aztec royal dish was *Guajolote Molé Poblano* – turkey with a fantastic chocolate and chilli sauce. It was this dish which earned the nickname 'Montezuma's Revenge', when the Spanish conquerors took Mexico in 1522. Montezuma II was the current Aztec Emperor and the Spanish, to whom the chilli was new, suffered the usual after-effects when they first tried the dish. Fortunately the dish survived, and the Spanish, having undoubtedly shot the cook, enhanced the molé by adding several more ingredients from the other side of the Atlantic. Garlic, onion, almonds, hazelnuts, pinenuts, raisins, banana, coriander, cinnamon, aniseed, cummin, cloves, pepper and sesame, now standard molé items, were all new arrivals at the time of the conquest. The Spanish Mexicans revered this molé as much or more than the Aztecs, and *Guajolote Molé Poblano* is now the national dish of Mexico.

Having compared Mexico and its food to that of the Old World, I subsequently found myself making a further comparison. Mexican food in Mexico is vibrant, colourful and appetising. Much use is made of maize in its various forms, beans, meat, cheese and spices (notably the chilli). Dishes resound with individual flavours. Sadly Mexican food in other parts of the world bears little resemblance to the real thing, greatly lacking in subtlety and suffering from the blandness of mass production. Chilli is either virtually absent or is merely used as a 'heat' provider rather than for its different flavours. Tortillas are sold as crisp packeted items, coated with antioxidants, rather than freshly made bread. The abundant use of maize flour (cornmeal) leads to a rather heavy aftertaste and beans have come to mean leaden stodge in the worldwide misinterpretation of the real Mexico.

CENTRAL AND LATIN AMERICA

The eighteen Central and South American countries, including Cuba, are all Spanish-speaking, with the exception of Brazil where the people speak Portuguese (see below).

The most important civilisation at the time of the Spanish conquest of the 1500s was that of the Incas of Peru, and, as already described, they were abruptly decimated. So few native Indians survived that little remains on record of their cuisine. However we do know that there were a number of similarities to the Aztec food of Mexico described earlier. For example, the Incas had a spice mixture, not unlike the molé, which the Peruvians called *locro*. Maize, tomatoes, potatoes and, of course, the chilli were in extensive use. Milk came from the llama which, along with the turkey, *coypu* (large rats) and the *cavee* guinea pig, were the main meat supply, and some very (to us) unpalatable recipes survive in various parts of Latin America. I'm told on good authority that here a popular and ancient recipe exists involving stewed rodent garnished with crispy deep-fried red ants. Today you will find pork, beef, chicken, fish, cheese and a Spanish/Mexican influence in their recipes and this book has a good selection from various Latin American countries.

As for the use of chillies, this varies from relatively little in some countries, such as Argentina and Chile, to profuse in Venezuela, Guatemala and Colombia. Experts are now confident that Bolivia was the birthplace of the chilli, and that it spread north and south across the continent tens of thousands of years before man arrived.

Chile, despite her name, is not a devout chilli-eating country, her climate being in the main too cold for chilli cultivation. However, one chilli sauce, *Color*, is worth trying to accompany any dish in the book, or to cook with, as *Color los Vegos* (Red Coloured Vegetables).

Brazil

Brazilian cuisine has a slightly different ancestry from that of her Latin American neighbours. We saw on page 11 how the Portuguese 'stumbled' across Brazil whilst sailing from Lisbon to the tip of Africa. They had agreed with the Pope not to encroach on Spain's New World but, as luck would have it, the exact line of latitude happened to pass through Brazil, so their occupancy of that territory was 'legal'. There they found widespread growth of chillies and exported them to Africa, India, China and beyond.

The Portuguese brought African slaves to Brazil and for this reason you will find a culinary connection with Africa and the West Indies, absent anywhere else in Latin America. Dishes like *Vatapa* (Coconut Shrimps) and *Mooqueca*, a chilli-marinated fish stew, are examples. *Leitão Recheado* is a delicious roast pork steeped in the traditional Portuguese marinade of red wine, vinegar, garlic and spices, to which chilli is added. Compare this with the Portuguese native *Porco com Vinho e Alhos* (Pork with Vinegar and Garlic) and their Goan *Vindaloo*. Brazil's *Caroco* (Avocado, Chilli, Egg and Tomato Dip) is an Incan recipe, as is *Picante de Papas* (Spicy Potatoes). *Anju* is a kind of Brazilian 'bread' using Portuguese-imported rice.

THE UNITED STATES OF AMERICA

The original inhabitants of the country were mostly nomadic, with few culinary traditions, following their buffalo herds around and living off the land. The arrival of the Spanish in Florida and California and the subsequent spread northwards of the Mexicans caused some Red Indians either to move or to settle and mix. The Pueblo Indians, for example, chose the latter, and built stone dwellings which are to be found on both sides of the Mexican border. Their food is largely influenced by Hispano-Mexican tastes, but their Red Indian Fry Bread, which I came across in Tucson, is a kind of deep-fried version of the Naan Bread of India. Being a wheat dough, however, it must be a post-conquest recipe.

American pioneers had more pressing matters to consider than the development of a national cuisine. The building of the wealthiest, most powerful and advanced nation on earth is the result of 200 years of hard labour.

That achievement perhaps explains the eat-to-live attitude of the early settlers and their modern descendants' love of fast food.

But not all Americans are content to settle for that, and a new gourmet vision is materialising. No cities are more cosmopolitan than those of America. There is no greater racial mix, for example, than in New York. This is reflected by its incredible range of restaurants. It is said that the cuisine of every nation on earth is available there, and, with 17,000 restaurants to choose from, who can doubt it?

Chilli has made an appearance on America's East Coast, as well as in California. But it is in the south-west states, led by Arizona, Texas and New Mexico, that the taste for chilli has become a raging passion.

Cajun and Creole Food

Louisiana has always, quite rightly, regarded itself as America's gourmet state. Its culinary heart is New Orleans, internationally known for its carnivals and feathered masks, its wrought-iron balustraded dwellings, its street cars, its jazz bands, its black ex-slave population with its African roots and fear of voodoo, and its proliferation of quality restaurants and pavement cafés.

The scene outside New Orleans could scarcely be more of a contrast. Louisiana is home to endless swamps, called the *bayou*, whose alligator-infested network of waterways is only understood by its inhabitants. The sugar cane and cotton estates are also never-ending, with their huge plantation houses, where you fully expect to see Rhett Butler and Scarlett O'Hara.

Louisiana is also home to the world's largest chilli sauce producers. Tabasco leads the pack, but other large brand names and attendant bottling plants are also present, such as Louisiana Gold (from Bruce Foods), Trappeys, Crystal, and scores of others.

The two culinary styles are Creole and Cajun. Creole originally meant a person of Spanish or French ancestry who was born in the Caribbean or in America. Subsequently it included a mix of Negro and white blood. In culinary terms, it refers to the 'haute cuisine' of the area. In the West Indies Creole cooking (also spelt 'Criole') refers to anything 'native'.

In New Orleans Creole cooking is synonymous with sophisticated cooking. Local produce, such as crawfish and chicken, rice and beef, are combined with French-inspired sauces and roux to create dishes which are as far removed from France as is the local pronunciation of each dish. *Fricassée*, chicken or veal in a white sauce, becomes Frik-eeair-sayee; *Courtbouillon*, the spicy stock, Coobee-you; and *Beignets*, fluffy light sugary doughnuts peculiar to New Orleans (Nawleens), Bay-nee-airts. Tabasco, by the way is pronounced Tair-biairs-cao. It all adds to the charm, and the food is as distinctive and delightful as the accent.

Cajun food owes its ancestry to a different set of circumstances. Groups of Southern French, called *Acadians*, migrated to Canada's Nova Scotia (New Scotland) in the early 1600s and established themselves as trappers until they were 'invited' to leave the area by the British. They went south. Unwelcome everywhere, they were obliged to keep on travelling until they reached the Gulf of Mexico and could go no further. There they found themselves in the uninhabited, inhospitable maze of the swampland bayou (bai-yee-oo). They put their trapping and fishing skills to good use and started to cultivate the difficult terrain in smallholdings. In time the Acadians acquired a deep Southern USA drawl and Acadians became *Cajuns* (caee-jarns).

Cajun food exemplifies their lifestyle; it is simply trappers' food. Like so many peoples from all over the world, they cooked what they caught, including alligators, turtles and frogs' legs. With French ancestry, however, it needed to be tasty, and garlic was the order of the day, as were onions. The indigenous bell pepper was discovered and revered and these three ingredients became so integral to Cajun cooking that their combination for the initial stir-fry is known in Cajun parlance as 'the holy trinity', to which chilli is often added.

THE WEST INDIES

The archipelago off Central America extends in a 1500 mile (2400km) area from Venezuela to Florida. The name given to it by Columbus and the Spanish conquistadors has stuck. In time the natives, including the Carib Indians, along with their traditions and culture, were virtually wiped out, as happened on the mainland. We do know that they used chilli in their cooking but we know little else. The subsequent Spanish occupants were ousted by other colonists, notably the British, who then used the fertile islands to grow crops. Grenada, for example, became the new home of mace and nutmeg. Allspice and chilli were indigenous to many islands, but it was sugar and cotton that were to become of major importance. To tend this crop, the British imported and utilised black slaves in shockingly inhumane conditions. Most were simply snatched from West Africa.

Slavery did not give the West Indians much opportunity to develop a national cuisine. Nevertheless, in a relatively short space of time, one did develop. It was influenced by Spanish, African and Asian Indian styles (the British introduced Indians for certain menial non-slave tasks in the islands). The resultant cuisine has a unique Afro/Spanish/curry base. Sugar, bananas, cotton, coffee, cocoa, coconut, spices and chillies are the main export crops. The West Indian diet also includes plantain, sourfruit, jackfruit, callaloo (local greens), yams, sweet potato and Christophines (small gourds). Native cooking is called Criole (or Creole). With its large Asian Indian population, you'll find an equally large number of dishes which are indistinguishable from those of the Indian subcontinent, such as *samosas*, *bhajis* and *curries*.

Jamaican Goat Curry is perhaps the area's most celebrated dish, although curry appears under a number of guises and names, such as *Stoba* in the Antilles and Curaçao, *Colombo* in Martinique and Guadeloupe, and *Pepper Pot* in Trinidad and Tobago. Even in largely Spanish Cuba there's a beef stew called

Picadillo Picante. No mention of West Indian food would be complete without *Jerk*. It's a sweet and hot marinade, now available as a bottled product. My *Jerk Veal* recipe shows how to make it. Spanish-influenced Puerto Rico provides a gorgeous starter in the form of *Croquetas de Chili y Queso* (Cheese, Carrot and Chilli Croquettes). Rice is cultivated on the islands and rice dishes – under the titles biriani and pullao – proliferate, indicating East Indian origin. Most celebrated of all, and probably worthy of the title of national dish, is *Rice and Peas. Rotis* (breads), such as *Chupatti, Puri* and *Paratha*, are all to be found. South-East London's new cafés, called roti houses, serve Caribbean curries with these breads.

Many types of chilli grow in the islands, the hottest of which is the Bahamian (or Scotch) bonnet, a variant of the hottest of the hot, the habanero. Its distinctive taste is usually present in the now widely available West Indian bottled sauces, which are decidedly not for the fainthearted. Those who adore such punishment can make their own by using the appropriate chillies in my red chilli mash recipe. Alternatively, you may wish to try *Stomachic Mandrum*, an Edwardian chilli recipe using Jamaican bird chillies and Madeira, and said to be 'an aid to digestion'.

AFRICA

We have seen how the Portuguese rounded the African coast during the sixteenth century. They established fortress bases, and eventually colonies, in several locations, such as the Cape Verde islands, Guinea, Nigeria, Angola and Mozambique. They imported the chilli and their cuisine, the influence of which will be found all over Africa, particularly in the latter two war-torn states today. Afro-Portuguese recipes are represented here by Angola's *Arroz de Coco* (Coconut Chilli Rice), Mozambique's *Piri-Piri Diabole* (Chilli Prawns, literally 'of the devil') and *Galinha Cafreal*, chicken marinated in lemon juice, garlic, chilli and salt, the namesake of its spicier descendant, the Indian

Goan *Cafreal*. Inexplicably, the Portuguese did not establish fortresses on the south coast between Angola and Mozambique, and this enabled the Dutch to colonise Southern Africa from 1652, until they were displaced by the British in 1806. Dutch linguistic and culinary influences still predominate, as illustrated by some of the area's classic national dishes, such as *Ingeledge Vis* (Pickled Fish), *Bredie*, a fish and gourd casserole, and *Bobotie*, a kind of vegetable pie topped with baked whisked egg.

Arab and Muslim culture and cuisine largely influenced the north-west African states, particularly those near the Gulf and the Red Sea. These included the Sudan, whose *Caruru*, stir-fried okra in a shrimp and coconut sauce, was exported from the Sudan by the Portuguese to Brazil. Ethiopia is represented by *Abay Wot*, the national dish, a deliciously spicy fish stew, *Inerja*, the local bread made from millet, and *Berbere*, Ethiopia's complex spice and chilli mixture which is but a short step from being a curry masala.

Africa's latter day colonists were France, Germany and of course Britain, who occupied much of the continent. Many British slaves were taken from West Africa and in consequence dishes found all over West Africa, like Sierra Leone's *Imojo* (Fish and Shrimp Salad), Ghana's *Amadan Ke Abobie*, made with plantains, tomatoes, chillies and black-eyed beans, Nigeria's Spinach and Sweet Potato *Palava*, and *Jollof* rice, with bacon and spices, will also be found in the West Indies.

Britain controlled Uganda, Kenya, and Tanganyika and Zanzibar (now Tanzania), planted coffee, tea and cotton crops and imported Asian Indians to run them. They also planted cloves on the island of Zanzibar. Today it is the world's largest clove exporter; hence the inclusion of the apt *Clove Rice* dish (*Zanzibari Chellow*). Despite problems in the 1970s the Asian community has remained strong in these countries, and curry is to be found everywhere. Most dishes are indistinguishable from their Indian ancestors, but the distinctive, Portuguese-influenced *Piri-Piri Curry*, a red chilli pepper hot beef dish, is one of the area's favourites.

CHILLIES

My mother always has three condiment pots on the table – the salt cellar, the pepper pot and another pepper pot containing extra hot chilli powder. Nearly everything, even her curries, get sprinkled with it. It is a habit she acquired from her years in India, and I learnt it from her when I was very young. One day, when I was about 12, my mum had a friend over for supper. Her name was Joy Adams. She had herself lived in India for many years and professed herself to be an old hand when it came to Indian food. Watching first my mum, then me, sprinkle chilli on the first course (tomato soup as I recall), Mrs Adams reached for the pot.

'Do be very careful – it's chilli powder,' said my mother.

'That's all right,' said Mrs Adams. 'I've been eating that stuff all my life,' and, as if to prove it, she sprinkled a minute amount on to her soup.

We all dipped into our bowls. Seconds later Mrs Adams was coughing and sneezing and spluttering. Her face and eyes went apoplectically red; all she was able to gasp was 'Water'. I remember being totally astonished. I had never seen the effect of hot food on the unsuspecting before. I don't remember any more. In fact I only recalled that scene now, 40 years later, as I was writing this piece. I'm sure Mrs Adams recovered, and that we all enjoyed the rest of the meal. But I offer this story as a warning. Chilli, particularly the very hot varieties, can create great discomfort, even in tiny amounts, for those not used to it. Fortunately that discomfort is short-lived and does no permanent harm. But what is it about chilli that makes it so hot? What, indeed, is chilli?

We are talking about the world's most popular spice. Chilli consumption, in tonnage, way exceeds its nearest rival, pepper, which itself way exceeds any other spice.

Chilli is the seed-carrying fleshy pod or fruit of a perennial shrub. It is a member of the *Solanceae* family, which also includes potato, tomato, tobacco and deadly nightshade! The botanical name for chilli is *capsicum*. Some etymologists claim it derives from the Greek word *kapto*, meaning 'bite' (a reference to its pungency no doubt). More likely, the word derives from the Latin word *capsa* or *capsula*, meaning 'case'. Certainly the words capsule and encapsulate are derived from the Latin.

Chilli is indigenous to Central and Latin America. Indeed it is now fairly certain that it originated in Bolivia. That ancestor, called the *chiltepin*, is to be found to this day growing wild, as far north as Arizona, on a shrub-like bush, with tiny, round, fleshy, red pods the size of peppercorns. It seems that distribution of the original chilli was in the hands, or rather the beak, of a thrush-sized bird, called the *Cardenal Torito*, whose droppings contained undigested seeds which grew into new plants. This explains why certain chillies are called bird chillies (see page 31).

There are five species of cultivated chilli. These are subdivided into thousands of varieties of chilli. Exactly how many exist may not ever be possible to determine. The reason is twofold. Firstly, chillies interbreed easily and fast. One variety breeding with another can create a third by the next season. Secondly, one particular variety can and does turn up in different parts of the world with many different names. This, of course, leads to confusion.

We can say with certainty that at least 3000 different chilli varieties exist, because the US Department of Agriculture Plant Introduction

Station in Georgia, USA (see page 300) has a collection of 3000 different capsicum seed varieties.

There is ample archaeological evidence to show that the ancient peoples of Central America grew chilli and used it in their food. Remains from before 7000 BC have been discovered near Mexico. There is also no doubt that the chilli was unknown outside America prior to 1492. The first recorded mention of it is in 1494 (by Chanca, the physician who accompanied Columbus on his second voyage to the New World). We have seen how rapidly the spice-eating world took to the chilli once it became available to them.

Had the Spanish discoverers used the two native words that were available, *aji* from the Aztecs and *chili* from the Incas, much confusion would have been avoided. Even the passage of 500 years has not rectified these misnomers. When the Spanish eventually realised that chilli was not pepper they began to use the Inca word *chili* but modified it to accommodate their spelling and pronunciation. It became *chile* (pronounced chee-lay). This word, but pronounced *chilee*, became the American standard. Europeans and others would pronounce it as tshyal (as in trial), sounding too much like child, so it became chilli in these places.

The principal attributes of the chilli are its piquancy and its hot taste, often described as 'burning'. Throughout this book, I will refer to chilli and chillies, not chilie, chillie or chilis, chillis or chilly (for this, perversely, means cold) hot peppers, or chili hot red peppers. The final spelling variant, chili, is often used to describe the cowboy dish *Chili (Con Carne)*. I quite like the current American vogue of calling chillies '*red hot chilie peppers*' – apart from having a nice rhythm it covers all options, leaving its reader in no doubt as to what is being referred to. The only snag is that green, yellow, brown, purple and white chillies have just as important a part to play as red! So I'll stick with chillies.

We saw on page 10 how Columbus was introduced to allspice berries. He promptly named these pepper, or, to be more accurate, *pimento* (pronounced pim-yento), the Spanish word for pepper. Even today allspice retains the name pimento.

Spread out a map of the world before you and draw one line of latitude 40° north and another 30° south. Between them you have demarcated the centuries-old chilli- and spice-eating lands. It has as much to do with climate as culture, and it is only very recently, in the last few decades in fact, that the 'developed' world has become aware of the chilli and the amazing variety of spices. Having discovered and exported the chilli all over the world, the Spanish and Portuguese and most Europeans back home ignored this culinary asset. Among the exceptions were Turkey, Greece and Hungary. The Ottomans' expanding sixteenth-century empire extended from India to Hungary. As it now included part of the ancient spice route, they took the chilli back home, and it became accepted, in moderation, in the cuisine of their empire. Following in the tradition of Columbus, the Greeks called the chilli by its old name *peperi* (pepper). The Latin name for pepper was *piper*. Modern Italians call chilli *pepperonci* and, whilst Italy grows her own chilli crops in the south, she also imports 20 tons of chilli per annum. The Slavic word is *paparka* and by 1570 a variation of chilli had become well established in Hungary where it was known as paprika. Hungary exports some 10,000 tons of paprika a year; Spain also grows paprika which she calls *pimiento para la pimenton* and she exports 20,000 tons each year.

The Constituents of Chilli

Chilli won Hungarian Professor Albert Szent Györgyi the Nobel Prize in 1937, following his discovery and identification of vitamin C. He used paprika in his tests and first named the unknown substance *ignose* (meaning 'ignorance', because he didn't know what he'd found). Later it became known as ascorbic acid, then vitamin C. It can only be found in fresh fruit and vegetables, and capsicum yields twice that of citrus fruit.

Other constituents of chilli include vitamin

A and alkaloids, called *capsaicin*. It is the latter which gives the painful burning sensation in the mouth. The effect is twofold: it causes the brain to activate the salivary glands to cleanse the irritation; it also releases endorphins, the body's natural painkillers. Because these give a person a feeling of pleasure and wellbeing, the brain begins to associate chilli with pleasure. As it becomes more used to the sensation, the brain releases more endorphins so the greater the buzz. Couple that with the fact that capsaicin is related to caffeine, nicotine and morphine, and it is little wonder that we become mildly addicted to spicy food, and that our tolerance of chilli heat increases. Fortunately for us curryholics and chili-heads, serious scientific research has been conducted in Western universities which conclusively proves that our addiction is harmless. Chilli eating has been referred to by some as 'mouth surfing', a term considered highly appropriate by those who indulge in such things.

For those who need reassuring, chilli has the following benefits. It counters the build-up of cholesterol, aids digestion, improves circulation, is a stimulant and antiseptic, is highly nutritious, and it is used in ointments for aching muscles. Chilli also has other uses. It is rubbed on to the hulls of ships to deter barnacles, and is carried by US police in spray canister form to fight criminals. Hens are fed red bell pepper mash to intensify the colour of their egg yolks. Spain's King Juan Carlos grows chillies in his garden, to enliven bland food. A jalapeño was the first chilli into space, carried there by astronaut William Lenoir in the shuttle *Columbia* in 1982. So popular is it now with the astronauts that a 2fl oz (50ml) bottle of Tabasco is standard issue in the food lockers.

The Scoville Scale

The Aztecs ranked chillies into six levels of heat, but it is the scale invented by American scientist Wilbur Scoville in 1912 which is used today. It measures chillies from zero points (nil heat) to a maximum of 300,000 points. At the bottom comes the bell pepper, with zero.

Tabasco clocks in at around 50,000 units, and Indian and Thai cayennes come in at around 125,000 units. But it is the mighty habanero which tops them all at a massive 300,000 Scoville units. The body is so astoundingly sensitive to capsaicin that 1 unit of capsaicin to 100,000 units of water is perceived to be 'painful' and even at a ratio of one to a million heat is sensed. The unitary measure is applied by a panel of tasters who note how far the chillies can be diluted yet still be tasted.

As for the painful effects of heat, chilli most affects the tongue and lips, whereas pepper burns under the tongue, ginger burns the throat, and mustard and horseradish burn the nose. Chilli lessens the taste of sour and bitter, and black pepper inhibits all tastes.

Capsaicin, the heat element in chilli, is found lining the fleshy walls of the seed pod. Contrary to popular belief, the seeds themselves are not the hottest part. They do carry capsaicin, but not as intensely as the flesh.

I do not stipulate the removal of chilli seeds except in the case of bell peppers, and certain fat mild chillies, where the seeds are very plentiful. In these specimens I recommend the removal of any white pith as well. In all other cases, it is too tedious to remove seeds. In any case the more you handle chillies, the more capsaicin you will get on to your hands. It is then that you can transfer it into your eyes and other equally sensitive body parts, even hours afterwards, no matter how many times you've washed your hands. Indeed, some unfortunate people apparently feel chilli burns on their hands for up to two days. It makes sense, therefore, to chop large batches of chillies at one go. Freeze what you don't use in an ice cube tray. (Take care not to use them at a later date for gin and tonic!)

Cultivation of Chillies

Chillies are very susceptible to disease, and crop failure is still very common, even when the most careful professional eyes are kept on them. Cross-pollination or interbreeding is also a problem, as is maintaining a standard level of heat from crop to crop. Chilli farmers will confirm that two differing species must be kept over 1 mile (1.6km) apart to guarantee no cross-breeding, and that if a hot chilli cross-breeds with a mild one, its next crop will be considerably milder. Furthermore, if a chilli is left unpicked from one year to the next, it will lose its heat intensity over time.

Chillies always start off green. As they ripen, most pods go yellow, then red. Some varieties go crimson, mauve, purple, black, brown, orange, pale green, pale yellow or white. They vary enormously in size, the largest being 10 inches (25cm), the smallest about $1/8$ inch (4mm) long. As for heat, neither size nor colour gives any indication of whether a particular chilli is hot or mild. Generally, the tinier it is, the hotter it is, but there is no cast-iron rule. Chillies are available fresh, in various colours, and dried.

We probably imagine that growing chillies hang down from their stalks. In fact, a number point upwards, and there are all manner of shapes. As well as long and narrow, chillies also come broad or flat, spherical, conical, egg-shaped, heart-shaped, bell-shaped, curved like a scimitar, or straight cylinder, blunt, or – most bizarrely – with a wrinkled hooded end (given the name Peter or penis pepper).

Chillies and Sex

As a matter of interest, the link between sex and chillies goes back thousands of years. Chillies were thought by the early Mayans, Aztecs and Incas to enhance virility and the Chinese believed the chilli contained aphrodisiac qualities. By the time the chilli reached the Old World, its reputation had become somewhat exaggerated. The Swahili word for chilli is *pili-pili*, which coincidentally (or not) means 'penis'. Curiously, the identical French Cajun word means the same thing! The painful rubbing of hot chilli on the male organ, in the erroneous belief that this would enlarge it, was practised by some tribal ancients. Conversely, some modern Muslims use chilli mash to punish young unmarried women who have become sexually active.

How to grow your own Chillies

You can use seeds from any fresh chillies and from dried chillies, providing they have not been cooked (ie: oven-dried). The seed is first sown in small pots or seed trays in a propagator, greenhouse or on a window-sill in late spring. When the seedlings are large enough to handle they should be transferred to 3 inch (7.5cm) pots to grow on to a size suitable for planting out (up to 10 inches (25cm) high). The plants should not be planted outside until all danger of frost has gone.

Planting can be done in large pots of good compost, growbags or in greenhouse borders. The growing tip may be pinched out to encourage the plant to bush out. Small white flowers will appear in profusion and chillies will soon follow. The plants will need regular watering, and feeding with liquid fertiliser, to ensure strong growth. After 2–3 months the crop can be picked in its green state. If red chillies are required they will have to be left on the plant to ripen, thus reducing the yield.

TYPES OF CHILLI

World wide, Mexico has the most varieties of chilli in daily culinary use. The USA comes second and India third. The colour photo on pages 34 and 35 shows 15 fresh chilli varieties plus 33 dried. Below I describe these and a few other chillies. It will help you to identify major types on the market, but you certainly will not need to stock all of them. (The numbers refer to those on the diagram.)

To cook the recipes in this book you can make do with five or six dry varieties and three or four fresh. Chilli suppliers are listed on page 300. The heat level numbers range from 0 (no heat at all) to 10 (maximum heat) and the heat scale used is described on page 29.

African Snub (23)
Virtually identical to **Jalapeño** (see below), these chillies are from Kenya. 2 inches (5cm) long by 1 inch (2.5cm) wide. Heat level **5**.

Aji (21)

Usually bright orange chillies from Brazil and Peru, but sometimes yellow or brown. Its aromatic taste makes it superb raw in salsas or salads. 3 inches (7.5cm) long by $^3/_4$ inch (2cm) wide. Heat level **7**.

Aji Amarilo (35)

Dried version of **Aji**, above.

Akola *(not illustrated)*

From Thane near Bombay, India, this small chilli is $1^1/_2$ inches (4cm) long by $^3/_4$ inch (2cm) wide. Heat level **3**.

Anaheim (17)

The Anaheim chilli is a variety which was cultivated as far back as 1900 for canning, in a factory in Anaheim, California. Developed from **Pasillas** (see below) in New Mexico, it was the ninth version, which was the ideal size for canning – a very precise 6 inches (15cm) long by $1^1/_2$ inches (4cm) wide and with minimal heat level. With its modest heat level it is widely used for all purposes. Heat level **2**.

Ancho and Ancho Chino (32, 39)

The green Mexican **Poblano** chilli when dried is known as the Ancho. In this form it is Mexico's most popular dried chilli. The Ancho Chino is smaller and more wrinkled than the larger, related Ancho, the former being 3 inches (7.5cm) long by 2 inches (5cm) wide, the Ancho being 4–6 inches (10–15cm) long by 3 inches (7.5cm) wide. Both are very dark brown, almost black, in colour, and have an aromatic fruity taste. Ancho aptly means 'wide', its heart shape creating one of the largest chillies. Heat level around **4**.

Banana Pepper

See **Hungarian Yellow Wax**, below.

Bedgi (41)

From the area west of India's Goa, the Bedgi or **Byadgi** is wrinkly and red and is often chocolate brown when dried. It is 2–3 inches (5–7.5cm) long and $^1/_3$ inch (8mm) wide. It is quite aromatic and has a heat level of **3**.

Bell Pepper *(not illustrated)*

Surely the most popular worldwide and mildest member of the capsicum family. It is also called **capsicum pepper, sweet pepper**, in Spain *pimiento* and in India *simla mirch*, and is also known by its colour, eg: **red pepper, green pepper** etc. They vary in shape from spherical to elongated and in size from about 2 inches (5cm) in diameter (miniature) to 6 inches (15cm) long by 3 inches (7.5cm) wide. Heat level **0**. A close relative to the bell pepper is the **Hungarian Sweet Pepper**.

Berebere *(not illustrated)*

An Ethiopian scarlet red chilli used to make the national dish (see page 165). The dried version is smooth, 3–4 inches (7.5–10cm) long by $1-1^1/_2$ inches (2.5–4cm) wide. Heat level **3**.

Big Jim *(not illustrated)*

This is the world's largest chilli. It is a cultivated version of the **New Mexican** chilli (see below, and see also **Anaheim**). It was developed in 1975, by one Dr Makayame, to be a huge, low-heat chilli produced on a disease-resistant plant. At first it was the size of a banana, but it soon became available at about 12 inches (30.5cm) long, and recent specimens have been reported at 17 inches (43cm).

Bird (48)

These are found all over Africa, where they are also called **Birds Eye, Congo, Mombassa, Pequin, Uganda** and **Zanzibar** chillies. They are very small conical chillies ranging from $^3/_8-^5/_8$ inch (1–1.6cm) long. They grow wild or semi-wild and are bright scarlet red. Their colour attracts mynah and other birds who eat them, with no apparent discomfort, distributing their seeds via their droppings. Some grow wrinkled, some smooth. All are very hot with a heat level of **8–9**.

Bombay Cherry (11)

Small, spherical, dark red chillies from central India, about $^1/_4-^1/_2$ inch (6mm–1.25cm) in diameter. Also available dried, they are attractive used whole in cooking. Heat level **4**.

Caribe Guero (24)

Guero is a term referring to all yellow chillies, and they are pale blond in colour. The Caribe variety is 2–2$\frac{1}{2}$ inches (5–6.5cm) long and 1–1$\frac{1}{4}$ inches (2.5–3.25cm) wide, and grows in Mexico and South West America (where it is known as the **Fresno** chilli) and of course in the Caribbean. While not grown there, it is available in Europe. It is ideal for salsas and salads, and though small, it is good for stuffing. Heat level **6**.

Casabel (33)

The word means rattle and it is one of Mexico's more intriguing chillies. It is more readily available dried, when its seeds rattle when shaken. The casabel measures 1–1$\frac{1}{2}$ inches (2.5–4cm) in diameter. With its deep reddy-brown colour and its slightly bitter tannic flavour, it looks and tastes good in virtually any dish. Heat level **4**.

Cayenne (4, 19, 40)

Undoubtedly the most widely used chilli in Indian and Indo-Chinese cookery, the cayenne derived its name from the Cayenne district of French Guiana, from whence the Portuguese transported it to Asia. It no longer grows in French Guiana and neither does it have much, if anything, to do with ground cayenne pepper (see page 39).

The cayenne chilli is long and thin with a sharp point, and there are numerous varieties ranging in size from 8 or more inches (20cm) long by $\frac{3}{4}$ inch (2cm) wide, down to miniature size (see **Thai Miniature** below) as little as $\frac{1}{2}$ inch (1.25cm) long by $\frac{1}{8}$ inch (3mm) wide. The varieties used prolifically in Indian cookery are generally between 4 inches (10cm) and 2 inches (5cm) in length. They are used raw whole, sliced or chopped, in chutneys, salads or as garnishes (see page 289 for the famous Thai chilli taste) or cooked in curries. Both their pungency and flavour suit these types of food admirably. Heat level **8–9**.

Chile Colorado

Its name means red chilli and it is a variety of **New Mexican** chilli (see below).

Chiltepin (46)

Most experts believe the Chiltepin or **Chiltecpin**, also called **Tepin**, is the original wild chilli – the plant from which all others have evolved. It is a tiny round berry slightly larger than a peppercorn. It is very decorative and bright scarlet in colour and, despite its high heat level, it is attractive to wild birds, who helped to distribute it across the prehistoric Americas. It is readily available in dried form from US mail order houses (see page 300) and its piquancy and tastiness make it suitable for any use.

Chipotle (25)

The Chipotle (pronounced cheepotlay) is not a type of chilli, it is a process. It is in fact the green **Jalapeño** chilli smoked and dried. Not only does it have a unique smoky flavour, but it has a nutty tannic taste as well. Many are canned but this reduces the subtlety of their taste. Chipotles average 3 inches (7.5cm) in length and 1 inch (2.5cm) in width. They have a heat level of **5**. Chipotles are superb in salsas and salads, indeed in any New World recipes.

De Arbol (20)

Literally meaning tree-like, the De Arbol (day-arbol) is a delicate, slender, cayenne dark-red variety. Long, thin and pointed and often curved, it is also referred to as *Cola de rata*, **Rat's Tail**, **Chilli Cow Horn** or **Bird's Beak** (see **Pico de Pajaro** below). They are 2$\frac{1}{2}$–4 inches (6.5–10cm) long by $\frac{1}{4}$ inch (6mm) wide, with a heat level of **7**.

Dutch Green (2)

Fatter than a cayenne and not as hot, the Dutch or **Holland Green** has been professionally cultivated from Indonesian cayennes to create a sweeter, less pungent, more marketable product. This has resulted in a pithy seedy inside (which needs discarding before use), and a medium-hot heat level of **6** which makes them suitable for use in salads and cooked dishes. At 5 inches (12.5cm) long by 1$\frac{1}{2}$ inches (4cm) wide, it can be stuffed.

Dutch Red *(not illustrated)*
Apart from the vibrant red colour and slightly sweeter flavour, this is the same as the **Dutch Green** (above).

Fresno
See **Caribe Guero** and **Kenyan**.

Goan (12)
A tiny red tepin-style chilli from Goa, India. It is used in the local fiery cuisine. Heat level **7**.

Guajillo (29)
The guajillo from Mexico is a beautiful russet red, translucent, thin-walled dried chilli, measuring between 4 and 6 inches (10–15cm) in length, and between 1 and $1^{1}/_{4}$ inches (2.5–3.25cm) in width. Most chillies grow hanging downwards (pendant). Guajillos grow upright, earning themselves an alternative name, **Mirasol** (looking at the sun). Its delicate flavour and mild heat level of **2–4** make it a favourite, especially for colouring, in all forms of New World cooking.

Gulbarga (26)
A town in central south India which grows a particular chilli which is sold (erroneously) as the **Kashmiri** chilli (see below). Consequently, it is called the **Mock-Kashmiri**. The Gulbarga, with its long thin wrinkled fleshy appearance (it is about 3 inches/7.5cm long by $^{1}/_{2}$–$^{3}/_{4}$ inch/1.25–2cm wide) does not remotely resemble the true Kashmiri, despite its nice crimson colour, and a similar heat level of around **4**. Nor does it have the flavour of the Kashmiri.

Guntur (36)
A district of India, north of Madras, with prolific chilli growing. The Guntur or **Andra** chilli is about 2 inches (5cm) long by $^{3}/_{4}$ inch (2cm) wide, with a sharp point. It has a good deep red colour when dried and, with a heat level around **6–7**, is the chilli most likely to be used as the major component in standard Indian chilli powder.

Habañero (14)
Originating from Havana, Cuba, the Habañero is the world's hottest chilli, measuring **10** (or 300,000 units on the Scoville scale, ie: 1 unit of Habañero can be detected in 300,000 units of water!). For the uninitiated even a tiny piece of Habañero would cause intense and prolonged oral suffering. For acclimatised chile-heads, it is one of life's great pleasures. Underneath the heat is a delicate plum-tomato apple-like flavour. The riper red ones have a sweetness that gives them a mouthwatering appeal.

Grown in Mexico and the Caribbean, this type of chilli is now becoming available in Great Britain. It has an irregular spheroid shape, with a small point, and is around 2 inches (5cm) long by $1^{1}/_{4}$–$1^{3}/_{4}$ inches (3.25–4.5cm) wide. It is available in green, yellow, scarlet and deep red. It has a number of close relatives such as **Scotch Bonnet** and **Rocoto** (see below). It is used mainly raw because it loses subtlety, but not heat, when cooked.

Hungarian Sweet Pepper *(not illustrated)*
Like the bell pepper, the Hungarian Sweet is fleshy and flavourful with no heat level (**0–1**). It is long (5–6 inches/12.5–15cm) but only 2–$2^{1}/_{2}$ inches (5–6.25cm) wide.

Hungarian Yellow Wax (16)
Originally from Europe, in America it is also called the **Banana Pepper**, a reference to its size and shiny yellow colour. This chilli grows up to 9 inches (23cm) in length and $1^{1}/_{2}$ inches (4cm) in diameter. It is not eaten in its green or red state, being rather unappetising, but in its pale yellow form it is sweet and succulent and ideal for stuffing. Heat level **3–4**.

Jalapeño (23)
The Jalapeño originated in Mexico – it is named after the Veracruz city of Xalapa – and is America's most popular chilli. It is between 2 and 3 inches (5 and 7.5cm) long and 1–$1^{1}/_{2}$ inches (2.5–4cm) wide at the top end, tapering to a point. It is fleshy and quite pithy and seedy inside (pith and seeds should be

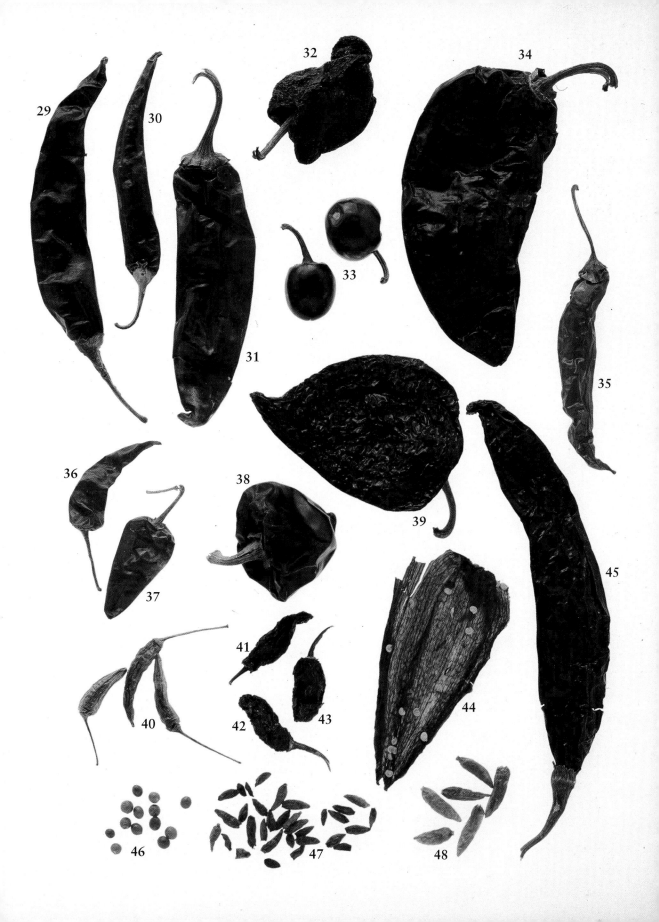

KEY TO PHOTO ON PAGES 34–5

The photograph shows the chillies at approximately 55% of their actual size.

1 New Mexican Green	25 Chipotle
2 Dutch Green	26 Gulbarga (Mock-
3 Spanish Green	Kashmiri)
4 Cayennes	27 Peperonci
5 Ornamental	28 Szechuan
Cayennes	29 Guajillo
6 Thai Miniature	30 Pulla
7 Serraño	31 New Mexico Dried
8 Sonepat	Red (Chile
9 Santaka	Colorado)
10 Scotch Bonnet	32 Ancho Chino
11 Bombay Cherry	33 Casabel
12 Goan Tepin	34 Mulato Primero
13 Tinelveli	35 Aji Amarilo
14 Habañero	36 Guntur
15 Tabasco	37 True Kashmir
16 Hungarian Yellow	38 Paprika
Wax (Banana	39 Ancho
Pepper)	40 Dried Cayenne
17 Anaheim	41 Bedgi
18 Spanish Red	42 Morita
19 Long Cayenne	43 Mora
20 De Arbol	44 New Mexico Dried
21 Orange Aji	Green
22 Kenyan	45 Pasilla
23 African Snub	46 Chiltepin
(Jalapeño)	47 Malawi Pequin
24 Caribe Guero	48 Uganda Bird

removed). Whether green or red, it is ideal for any use, raw or cooked.

African Snub, **Kenyan** and **Caribe** chillies are much more readily available in Europe and are virtually indistinguishable from Jalapeños, with a similar heat level of **5**.

Kashmir (37)

The true Kashmir chilli is native to the northern-most state of India and is much in demand for its bright crimson colouring, a quality it imparts to cooking. So much is the Kashmir chilli (**Kashmiri Mirch**) in demand that there is not enough total annual crop, to go round, and pretenders or mock-Kashmir chillies are passed off in its place (see Gulbarga above). The true Kashmiri chilli is deep crimson with a smooth, shiny, thin skin when dried. It is about 2 inches (5cm) long by 1 inch (2.5cm) wide and has a fruity flavour and a low heat level of around **4**.

Kenyan (22)

A smallish chilli about 2 inches (5cm) long and 1 inch (2.5cm) wide, gently tapering to a rounded point. It is almost identical to Mexico and America's **Fresno** chilli, although the Kenyan is around **5** on the heat scale (about $1^1/_2$ points lower than the Fresno). It can be substituted for the **Japapeño**.

Manzana
See **Rocoto**.

Mora (43)

The **Chipotle** is the smoked, dried green **Jalapeño**. The Mora is the red equivalent. It is considerably wrinkled and browny-red in colour. Mora means 'blackberry' and its fruity aromatic flavour is highly suitable for salads, sauces and salsas. Sizes range from $1^1/_2$–$2^1/_4$ inches (4cm–5.5cm) in length and $^1/_2$–$^3/_4$ inch (1.25–2cm) wide. Heat level is around **5**.

Morita (42)

A small version of the **Mora** (above), between 1–$1^1/_2$ inches (2.5–4cm) in length and $^3/_8$ inch (1cm) wide.

Mulato (34)

When the Mexican **Poblano** chilli (see below) ripens and turns reddy-brown and is dried, it is called the Mulato. It is an important chilli in Mexican cooking, especially for the chocolate molé (see pages 22 and 134) along with the **Ancho** and **Pasilla** chillies. The Mulato is 4–6 inches (10–15cm) long and 2–3 inches (5–7.5cm) wide. It is the smoky, liquorice, aromatic flavour, as well as its chocolate-black colour which gives it its appeal. Heat level **2–4**.

New Mexican Green (1)

This variety of chilli has been cultivated for reliability, disease resistance, fleshiness, minimal heat (its level is **3–5**) and size. It grows between 6 and 9 inches (15 and 23cm) long and $1^1/_2$–2 inches (4–5cm) wide. It is the perfect subject for stuffing but is equally at home in other cooking. It is also available in its riper red form, when it has a sweeter taste.

New Mexican Dried Green (44)
The fresh **New Mexican Green** chilli (above) is roasted, peeled and dried and is sold as 'the green chilli' or the 'Californian chilli'. Use it in stews and soups, or soak it and use in salsas for a pleasant smoky taste. Heat level **3–5**.

New Mexican Dried Red (31)
Also called **Chile Colorado** (red chilli) and **Californian Chile** (see **New Mexican Dried Green**, above). In dried form it shrinks a little to 5–7 inches (12.5–18cm) long by $1^{1}/_{2}$–2 inches (4–5cm) wide. It is translucent and with a similar **3–5** heat level. Used year round for cooking, it is also used to make American chilli powders and for ristras (strings of chillies used for decorative purposes).

New Mexican Eclipse, Sunrise, Sunset
(not illustrated)
All three are the same type of chilli which has been given pretty marketing names depending on its colour: Eclipse being the dried chilli which is purply brown; Sunrise is yellow, and Sunset is orange. The heat level is around **2–4**.

New Mexican Miniatures *(not illustrated)*
Dried baby versions of the immediately preceding chilli. They are the same size and appearance as the **Cayenne** (see above) but the heat level is **2–3**.

Orange Aji
See **Aji**.

Ornamentals (5)
These are miniatures grown as pot plants for decoration, though many can, of course, be eaten. They are generally small (**Pequins** and **Tepins** etc.) and come in a variety of pretty colours. **Chinese Multicolours** are, for example, tiny plum-like chillies varying from crimson to mauve, and **Black Plum** are tiny, purple and egg-shaped.

Paprika (38)
Paprika is the Hungarian word for pepper, but today it has come to mean a particular flavourful spice (see page 40). The actual chilli is a fleshy pod, cultivated in Hungary over the centuries to give maximum flavour, a deep red colouring and variable heat levels. The heat level most popular today is **0–1**. The pod is quite broad and can be pointed, elongated, heart-shaped or aubergine-shaped. It is not related to the **Hungarian Sweet Pepper** (see above), but is related to the Spanish paprika pod called **Pimiento** (see below).

Pasilla (45)
This dried chilli is one of Mexico's most highly regarded, along with the **Ancho** and **Mulato** chillies. All are used in chocolate molé (see pages 134–7). The Pasilla is also called **Chili Negro** (black chilli). In fresh form it is known as the **Chilaca**, and it turns from dark green to purply dark brown as it ripens. Pasilla means small raisins, alluding to its grape-like flavour and not its size. The Pasilla, sometimes wrongly called **Mulato** (see above), grows between 6 and 9 inches (15–23cm) in length and 1–$1^{1}/_{2}$ inches (2.5–4cm) in diameter. Its heat level is **3–5**.

Peperonci (27)
A chilli from Europe, it is to be found in Italy, Sicily and Sardinia. Dried, it is wrinkly, curved and russet red, 2–4 inches (5–10cm) long and $^{1}/_{2}$ inch (1.25cm) wide. Peperoncis are used in sauces and they are often bottled in olive oil. Heat level **5**.

Pequin (47)
Also spelt **Piquin**, and pronounced peekin, it simply means small, and refers to the tiniest chillies – which are almost invariably among the hottest with a heat level of **8–9**. There are many varieties, some round (see **Chiltepin**) and some conical. Others are called **Chile Bravo, Chile Mosquito, Chile Pequeño, Bird** and **Birds Eye**, and **Tuxtla**.

Peter Pepper *(not illustrated)*
Often given the name **Penis Pepper**, this is an ornamental chilli, bred for fun and for its phallic appearance. Red or green with a length between 3 and 4 inches (7.5–10cm), it

ends in a rounded dome, which is inset inside the main sheath of the chilli. Extremely rare.

Pico de Pajaro *(not illustrated)*
With the delightful name 'the beak of the bird', this bright orangey-red, small chilli is 1 inch (2.5cm) by $^1/_4$ inch (6mm), and is curved, just like a bird's beak. Its heat level is 6–7. It is nice used whole in salsas.

Pimiento *(not illustrated)*
Spanish paprika is different from the Hungarian variety (see **Paprika** above and page 40). It is more heart-shaped, smaller (maximum size is 4 inches/10cm long by 2$^1/_2$ inches/6.5cm wide), and has a little less savoury flavour than the Hungarian version. When ground it is called **pimiento para pimenton** in Spanish. Heat level **0**.

Piri-Piri *(not illustrated)*
This is an African term meaning chilli. Also called **Peri-Peri** or **Pili-Pili**. Be careful before you start asking certain Africans or Cajuns for Pili-Pili: in both Swahili and Cajun French it means penis!

Poblano *(not illustrated)*
An important and popular Mexican chilli, but although used locally fresh, we only see the dried form. It makes two dried chillies.

Pulla (30)
A smaller dried relative of the Mexican **Guajillo** (see above), measuring 4–5 inches (10–12.5cm) long by $^3/_4$ inch (2cm) wide. It is deep red, thin fleshed and attractively translucent with a fruity aromatic taste. Easily available dried, it can be used for all purposes. Heat level **6**.

Rocoto *(not illustrated)*
A chilli much prized in its native Mexico City for use in salsas. Its size and shape are like a hen's egg. Its heat level is around **8** and it has a marvellous apple-like flavour (hence its other name, **Manzana-apple-chilli**). It has one further unique feature – its seeds are black, which makes it most attractive in salsas.

Sadly, it is hard to get outside of its native Mexico and Peru.

Santaka (9)
A deep red erect Japanese chilli. Not unlike the **Serrano** (see below).

Scotch Bonnet (10)
Very closely related to the Habañero chilli (see above), the Scotch Bonnet (or **Bahamian, Bahama Mama, Jamaican Hot** or **Martinique Pepper**) is just about as hot (**9–10**) and has a similar apple–cherry tomato flavour. Like the Habañero, it is spherical, although rather more squashed in shape, and it is smaller (1$^1/_4$–1$^1/_2$ inches/3.25–4cm) in diameter. Native to the Caribbean, it is available in the UK in green, yellow, orange and red as well as multi-toned. It is great for salsas and sauces.

Serrano (7)
The Serrano, meaning 'from the mountains', is native to Mexico and south-west America. At **6–7** on the heat scale, it is widely believed to be the hottest chilli by many Americans who adore it in its red or green form (see **Habañero** and **Cayenne**). It can be best described as bullet-shaped. Two similar-sized species are widely available, **Balin** (pellet) and **Tipico** (typical) in the USA. Both are quite small – only 1–2 inches (2.5–5cm) in length and $^1/_2$–$^3/_4$ inch (1.25–2cm) wide. A larger, double sized species (**Largo**) is only found in Mexico. Serraños have yet to be exported or cultivated outside the New World.

Serrano Seco *(not illustrated)*
The dried version of the red **Serrano**, it is actually deep orange in colour. Dimensions and heat level are the same as **Serrano**. Widely available, and the only substitute for the fresh item for those outside the New World.

Sonepat (8)
A dried yellow/orange chilli from India's Punjab, used for imparting a yellow colour to curries. Heat level **5**.

Spanish Green (3)
Virtually identical to **Dutch Green** (see above).

Spanish Red *(not illustrated)*
Virtually identical to **Dutch Red** (see above).
Also called **Brazilian Red**.

Szechuan, Sichuan (28)
Not introduced to China until the sixteenth
century, chillies are now fundamental to the
cooking of China's western province. A
number of chillies now grow there, including
Ngau kok tsiu (a type of **De Arbol**), **Fan
chiew tsiu** (a Dutch type), **Tse tin tsiu** (a
Mirasol type). The hottest, which is simply
called **Szechwan** in the West is probably a
Cayenne type. In China it is called **Tsim tuk
laat tsiu** or **Rajiano**. It is pungent, with a heat
level of **8**, and grows between 2–4 inches
(5–10cm) in length and $^1/_4$–$^1/_2$ inch
(6mm–1.25cm) wide.

Tabasco (15)
The Tabasco chilli derived from a state of that
name in south-east Mexico, where the land is
mostly flat and marshy, and it is hot and
humid with extensive jungles. The Tabasco no
longer grows there, but will be found in New
Iberia, Louisiana, the home of the famous
sauce company of the same name where it has
grown since at least 1850. Tabasco chillies are
also grown by the sauce makers in Venezuela,
Guatemala and elsewhere.

The Tabasco grows pointing upwards, is
bright red when picked, $1^1/_2$ inches (4cm) long
by $^3/_8$ inch (1cm) wide, and has a heat level
of **9**.

Tepin
See **Chiltepin**.

Thai Miniature (16)
This minute variety of cayenne is loved by the
Thai nation. Called, in Thai, **Priki nu**, it is
used green or red in Thai curries and sauces.
The heat level is **8–9**.

Tinelveli (13)
A small cherry type chilli, also called
Tirinevelly, from the deep south of India.
About $^1/_3$ inch (8mm) in diameter, it is conical
in shape and has a heat level of **6**.

Uganda Bird
See **Bird**.

Wax
Very shiny chillies are often grouped together
under the name Wax. Some examples include
**Hungarian Wax, Caloro, Torrido, Santa Fe
Grande** and **Gold Spike**. Sizes vary, as do heat
levels and colours.

CHILLI POWDERS AND PAPRIKA POWDER

As with chillies here is another area of massive
confusion, especially to the uninitiated. What
goes into the packet is entirely at the discre-
tion of the processor. Consequently, a packet
of chilli powder, for example, may contain a
mixture of chilli and other spices, it may
contain some salt, even some flour. Whatever
it contains, fortunately the law requires the
processor to declare the ingredients on the
packet. So my first piece of advice is to read
the packet. What the packet will not tell you,
however, is what type of chilli has been used.
Nor does it tell you its heat level.

Some UK processors do go so far as to sell
two grades: chilli powder and extra-hot chilli
powder. At least eight different brand names
are available and each one's heat level is different, ranging from 5 to 8 for the standard
chilli powder, to 8 to 9 for extra hots (which
are made from **Uganda** or **Malawi Bird
chillies**). Indian chilli powders (made and sold
in India) are no more reliable. Even
powdered, branded Kashmir chilli powders do
not necessarily contain **Kashmir chillies** (see
page 36).

Cayenne Pepper
A further confusion applies to cayenne pepper.
It would seem logical to assume that it is a hot
chilli powder made exclusively from **Cayenne**
chillies (see page 32). However, it is generally
not Cayennes that are used. In India it is made
with **Bird chillies** but is mixed with 25 per
cent salt. British manufacturers used to add
spices to hot chilli, but now this practice has
stopped, and whilst there is no stipulation as
to what chillies are used, the heat level must

be at least **8**. Cayenne pepper in America is also called red pepper, or red dust. This is a generic term equivalent to the British or Indian chilli powder. Again there is no stipulation as to which chilli can be used, so the powder can vary from mild to hot.

Chili Powder

Chili powder (spelt with one 'l') is a mixture indigenous to the USA, specifically blended to cook chili-con-carne. Its invention is attributed to one Willie Gebhert as far back as 1892. There are now almost as many mixes as there are chili cooks and obviously the contents vary quite markedly. Typically, a chili powder will contain one or more mild chillies (such as **Anaheim**), and it should be at least 80 per cent chilli. Often it is not, and salt can make up as much as 40 per cent of the total. Other ingredients might include powdered garlic, oregano, cummin, flour, sugar, citric acid and chemicals. As with all such factory blends, it is better by far, and cheaper, to make your own. See chilli recipes on page 45.

Crushed Chillies or Caribe

Other chilli products include what are called crushed chillies in Britain, and chile in the USA, where it is also called red grit, pizza pepper, peperone rosso, red flakes, coarse chile, caribe or, simply, chile seeds. And that is exactly what it is. It can be hot or mild, so again experimentation will be needed before you find a make you like.

Chile Molido

Mexican and American specialist producers wanting to give their customers satisfaction and reliability now produce powders from specific chillies. Called Chile Molido (from the Spanish meaning ground) these are guaranteed to contain the chilli specified on the packet, with no blending or adulteration with salt, flour or anything else. Heat levels are stated and also guaranteed. You can obtain molidos made from many of the Mexican and American chillies. Furthermore, it is often available in either red or green form. See page 300 for suppliers' addresses.

Paprika

Paprika is the Hungarian name for pepper. Chillies were first introduced there by Ottoman Turks in the sixteenth century. Over the centuries, a type of pepper was cultivated, especially in the Szeged and Kalocsa districts. At first paprika was deep red in colour and very pungent. Over the years the pungency has been bred out of Hungarian paprika, so what we now expect is a tasty deep-red powder used for flavouring and colouring purposes, but not for heat. However, what we actually get may be wide of the mark; paprika may be mild or it may be hot. It can range in colour from rust to crimson, and it may have unspecified additions. The worst paprika will even be bitter. The reason is that, being a major crop, numerous other countries have become producers.

Spain's paprika, called *pimiento para pimenton* is made from a different pepper to Hungary's, but ranks as second only to Hungary's in flavour and quality.

The real thing, from Hungarian or Spanish peppers, is undoubtedly the best.

As with everything else, expect to pay the most for the best, but be sure it is the best you're paying for. Once you've found your favourite brand the best thing is to stick with it (or them).

SPICY WORKSHOP

This chapter contains useful information on kitchen equipment, cooking techniques and particular ingredients, and basic recipes that crop up again and again. There are also recipes for aromatic spicy mixtures such as Indian Garam Masala, Japanese Seven-Taste Pepper, Chinese Five-Spice and Ten-Spice powders, Afghan Char Masala and Arabian Baharat. These spice mixtures are used as condiments. For example, aromatic salt (salt combined with spices) enhances virtually any dish the world over. We also examine how to roast and grind spices, how to make curry masalas (mixtures) and pastes, how to clarify butter to make ghee, how to make tamarind purée and how to deal with coconuts. We make a very tasty, spicy, clear cooking stock with the rather off-putting name of Akhni, and see how to fry onions until they are crispy brown (onion tarka).

POTS AND PANS

I could not manage without woks or karahis (see Glossary) and my preference is carbon steel. They are relatively inexpensive and I have a range of woks and karahis, from small (8 inch/20cm) to large (16 inch/40cm). As for cleaning, I prefer to scrub them thoroughly after use (which tends to remove the blackened patina a bit, but is more hygienic). It doesn't matter how much you scrub a wok/karahi it will never be absolutely clean. The problem of rust is very easily overcome by wiping the pan dry with kitchen paper (if you use a tea towel it will be stained). As soon as you've washed it, place it empty on your stove at high heat for 1–2 minutes until it starts to 'blue'.

The other vital piece of cooking equipment is a large flat frying pan in which you can cook omelettes, pancakes and flat breads. Again, the heavier the better. The Indian *tava* (identical to the Mexican *comal*) is not mandatory but it does all those jobs efficiently and (in heavy carbon steel) is inexpensive.

HANDLING CHILLIES

The hotter the chilli the more capsaicin it contains. This, the 'heat' component, is easily detected by sensitive parts of the human body. Furthermore it is very resistant to washing. Even after several soapy scrubs, detectable amounts of capsaicin will remain on hands which have chopped habanero chillies, even after 24 hours. The sensible advice is to wear a pair of disposable plastic gloves. Even if you are macho enough to cope gloveless with the effects of capsaicin, consider its effect if you come into contact with others who are more sensitive. Never, never touch your eyes after handling chillies – the resulting stinging is far from pleasant.

ROASTING CHILLIES AND BELL PEPPERS

This is a common practice in Mexico and America, particularly with the fleshier species. Roasting enhances flavours, releasing volatile oils, and both softens the chilli or pepper and enables the skin to be removed more easily. The net result is a sweeter taste with smoky overtones.

Suitable types of chillies for roasting include any which are large and fleshy, such as **New Mexican, Dutch, Yellow Wax, African Snub, Kenyan** and **Jalapeño**. Bell peppers are also suitable. Recipes in this book indicate when roasting is required.

Some dried chillies are commercially roasted (smoked). These include the **Chipotle, New Mexican Dried Green, Mora** and **Morita,** and these can be used as substitutes where a recipe asks for roasted chilli.

Roasting requires minimal effort:

1. Cut the chilli(ies) in half and remove and discard all pith and seeds.

2. Place skin side up on the grill rack, and grill at the halfway position at medium heat.

3. Keep an eye on the chillies as sizes, and therefore roasting times, vary. As soon as they develop black heat spots, withdraw the grill rack, leave the chilli until cool enough to handle, then peel or scrape the flesh from the skin. Discard the skin. Use the flesh at once, or freeze it.

SOAKING DRIED CHILLIES

Place the dried chillies in a bowl and pour over boiling water. Leave to soak for 20 minutes then drain and use as required.

MARINATING MEAT, POULTRY AND FISH

The longer you marinate fresh meat or poultry, the more the flavours will impregnate it. For meat and poultry I recommend a marination of between 24 and 60 hours.

Use only meat or poultry that you can be certain is very fresh. Only with a fresh subject can you be certain that it is safe to leave it uncooked for a further 24–60 hours. Secondly, and equally crucial, you must use the fridge.

Marinating fish and shellfish requires very much less time simply because marinades penetrate the flesh much faster and, more importantly, fish deteriorates much faster than meat, so that even 24 hours in the fridge would be too long. Generally a marination as short as 1 hour for soft flat fish, or up to 6 hours for thick fish or shell-off seafood, is ample. As with meat, use only the freshest fish or shellfish.

1. Use a bowl of sufficient size to be virtually filled with the subject and the marinade.

2. Use a ceramic, glass or enamelled, stainless steel or non-stick surface bowl, but do not use one made of aluminium, cast-iron, or untreated steel or metal, or the acids from the marinade (especially vinegar and dairy items) will corrode the surface and add a horrid metallic taste to your finished cooking.

3. Make the marinade up first, and put it into your bowl.

4. Prepare the ingredient to be marinated (the subject) by removing skin, fat, scales, fins and any other unwanted matter.

5. Wash and dry the subject and make small gashes in the surface to allow the marinade to penetrate into a greater surface area. Unless you like impregnating your fingers with garlicy flavours, I recommend that at this stage you put on a pair of thin disposable plastic gloves.

6. Once stage 5 is completed, place the subject, without delay, into the bowl, massaging the marinade into the subject with your hands. Be sure that the subject is evenly coated, especially on top.

7. Cover the bowl with plastic film and place it in the fridge for between 24 and 60 hours (less for fish and seafood).

8. Every 12–15 hours take it out and spoon excess marinade on top. Re-cover and replace in the fridge.

9. It is best to bring it out of the fridge to allow the subject to return to room temperature before cooking.

10. At the end of stage 6, it is possible to freeze the marinade and its subject. The marination process does work to a reasonably effective degree in the freezer. Remember to allow plenty of time for the subject to thaw and come back to room temperature before cooking.

GHEE

Ghee is a clarified butter which is very easy to make and gives a distinctive and delicious taste. When cooled and set, it will keep for several months without refrigeration, as does dripping. If you want to make vegetable ghee, simply use pure vegetable block margarine instead of butter.

2lb (900g) any butter

1. Place the butter blocks whole into a medium non-stick pan. Melt at a low heat.

2. When completely melted, raise the heat very slightly. Ensure it does not smoke or burn, but don't stir. Leave to cook for about 1 hour. The impurities will sink to the bottom and float on the top. Carefully skim off the floating sediment with a slotted spoon, but don't touch the bottom.

3. Turn off the heat and allow the ghee to cool a little. Then strain it through kitchen paper or muslin into an airtight storage jar. When it cools it solidifies, although it is quite soft. It should be a bright pale lemon colour and smell like toffee. If it has burned it will be darker and smell different. Providing it is not too burned it can still be used.

NITER KEBBEH
Spiced Ghee

This is a remarkable clarified butter. It is unique because it is given flavouring by cooking spices in the clarification process. It is only made in Ethiopia, where they cook everything savoury with it. Like my aromatic salt, I find that *niter kebbeh* can be used to enhance many a dish whether Ethiopian or not. Use a non-stick saucepan or you'll be scraping and cleaning until this time next year.

2lb–2lb 3oz (900g–1kg) any butter
8–10 garlic cloves, crushed
2×2 inch (5cm) cubes ginger, grated

1 inch (2.5cm) cube fresh turmeric root, grated (chef's tip, page 183) or 1 teaspoon ground turmeric
4oz (110g) onions, finely chopped
1×4–6 inch (10–15cm) cinnamon quill
6 green cardamom pods, halved
6 cloves

Follow the recipe for ghee, and add the remaining ingredients to the melted butter at stage 2.

COCONUT

Coconut is widely used in Indian and other Asian cooking. There is absolutely no substitute for fresh coconut. Equally, there is nothing as tedious as preparing fresh coconut. We're all familiar with the hairy brown hard 'nut'. If only there was an easy way to prepare it. Now there is. You can buy frozen shredded coconut flesh in Chinese shops.

Cooks only use three parts of the coconut: the liquid inside, coconut water, as a drink or as cooking stock; the white flesh; and coconut milk which is made from the flesh.

When buying a fresh coconut, shake it to ensure it is full of liquid. The more liquid it has, the fresher it is. Don't use coconuts without liquid or with mouldy or wet eyes.

To Open a Coconut

1. Make a hole in two of the three eyes with a clean screwdriver or corkscrew. Drain off and keep the liquid (**coconut water**) for stock.

2. Bake the empty coconut in the oven at 400°F/200°C/Gas 6 for 15 minutes.

3. While still hot, crack it with a hammer or something heavy.

4. Remove the outer husk and discard.

5. Break the inner parts into manageable pieces. Pare off the dark inner husk, using a small knife or a potato peeler.

6. Use the flesh in chunks, puréed or grated. Freeze any spare.

Ready-to-use Coconut Products

Desiccated coconut is one substitute for fresh coconut, and can be used by adding it dry to your cooking, or by simmering it in water and straining it to create coconut milk. **Canned coconut milk** is much richer and thicker, and a fairly new product is **coconut milk powder**. This is very finely ground, dried coconut flesh – which has a creamier taste than desiccated, and mixes well with water without any lumps. It is a boon to convenience cooks. To use, either add directly during cooking or add water to make a paste.

The familiar 7oz (200g) rich block of 'creamed coconut' is a combination of freshly grated coconut flesh and coconut oil, which sets solid. It must be kept in the fridge. To use, boil a little water, cut off the amount required and melt it in the hot water. If you try to fry it without water it will burn.

TAMARIND PURÉE

Tamarind, also known as the Indian date, is a major souring agent, particularly in southern Indian cooking. The tamarind tree bears pods of about 6–8 inches (15–20cm) long which become dark brown when they ripen. These pods contain seeds and pulp, which are preserved indefinitely for use in cooking by compression into a rectangular block weighing about 11oz (300g).

To use tamarind, soak the block overnight in twice its own volume of hot water – about 23fl oz (650ml) per 11oz (300g) block. The next day pulp it well with your fingers, then strain through a sieve, discarding the husks. The brown liquid should be quite thick, and there will be plenty of it. Freeze any spare.

Alternatively, for a small portion, cut off about an eighth of the block – a piece about $1^1/_2$ inches (4cm). Soak this in about $3^1/_2$fl oz (100ml) water for 30 minutes or more. Pulp and strain as above. Lemon or vinegar or mango powder can be used as substitutes, but give completely different flavours.

ONION TARKA

The *tarka* is the traditional crispy brown onion garnish sprinkled over several of the dishes in this book. I like to make a reasonable size batch. If cooked correctly these dry crispy pieces will keep, like biscuits, in an airtight tin. To get them crispy, the trick is to dry the onion in a low oven, then to fry them at medium heat. Serve hot or cold.

MAKES about 5oz (150g) dry tarka

8oz (225g) onions, peeled
6–8 tablespoons vegetable or sunflower oil

1. Finely slice the onions into matchsticks about $1^1/_2$ inches (4cm) in length.

2. Preheat the oven to 210°F/100°C/Gas $^1/_4$.

3. Spread the onion sticks on a baking tray and place in the oven for anything between 30 and 45 minutes. Check a few times that they aren't burning.

4. They should now be quite dehydrated, so heat the oil in a karahi or wok.

5. Add the onion sticks and stir-fry for a few minutes, until they go golden brown. A little blackening is fine, but control things to prevent an all-black situation.

6. When you have the colour you like, strain off the oil (keep it for subsequent cooking). Drain the onions on absorbent paper.

AKHNI STOCK

Sometimes called *yakhni*, this aromatic clear liquid is an all-purpose vegetable stock. It probably originated in ancient Persia, and variations on it are used all over the Middle East and the curry lands as far east as Thailand. I've found that it goes well with a great many dishes from the Third World, although I would omit ginger when using akhni in any recipe which doesn't itself use ginger or galingale.

You can freeze it or keep it in the fridge for

a couple of days, but it is essential to re-boil it after this time; it will be safe for several re-boils, but use it finally in a soup or other cooking. Add the brine or water from tinned vegetables to your stock. You can top it up with fresh or leftover ingredients as required.

MAKES 1¹/₂–2 pints (900ml–1.2 litres)

6 tablespoons soy or sunflower oil
6–8 garlic cloves, crushed
2oz (50g) cube ginger, grated (optional)
1lb (450g) onions, chopped
1 teaspoon aromatic salt (page 46)

Spices (whole)

10 cloves
10 green cardamom pods
2×6 inch (15cm) cinnamon quills
6 bay leaves

1. Heat the oil and stir-fry the whole spices and the garlic for 30 seconds. Add the ginger if it is being used and continue to stir-fry for a further 30 seconds. Add the onions and stir-fry for about 5 more minutes.

2. In a 5–6 pint (2.75–3.5 litre) saucepan, bring the water to the boil, add the fried ingredients and the aromatic salt.

3. Simmer for at least 1 hour with the lid on, until the stock has reduced by two-thirds to half.

4. Strain off and discard the solids.

SPICES

Storing spices

Whole spices retain their flavour longer than ground, for one year or more sometimes. Ground spices give off a stronger aroma than whole, and of course this means their storage life is that much shorter. Three months is about right for most ground items. So plan your larder accordingly, and buy little and often and grind freshly. Keep the spices out of sunlight (better in a dark cupboard) and in airtight labelled containers. Clean coffee or jam jars are excellent.

Grinding spices

It is better by far to grind your own whole spices whenever you can. Firstly you can be sure of the quality and contents, and secondly they will be fresher and tastier. The traditional method is by mortar and pestle, but you can use an electric coffee grinder or the new electric spice mill. Use small quantities to prevent overloading the motor.

I have long been a proponent of the Kenwood spice mill, the simple attachment which works with their Chef unit. Indeed I helped Kenwood with its development trials. I have done so again with Kenwood's redesigned unit. It successfully grinds all spices and roots, wet or dry, to a medium-textured paste. But, for the purist, the optimum tool hails from India. It is the Ultra Grind Electric Stone Grinder, and its results are simply indistinguishable from hand grinding (wet or dry) while taking a fraction of the time. It's great for making stone-ground flour too. The Curry Club sells these units (see page 300).

Don't try to grind dry ginger or turmeric. They are too fibrous for most small grinders, and commercial powders are adequate. Peppers – chilli, paprika and black or white pepper – are tricky, and commercially ground powders will suffice. The oilier spices such as cloves, nutmeg, brown cardamoms and bay leaves are easier to grind if roasted first.

In the recipes, when a spice is referred to as 'ground', this means factory ground. Where it requires the spice to be home-ground (usually after roasting), the recipe clearly states this.

Roasting whole spices

Whole spices contain essential or volatile oils. It is these which we can smell when handling a spice, and it is these which we must release when we cook with spices.

Roasting whole spices is my favourite way of releasing their essential oils. A roasted whole spice tastes quite different from a raw one and the release of flavour is pleasantly overwhelming.

The roasting process is simple and can be done in a dry pan on the stove, in a dry electric frying pan, under the grill or in the oven at 325°F/160°C/Gas 3 for about 10 minutes. Each spice should be heated gently until it gives off its aroma. The spice should not blacken, a light brown at most is sufficient. The original oil of the spice must not be totally cooked out or it will lose its flavour. A little experimenting will soon show you how to do it. In some recipes pre-roasted spices are important.

Blending spices

This sounds rather grandiose. In fact it's simple. Every mixture is called a blend. Generally we mean ground spices, and of course the best-known blends of all (with the worst reputation) are curry powders. 'Curry powder' gives a totally wrong image and is generally despised by cooks in all the curry lands, who call any mixture of spices the 'masala'.

In the following recipes, you can adjust the quantities of spices used to your own taste. I've added metric weights (in grammes) to some because it is easier to be accurate with very small quantities. **Spoon measures of spices are heaped.**

AROMATIC SALT

Throughout this book, recipes call for aromatic salt. This is salt, preferably sea salt, to which is added a light spice mixture. Ordinary salt can be used in its place, but the spicing adds delicacy and subtlety to a recipe.

Here are two versions, the first being light and aromatic, the second containing spicier tastes as well as nuts. Finely grind a reasonable size batch and store in a screw-top jar.

1. Lightly Spiced Salt

4oz (110g) coarsely granulated sea salt
1 teaspoon powdered cinnamon
1 teaspoon ground allspice

2. Spicier Aromatic Salt

Add to the above lightly spiced salt:
$1/2$ teaspoon ground fenugreek seeds
1 teaspoon dried mint
1 tablespoon ground almonds
$1/2$ teaspoon ground turmeric

NG HEUNG FUN/WU HSIANG FEN
Chinese Five-Spice Powder

This is the Chinese version of garam masala (page 47). It is aromatic, especially when roasted, and it adds a warm glow to Chinese cooking. Indeed you can add it to virtually any savoury dish. It can be used either whole (in which case omit stage 4) or ground, 1–2 teaspoons being sufficient. This recipe will give you enough for several dishes. Making it little and often is best.

MAKES about 5oz (150g)

1oz (30g) each of:
cinnamon quill
cloves
fennel seeds
star anise
Sichuan peppercorns

1. Mix the five spices together.

2. Preheat your wok (keeping it dry). Add the spices and dry-fry, stirring, for about 1 minute to release the volatile oils.

3. Allow the spices to cool completely.

4. Grind to a fine powder. Keep in an airtight jar. Use within 6 months for maximum flavour.

WEI FEN/BAA KUK TEE
Chinese Ten-Spice Powder

Also called Chinese Taste Powder, this combination of flavourings is used as a sprinkling or dipping condiment. You can vary the proportions of the ingredients to suit your taste.

MAKES about 5oz (150g)

2oz (50g) Chinese five-spice powder (page 46)
2oz (50g) sea salt, finely ground
1oz (30g) caster sugar
1 teaspoon (5g) liquorice powder
1/2oz (15g) chilli powder
1 teaspoon (5g) dried chives

1. Mix all the ingredients together thoroughly.

2. Store in an airtight jar. Use within 6 months for maximum flavour.

SHICHINI TOGARASHI
Japanese Seven-Taste Pepper

This is a most popular Japanese seasoning. The actual seven ingredients vary from recipe to recipe, as does the heat level. Chilli should figure prominently. Sansho pepper can be obtained from specialist Japanese stores. In its absence use Sichuan pepper.

MAKES about 1oz (30g)

Equal parts (1 teaspoon of each is plenty):
sesame seeds
poppy seeds
nori seaweed
grated orange peel
chilli powder
black pepper
sansho pepper

1. Heat the seeds, seaweed and orange peel in a wok for 1 1/2–2 minutes.

2. Allow to cool, then mix with the chilli powder and ground peppers.

3. Grind to a fine powder. Keep in an airtight jar for 3–6 months.

GARAM MASALA

This aromatic mixture of spices is used in Indian cooking as a condiment and to enhance curries. Sprinkle over 2–3 tablespoons towards the end of the cooking time so that the aromatics are not lost.

Garam means 'hot' and masala means 'mixture of spices', and there are as many recipes as there are cooks who make it. This one is my favourite.

MAKES about 7oz (200g)

5 tablespoons (70g) coriander seeds
3 tablespoons (50g) cummin seeds
1 1/2 tablespoons (25g) black peppercorns
3 × 2 inch/5cm pieces (15g) cassia bark
1 tablespoon (15g) cloves
1 tablespoon (15g) brown cardamom pods
1 nutmeg
4–6 bay leaves
1 teaspoon (5g) ground ginger

1. Mix together all the spices except the ground ginger.

2. Preheat your wok or karahi (keeping it dry) on the stove. Add the spices and dry-fry, stirring, for 1–2 minutes. Do not let the spices burn. They should give off a light steam.

3. When they give off an aroma remove from the heat, cool and grind in batches.

4. After grinding, add the ginger, mix thoroughly and store in an airtight jar.

AROMATIC GARAM MASALA

This recipe, which comes from Kashmir, high in the Himalayan mountains, omits hot spices and concentrates on aromatics.

MAKES about 7oz (200g)

4¹/₂ tablespoons (60g) coriander seeds
2¹/₂ tablespoons (40g) white cummin seeds
5 teaspoons (25g) aniseed
5×2 inch/5cm pieces (25g) cassia bark
1¹/₂ tablespoons (25g) green cardamom seeds
  (not pods)
1 tablespoon (15g) cloves
1¹/₂ teaspoons (5g) dried mint
4–6 (2g) bay leaves
1 tablespoon (2g) dried rose petals (optional)
1 teaspoon (¹/₂g) saffron strands (optional)

Dry-fry, grind (see page 45) and store in an airtight jar, as in the previous recipe.

CHAR MASALA

Char in Hindi, Urdu and Pashto means 'four', and *masala*, our familiar 'mixture of spices'. This can be used as a substitute for garam masala if you wish to have a very fragrant mixture of spices with no heat.

The four spices are usually the same, though the proportions can vary.

MAKES about 2oz (50g)

4×2 inch/5cm pieces (20g) cassia bark
4 teaspoons (20g) white cummin seeds
2 teaspoons (10g) green cardamom seeds (not
  pods)
2 teaspoons (10g) cloves

Dry-fry, grind (see page 45) and store in an airtight jar.

PANCH PHORAN

This is a Bengali mixture of five (*panch*) 'spices'. There are several possible combinations, but this is my favourite.

The mixture is always stir-fried in ghee or oil to bring out the aromatics. I've used it in some of the recipes in this book, such as *Dhal Nehri* and *Sindhi Luki Masale Dar*. There is nothing to prevent you using it in others of your choice.

Simply mix together equal parts (1 teaspoon of each is plenty):

white cummin seeds
fennel seeds
fenugreek seeds
mustard seeds
wild onion seeds

BAHARAT

This is the Arab version of garam masala. The origins of the mixture go back at least 1500 years, to the time when the Arabs retained the Mediterranean monopoly of spices. The addition of paprika to the mixture is relatively recent and it enhances both colour and taste.

Use baharat as a condiment or garnish, sprinkling it on to your food as required, or use it as an initial cooking spice, for example in the recipe on page 198.

MAKES 6oz (175g)

4 tablespoons coriander seeds
3 tablespoons cummin seeds
2 tablespoons Hungarian paprika
1 tablespoon ground cinnamon
1 tablespoon ground white pepper
2 teaspoons ground cloves
2 teaspoons ground nutmeg

1. Heat your wok or karahi on the stove. Add the coriander and cummin seeds and dry-fry, stirring, for a couple of minutes. Do not let them burn. They should give off a light steam.

2. Cool and finely grind these spices (see page 45), then mix in the remaining ground spices.

3. Store in the dark in an airtight jar. Use within six months.

MILD CURRY BLEND

This spice mixture is the basis for mild curry paste (see page 49).

MAKES about 9oz (250g)

4¹/₂ tablespoons (60g) coriander seeds
2 tablespoons (30g) white cummin seeds
4 teaspoons (20g) fenugreek seeds
5 teaspoons (25g) gram flour (besan)
5 teaspoons (25g) garlic powder
4 teaspoons (20g) paprika
4 teaspoons (20g) turmeric
4 teaspoons (20g) aromatic garam masala
  (page 47)
1 teaspoon (5g) dry ground curry leaves
1 teaspoon (5g) asafoetida
1 teaspoon (5g) ground ginger
1 teaspoon (5g) chilli powder
1 teaspoon (5g) yellow mustard powder
1 teaspoon (5g) ground black pepper

1. Dry-fry and then grind (see page 45) the first three spices.

2. Mix together well with the rest of the ingredients and store in an airtight jar.

3. For an extremely mild curry powder, omit the last four spices.

4. For extra flavour, add 2 tablespoons white sugar and/or 1 teaspoon salt during the blending.

MILD CURRY PASTE

Many recipes in this book require mild curry paste. You can buy bottled curry paste and the Curry Club makes curry pastes to my recipes. On the other hand you may like to have a go at making your own. It's not at all difficult and the results are better than commercially produced ones simply because the thorough cooking process releases the volatile oils in the spices and removes the raw tastes.

If you use a factory-made curry paste, always re-cook it in oil. This ensures that the rawness (which is inevitable when factories use 500 litre vats) is cooked out.

You can use all the previous quantity mild curry blend to make a large batch of paste. Using vinegar (rather than all water) to make the paste will enable you to preserve it in jars. As with all pickling, sterilise the jars first (see page 286). Top off the paste in the jar with hot oil and inspect after a few days to see that there is no mould. If there is a little, scrape it off and repeat stages 3–5 using more oil.

If you don't wish to make and store a large batch of paste, make just enough for one dish for four people. Where a recipe says '1 tablespoon mild curry paste', measure 1 heaped tablespoon mild curry blend (see page 48) and mix it with water to make a runny paste. When you add it to the recipe make sure that it fries long enough to cook out the rawness.

MAKES about 1¹/₂lb (675g)

1 quantity mild curry blend (page 48) or
  commercial curry powder
6–8fl oz (175–250ml) vinegar (any type)
6–8fl oz (175–250ml) vegetable oil

1. Put the mild curry blend spices in a bowl.

2. Add the vinegar and enough water to make a creamy paste.

3. Heat the oil in a karahi or wok.

4. Add the paste to the oil. It will splatter a bit so be careful.

5. Stir the paste continually to prevent it sticking until the water content is cooked out.

GARAM MASALA PASTE

This is an amalgamation of cooked mild curry paste and dry-roasted garam masala. It produces a nutty dark brown curry paste which gives an especially aromatic result.

MAKES about 7oz (200g)

5oz (150g) mild curry paste (above)
2oz (50g) garam masala (page 47)

1. Cook the curry paste according to the recipe above, and the garam masala according to the recipe on page 47.

2. At any time (months, days, minutes) the two can be combined and the paste is immediately ready to use. It will store indefinitely.

APPETISERS

Appetisers are to be found the world over. In Turkey and the Middle East they're called *mezze*. In Mexico they are *antichuchos* ('little whims') or *batanas*, substantial snacks. In Spain they are *tapas* and in France *hors d'oeuvre*. Brazilians call them *saladhinos* ('salty things').

Most of us enjoy appetisers as part of a meal. We expect them at a restaurant or dinner party. The theory is that appetisers are designed to stimulate the appetite to prepare it for a meal to follow. So they should be teasingly small, leaving the diner rampant for more good things. That's the theory anyway!

In practice, it is all too easy for the cook or restaurant to over-provide, and for the diner to over-eat at this stage of the meal, when most hungry. According to the sixteenth-century French writer Rabelais, 'Appetite comes with eating', so I hope that, taken in moderation, my appetisers will prove Rabelais right, and that they will set you up to enjoy all the dishes which follow. Of course, all appetisers can be enjoyed in isolation as a snack or a meal. In Turkey and the Middle East, for example, appetisers (or *mezze*) served at one meal can total dozens.

No matter how you choose to follow this selection of appetisers, I wish you Bon Appétit!

OPPOSITE *Clockwise from top: Japanese horseradish, Tempura (king prawns and chillies in batter, page 73), Asparagus and Red Soy Soup (page 85), Spicy Japanese Fish Balls with their dipping sauce (page 74)*

CROQUETAS DE CHILI Y QUESO
—— *Cheese, Carrot and Chilli Croquettes* ——

PUERTO RICO

This recipe could have originated anywhere. In fact it is from Puerto Rico, the charismatic Hispanic island in the Caribbean. Serve as a starter with a dip such as Guacamolé (see page 58) or as an accompaniment to a main course dish like *Leitao Recheado* (page 108).

MAKES 8

INGREDIENTS

1lb (450g) grated carrot
2–4 fresh green chillies
3 eggs
5oz (150g) cottage cheese
1/2 teaspoon aromatic salt (page 46)

1 tablespoon chopped fresh
  coriander
plain white flour or cornmeal
7oz (200g) breadcrumbs
corn oil

METHOD

1. Purée the carrot and chillies in a food processor using minimal water. Add 2 eggs, the cottage cheese, salt and fresh coriander.

2. You should have a mouldable paste, not too wet. Add just sufficient flour or cornmeal to achieve this if necessary.

3. Divide the mixture in half. Take one of these halves and divide it into four. Shape each lump into a small sausage shape.

4. Beat the remaining egg and put it in a flat dish. Put the breadcrumbs on a flat dish.

5. Roll the first croquette in the egg, then roll it on the breadcrumbs, covering it completely. Repeat with the others.

6. Heat plenty of oil in a large frying pan. Fry the croquettes, turning them immediately to ensure that they are coated with oil. Fry for 6–8 minutes, until they are golden, turning frequently, and serve.

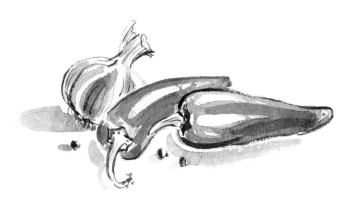

KILAWIN
—— *Marinated Fish* ——

PHILIPPINES

This raw fish marinated in lime juice makes a fascinating comparison with the *ceviche* from Latin America (page 56). Both territories were Spanish and it is likely that the recipe was transported across the world from Mexico to the Philippines. There they added spices and flavourings typical of the East Indies – cloves, nutmeg, coconut and fish sauce.

SERVES 4

INGREDIENTS

1lb (450g) Dover sole, filleted and skinned
6 tablespoons coconut milk powder (page 44)
$1/_2$ teaspoon ground cloves
a pinch of grated nutmeg
1 teaspoon patis or nam pla fish sauce (chef's tip, page 172)
aromatic salt (page 46) to taste

MARINADE
14fl oz (400ml) freshly squeezed lime juice
2 garlic cloves, crushed
1–3 green cayenne chillies, chopped

GARNISH
4 lime wedges
1 red pepper, cut into strips

METHOD

1. Mix the **marinade** ingredients together.

2. Wash and dry the fish fillets, and cut into small pieces.

3. Place the pieces of fish close together in a well-fitting non-metallic flat dish. Pour the marinade over the fish.

4. Cover and refrigerate for up to 8 hours.

5. Remove the fish from the marinade and place it on a bed of green salad.

6. Mix the coconut milk powder with the marinade, ground cloves, nutmeg, fish sauce, salt and enough water to make a creamy dressing.

7. Pour this over the fish, garnish with the lime wedges and red pepper, and serve.

OSTIONES EN ADOBO
—— *Spiced Oysters* ——

COLOMBIA

In this Colombian recipe fresh oysters are coated with an *adobo* (a spice mixture) and grated cheese and then grilled.

SERVES 4 as a starter or 8 as an appetiser

INGREDIENTS

24 fresh Grade 1 oysters (any type)
  in their shells
butter
4oz (110g) grated Cheddar cheese

$1/2$ teaspoon ground cummin
$1/2$ teaspoon ground coriander
$1/2$ teaspoon aromatic salt (page 46)
$1/2$ teaspoon sugar

ADOBO
6 tablespoons thin chilli sauce
  (page 287)
1 teaspoon Hungarian paprika

GARNISH
fresh coriander
black caviar
1 lime

METHOD

1. Preheat the grill to medium heat. Mix the **adobo** items together to make a paste.

2. Open the oysters (see chef's tip).

3. Paint enough paste on to each oyster to cover it. Put a dot of butter and some grated cheese on top.

4. Put the oysters on the grill pan in the midway position and raise the heat a little.

5. Slowly grill for a few minutes (it depends on the size of the oysters) until cooked.

6. Serve, garnished with the fresh coriander, caviar and a squeeze of lime juice.

Chef's Tip

OYSTERS
Oysters can be opened with a strong-bladed kitchen knife or you can purchase a specially designed oyster knife. If the oysters are to be cooked I find an easier method is to place them on the grill pan rack at the lowest point under a lowish grill. The heat will soon open them up. At this point, remove the top shell.

FACING PAGE *Clockwise from top: Avocado, Chilli, Egg and Tomato Dip (page 60) served with tortilla chips, Mixed Bean Sprout Combo (page 68) and Spiced Oysters (above)*

CEVICHE

—— *Marinated Fish* ——

MEXICO

Ceviche is a spicy fish dish found in Mexico and most of Latin America. The fish is raw but, before you turn away thinking it's not for you, give it a try – it's delicious. Choose thin juicy fillets of fish (haddock or mackerel are fine, red snapper is traditional). Simply marinate for a few hours and serve chilled as a stylish starter with a green salad.

SERVES 4

INGREDIENTS

*1lb (450g) fish (see above), filleted
and skinned
2–4 shallots or baby red onions
1 or more tablespoons red chilli
mash (pages 286–7)
2½fl oz (75ml) fresh orange juice*

*2½fl oz (75ml) lemon juice
2½fl oz (75ml) lime juice
½ teaspoon salt*

GARNISH
*whole fresh coriander leaves
fresh lime leaves*

METHOD

1. Wash and dry the fish fillets, and cut into small pieces.

2. Slice the shallots or onions into thin rings.

3. Mix the chilli, fruit juices and salt together to make the marinade.

4. Place the pieces of fish close together in a well-fitting non-metallic flat dish. Pour the marinade over the top, ensuring that it covers the fish. Top with the onion rings.

5. Cover and refrigerate for up to 8 hours (see page 42). During this time the citric acid will penetrate and soften the fish – in effect 'cold cooking' it. When the flesh becomes fully opaque it is ready to eat.

6. Garnish with fresh coriander and lime leaves, and serve with tortilla chips.

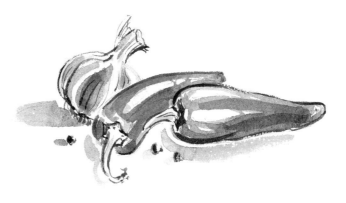

ANTOJITOS

—— *Spicy Heart Appetisers* ——

MEXICO

Literally meaning 'little whim', the *antojitos* of Peru, or *antichuchos* of Mexico, are very popular appetisers sold at street kiosks. Any sort of offal – liver, brain, kidney – can be an *antojitos*. Heart is the subject of this one. Originally (before the Spanish) it was llama heart. Here I use lamb's heart. Marinate it for up to 60 hours and serve as a party appetiser or pre-starter on cocktail sticks.

SERVES 4

INGREDIENTS

8oz (225g) lamb's heart

MARINADE
2 tablespoons red chilli mash (pages 286–7)
$^1/_2$ teaspoon ground cummin
1 garlic clove, crushed
1 tablespoon corn oil

1 tablespoon finely chopped fresh coriander
$^1/_2$ tablespoon finely chopped fresh oregano or 1 teaspoon dried oregano
4fl oz (120ml) red wine
2fl oz (50ml) lemon juice
$^1/_2$ teaspoon salt

METHOD

1. Dice the heart into $^1/_2$ inch (1.25cm) pieces.

2. Mix together the **marinade** ingredients in a large non-metallic bowl and add the heart. Cover and refrigerate for up to 60 hours (see page 42).

3. When ready to cook, preheat the grill to medium heat.

4. Thread each heart piece on to a cocktail stick. Then place all the pieces on the grill rack at the midway position in the grill. Cook until ready (5–8 minutes, depending on the size of the pieces).

5. After about 3 minutes, remove the rack from the grill and pour over all the remaining marinade. Finish cooking.

6. Serve on cocktail sticks with green or mixed salad and a squeeze of lemon juice.

CHILAQUILES
—— Fried Tortillas with Chilli Sauce ——

MEXICO

Pronounced Chiller-killees, and very popular in Mexico, this dish can be made using packet tortilla chips. This version contains *chorizo* (Spanish sausage) and is topped with melted cheese. Other versions contain prawns or chopped avocado. Serve with salsas (pages 290–292).

SERVES 4

INGREDIENTS

6oz (175g) salsa roja *(page 290)*
6oz (175g) salsa verde *(page 292)*
8oz (225g) chorizo, *chopped into bite-size pieces (page 105)*
4 rashers cooked crispy bacon, crumbled
salt

1lb (450g) packet tortilla chips
4–6 tablespoons sour cream
4oz (110g) Mozzarella cheese, chopped
whole fresh coriander leaves
freshly ground black pepper

METHOD

1. Put the two salsas, the chorizo and the crispy bacon together in a pan. Mix them together, heat, and add salt to taste.

2. Just before serving, preheat the grill, add the tortilla chips to the warm salsa mixture in a serving bowl, and top with the sour cream. Put the cheese on top.

3. Place under the grill just long enough for the cheese to melt. Garnish with the coriander and a grind of black pepper. Serve at once.

GUACAMOLÉ
—— Avocado Dip ——

MEXICO

The avocado originated in Latin America. The Aztecs considered it sacred and used it as an aphrodisiac. Only Aztec males were permitted to eat avocado whose name derives from the Aztec words *ahuactl* ('testicle') and *cuahuitl* ('tree'). The word *Guacamolé* (pronounced Gwak-ar-moal-lay) derives from these words to which the word *molé*, meaning 'mixture', is added.

This is a delicious creamy green purée, ideally served with salad or crudités. If guacamolé is made too early the surface goes black, but it is so easy to make that it should really be left until the last minute.

SERVES 2

INGREDIENTS

1 green jalapeno or Kenyan snub
 chilli
1 garlic clove
1 tablespoon chopped onion
1 small green tomato
1 teaspoon chopped fresh
 coriander

1 ripe avocado
salt

GARNISH
a few fresh coriander leaves
2 lemon or lime wedges

METHOD

1. Coarsely chop all the ingredients, except the avocado, and mulch them down in a blender or food processor. This can be done in advance.

2. Just before serving, halve the avocado and remove the pit. Scoop out the flesh (keeping the shells) and add it to the other ingredients. Mulch to a fine purée and add salt to taste.

3. Serve in the shells, garnished with the fresh coriander leaves and a wedge of lemon or lime.

Note: A milder variation is to add 2–3 tablespoons natural yoghurt or cream cheese at stage 1.

AGUATES RELLENOS CON CANGREJO
—— Crab-Stuffed Avocado ——

PERU

This attractive Peruvian recipe uses ripe soft avocado, mixed with sour cream, crab meat and chilli. Serve with a green salad.

SERVES 4

INGREDIENTS

2 ripe avocados
2 tablespoons sour cream
1 teaspoon green chilli mash
 (page 287)

4 tablespoons white crab meat
a few sprigs of fresh parsley

METHOD

1. Halve the avocados and remove the pits.

2. Scoop out the flesh and keep the shells. Chop the flesh, mixing it with the sour cream, chilli mash and crab meat.

3. Refill the avocados, piling the mixture into the shells. Garnish with fresh parsley, and serve chilled.

CAROCO
—— *Avocado, Chilli, Egg and Tomato Dip* ——

BRAZIL

This is a rather special Brazilian version of Guacamolé. In fact the easiest way to make it is to add the extra ingredients to a ready-made Guacamolé, as described in the recipe on page 58. I've used quails' eggs because they are so attractive and delicate, but you can substitute a small hen's egg if you prefer.

SERVES 2

INGREDIENTS

1 quantity Guacamolé (page 58)
¹/₂ teaspoon olive oil
3 quails' eggs, hard-boiled, 2 quartered, 1 sliced
2 black olives, pitted and quartered
2–3 cherry tomatoes, chopped

GARNISH
4–8 thin strips cooked tinned anchovy (optional)
2–4 thin strips sun-dried tomato (chef's tip, page 76)
a few fresh coriander leaves
2 lime wedges

METHOD

1. Make the Guacamolé to the end of stage 2 (page 59).

2. Mix into the purée the oil, the 2 quartered eggs, the olives and tomatoes.

3. Serve in the avocado shells, garnishing with strips of anchovy (optional) and sun-dried tomato, some sliced egg, a few fresh coriander leaves and the wedges of lime.

Note: You can also add cooked peeled shrimps to the purée and/or as garnish 2–3 chopped sun-dried tomatoes in oil.

PAN-ROASTED PEANUTS

INDONESIA

These are delicious in their own right as an appetiser, to serve with drinks. They also appear cooked in some of my recipes such as *Caruru* (page 168) or as a garnish. The most tedious part of the job is removing the clinging pink skins. Other nuts, such as cashews, can also be pan-roasted.

MAKES 5oz (150g)

INGREDIENTS

5oz (150g) shelled peanuts   *some chilli powder (optional)*

METHOD

1. Preheat a karahi or wok on the stove. Put the peanuts in and dry-fry for about 3 minutes. Be careful though. Depending on the heat, some may start blackening before this.

2. To stop the roasting, transfer them at once to a cold pan. With luck, the skins will have come away – but never, it seems, all of them. When they're cool enough, rub them together to loosen the remaining skins. Then pick the nuts out and sprinkle with chilli powder (if using).

3. They should keep in an airtight jar for 3–4 weeks, but they'll probably get eaten much sooner.

KAUSHWE-KYAW

—— *Chicken and Shrimp Noodles* ——

BURMA

Burma, a forgotten land locked away under a dictatorial regime, provides the missing link between Indian and Chino-Thai cooking, as shown by this typically simple noodle dish, spiced with garam masala.

These noodles can be made in advance in minutes, refrigerated and served cold. I always serve other starters with them, using them as a bed for *Kokis* (page 69) or *Kuroke* (page 74) or *Teochew Satay* (page 62).

SERVES 4 as part of a starter

INGREDIENTS

3¹/₂ oz (100g) egg noodles
4oz (110g) cooked chicken meat, in large shreds
5oz (150g) cooked baby shrimps, shell on
2 teaspoons garam masala (page 47)

1–3 fresh red chillies, chopped
2 tablespoons walnut or pistachio nut oil
1 tablespoon whole fresh coriander leaves
1 tablespoon chopped fresh mint
¹/₂ teaspoon aromatic salt (page 46)

METHOD

1. Put the noodles in a pot of boiling water and turn off the heat. After 1–2 minutes stir and carefully loosen the noodles. Repeat a few minutes later, by which time they will be fully softened.

2. Drain and cool.

3. Mix all the remaining ingredients with the noodles. Chill and serve.

TEOCHEW SATAY
—— *Grilled Pork Strips with Peanut Sauce* ——

MALAYSIA

Of Persian origin, being based on kebabs, this popular snack is found all over Malaysia and Indonesia. Thin strips of chicken or meat, in this case pork, are marinated in spices, grilled and served with a peanut sauce.

MAKES 10

INGREDIENTS

1lb (450g) lean leg of pork, off the bone
10×8 inch (20cm) bamboo skewers

MARINADE
4 tablespoons tamarind purée (page 44)
2 tablespoons fresh lemon juice
1 teaspoon cummin seeds, roasted and ground
2 teaspoons coriander seeds, roasted and ground
1 teaspoon chilli powder
^{1}/$_2$ teaspoon lemon grass powder
^{1}/$_2$ teaspoon Chinese five-spice powder (page 46)

PEANUT SAUCE
6 tablespoons smooth peanut butter
2 teaspoons ketjap manis (chef's tip, page 192)
4 tablespoons coconut milk powder (page 44)
1 teaspoon sambal manis (page 288)
^{1}/$_2$ teaspoon aromatic salt (page 46)
1 teaspoon garlic powder
^{1}/$_2$ teaspoon Chinese five-spice powder (page 46)
1 teaspoon blachan shrimp paste (chef's tip, page 172, optional)
4 tablespoons light oil

METHOD

1. Cut the pork into strips approximately 1^1/$_2$×^{3}/$_4$×^{1}/$_2$ inch (4×2×1.25cm). Beat these to about 2^1/$_2$×1^1/$_4$×^{1}/$_4$ inch (6.5×3.25×0.6cm).

2. You should get at least 16 strips, plus some small offcuts (beat these out too).

3. Mix the **marinade** ingredients together in a large bowl. Immerse the pork strips, cover and refrigerate for up to 60 hours (see page 42).

4. Soak the bamboo skewers in water for 1 hour. This gives them a greater resistance to burning during cooking.

5. Mix the **peanut sauce** ingredients (except the oil) together with enough water to make a pourable paste. Heat the oil and stir-fry the paste continually for 2^1/$_2$–3 minutes to cook out the water and reduce the sauce. Remove from the heat and keep warm.

6. Thread two pieces of meat on to a skewer, leaving space between the pieces. Repeat with the other skewers. Put the offcuts on to two additional skewers. Stir any surplus marinade into the sauce.

7. Preheat the grill to medium heat. Put the skewers on the grill rack over the grill pan. Place this in the midway position. Cook for 4–5 minutes, turning once.

8. Quickly reheat the sauce and serve in a small bowl with the skewers on a bed of salad and spring onion leaves.

BELOW *Thai Spring Rolls (page 70) served with Sweet Chilli Sauce (page 288) and Grilled Pork Strips with Peanut Sauce (opposite)*

KARI PATIS
—— Curry Patties ——

SRI LANKA

These little Sri Lankan vegetable curry-filled patties (about 3 inches or 7.5cm in length) are just the ticket at any time of day or night – for a snack, a picnic or a party. They're quite easy to make and can be frozen before or after baking. Leftover filling can be used in a curry.

MAKES 20

INGREDIENTS

14oz (400g) packet frozen puff pastry (or home-made)

FILLING
3 tablespoons niter kebbeh (page 43) or ghee (page 43)
2–4 garlic cloves, crushed
1 inch (2.5cm) cube ginger, grated
1–2 fresh green cayenne chillies, chopped
4 tablespoons dried onions (chef's tip)
4 tablespoons coconut milk powder (page 44)
3–4 fresh spinach leaves, chopped

1 tablespoon chopped fresh coriander
5–6 tablespoons cooked dhal
4oz (110g) mashed potato
2–3 chopped devilled chilli cashew nuts (page 65)
1 teaspoon ground aromatic salt (page 46)

SPICES
1 teaspoon cummin seeds
1 teaspoon mustard seeds
1/2 teaspoon ground turmeric
10 curry leaves

METHOD

1. Heat the niter kebbeh or ghee in a karahi or wok. Stir-fry the **spices** for 20 seconds, add the garlic and ginger and stir-fry for 30 seconds more. Add the chillies and dried onions and stir-fry for 30 seconds.

2. Add the coconut milk powder, spinach, fresh coriander and the dhal and enough water to make a thick mixture. Stir-fry for 1–2 minutes, to reduce a little.

3. Remove from the heat. Mix in the mashed potato, nuts and salt and leave to cool completely. Preheat the oven to 425°F/220°C/Gas 7.

4. Thaw the pastry, then cut it into four equal pieces. Roll each piece to 1/8 inch (3mm) thickness and about 6 inches (15cm) square. Using a 3 inch (7.5cm) round pastry cutter, cut out 4 discs.

5. Repeat with the other pieces of pastry until you have 16 discs and some spare pastry.

6. Roll out the spare pastry and cut as many more discs as you can – it should make four more.

7. Put 1–2 teaspoons filling on to one half of the first disc. Fold it over and press it closed. Repeat until all the patties are made.

8. Place them on a flour-dusted baking tray and bake for 10 minutes. Inspect. They should be almost perfectly golden. If not, bake for a few more minutes. Serve hot or cold with chutneys.

Chef's Tip

DRIED ONIONS
Dried onion flakes are available in two forms: unfried and fried. I find both versions very useful as they save 15 minutes of stir-frying.

Usually I just add them dry to my cooking. I ignore the manufacturer's instructions to soak them first in water. However, when frying, dried onions will burn very fast. Stir-fry continuously and briskly and when the desired colour is reached add a little cold water to stop them cooking.

KAJU BADAN
—— Devilled Chilli Cashew Nuts ——

SRI LANKA

These are excellent with an aperitif or as a garnish for many of the spicy dishes in this book, such as *Kari Patis* (see opposite). Buy an 18oz (500g) packet of shelled uncooked cashew nuts and prepare all of them. They will keep for ages in an airtight jar.

MAKES 18oz (500g)

INGREDIENTS

6–7 tablespoons vegetable or corn oil
18oz (500g) bag of cashew nuts
aromatic salt (page 46) to taste
chilli powder to taste

METHOD

1. Heat the oil in a karahi or wok over a high heat.

2. Carefully add all the nuts. Lower the heat to medium, and stir-fry briskly and continuously until the nuts start to go golden.

3. Strain the nuts (keeping the oil for future use) and put the hot nuts into a bowl. Immediately sprinkle over the salt and chilli powder to taste. Allow to cool. Eat at once and/or store in an airtight jar.

Note: At stage 2 keep turning the nuts to prevent patchy burning and watch out – they suddenly go golden. They also continue to change colour after you've strained them. So under rather than overcook.

SINGHODAS
Gujerati Samosas

INDIA

Singhoda is the Gujerati name for samosa, that well-known, well-loved triangular patti. In the Indian state of Gujerat they would fill the *singhoda* with a mild sweetish filling. You can recreate this by omitting the chilli and adding sultanas and brown sugar. Either way this filling is made almost instantly and requires no cooking. Use ready-made filo or spring roll pastry and your work is made easier. Swap the fillings between this and the *Kari Patis* (see page 64) as the mood takes you.

MAKES 24

INGREDIENTS

1 packet spring roll or filo pastry
plain white flour
oil for deep-frying

FILLING
4oz (110g) canned chickpeas,
 crushed
7oz (200g) canned hummus
4 tablespoons dried onions (chef's
 tip, page 65)
2–4 garlic cloves, crushed

1 tablespoon chopped fresh
 coriander
5–6 dry or fresh curry leaves,
 chopped
1–3 fresh red cayenne chillies,
 chopped
2 tablespoons coconut milk
 powder (page 44)
1 tablespoon desiccated coconut
1 teaspoon mustard seeds, roasted
1 teaspoon aromatic salt (page 46)

METHOD

1. Mix the **filling** ingredients together in a bowl to make a thick, dryish but cohesive mixture, using a little water as needed.

2. Now to the pastry (see chef's tip, page 71). Open the packet and pull out enough sheets to create 24 rectangles about 8×3 inches (20×7.5cm) for normal size samosas. While you are working on one sheet cover the rest with a clean, damp tea towel to keep them moist and pliable. If you are feeling ambitious you can make dainty cocktail samosas. Try 4×1½ inch (10×4cm) rectangles. They will take much longer to make but the results are ideal for a party. Simply scale down the filling quantities to a quarter of the normal size version.

3. Mix some flour with enough water to make a glue-like paste to stick each samosa together.

4. Take the first rectangle. Place 1 teaspoon of filling on it (see right). Make the first diagonal fold, then the second and third.

5. Open the pouch and top up with some more filling. Do not overfill, or it will burst during cooking.

6. Brush some flour and water paste on the remaining flap, sticking it over the opening to seal in the filling. Trim off the excess. Repeat with all the others.

7. Cook in a deep-fryer at 375°F/190°C (chip-frying temperature) for 8–10 minutes.

8. Serve with chutney.

Note: Samosas can be frozen before or after cooking.

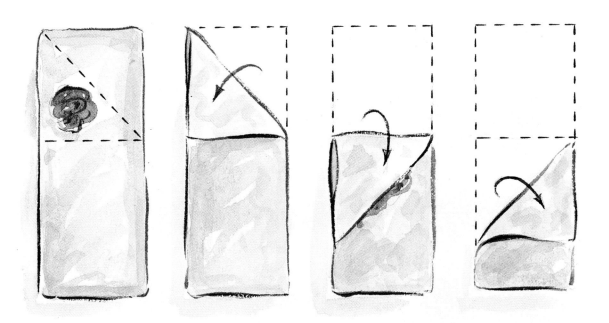

MOONG CHANA SALAT
—— *Mixed Bean Sprout Combo* ——

INDIA

I came across this fresh light dish of spiced mixed bean sprouts at the Seaview Bar at Bombay's Taj Mahal Hotel. Many supermarkets now sell packets containing a mixture of moong, chana, chickpea and other bean sprouts. Alternatively, you can grow your own (see chef's tip). Served cold, it makes a great salad dish or an accompaniment.

SERVES 2

INGREDIENTS

5oz (150g) mixed bean sprouts
2 tablespoons paneer (page 228), cut into $1/4$ inch (6 mm) cubes
1 teaspoon very finely diced red bell pepper
1 teaspoon very finely diced green bell pepper

$1/2$ teaspoon diced green cayenne chilli
2–3 tablespoons Pat's Spicy Vinaigrette (page 296)
salt to taste

METHOD

Mix all the ingredients together in a bowl and serve chilled.

Chef's Tip

GROWING BEAN SPROUTS

Fresh bean sprouts are high in vitamins and low in calories. They taste great too. Any dried whole lentils or pulses will work. It takes 5–7 days to sprout the beans. Don't buy packet seed from seed growers, as it's far more expensive than the identical item from a food shop.

1. Thoroughly clean a $1/2$ pint (300ml) glass jar.

2. Put about 2oz (50g) lentils (one type or mixed) in the jar.

3. Fill the jar with warm water and let it stand for 10 minutes.

4. Drain all the water away, cover the jar and place it on its side in a dark, warm place – preferably at about 75°F (23°C).

5. Repeat the warm water soak and rinse process (stages 3 and 4) at 12-hourly intervals for 5–7 days, after which the sprouts will be ready to eat.

Note: Kept in the dark the sprouts will be white. If you wish to have green sprouts (which taste the same) move them into a light (warm) place after 2 days.

KOKIS

—— *Coconut Fritters* ——

THE MALDIVES The Maldives are a group of 'desert islands' off southern India. If ever I were on a desert island and was asked to name the one luxury item I'd like to have with me it would be an everlasting supply of *kokis*. They are a kind of savoury waffle made in pretty moulds. These are dipped into the batter. If you have a waffle mould use that. Otherwise just spoon dollops into a deep-fryer. Plain rice is satisfactory but flavoured left-over rice is even better.

SERVES 4

INGREDIENTS

3oz (75g) rice flour
3oz (75g) coconut milk powder
   (page 44)
3oz (75g) cooked rice
1 egg
$^1/_2$ teaspoon ground turmeric

3 tablespoons fresh lime juice
1–3 teaspoons red chilli mash
   (pages 286–7)
1 teaspoon aromatic salt (page 46)
oil for deep-frying

METHOD

1. Simply mix all the ingredients (except the oil) in a bowl with just sufficient water to make a thick batter.

2. Preheat the oil in a deep-fryer to 375°F/190°C (chip-frying temperature).

3. If you have a *koki* or waffle mould, dip it three-quarters of the way into the batter. Lower it into the hot oil. The *koki* should slip off into the oil. Add the remaining *kokis*, waiting a few seconds between each to keep the oil temperature stable.

4. Alternatively, lower a tablespoonful of batter into the hot oil. Wait a few seconds and repeat, until you have used all the batter.

5. Deep-fry for about 8 minutes and serve with Trevor Pack's Chilli Chutney (see page 295).

HAE-KOON
—— Thai Spring Rolls ——

THAILAND

These are spring rolls, Thai-style. Traditionally made from thin slices of bean curd, you'll now find them in Thailand made from spring roll pastry, as we make them here. Serve with green salad and Thai Hot Chilli Sauce (page 289) or Vietnamese Chilli Dip (page 290).

MAKES 24

INGREDIENTS

24 sheets spring roll or filo pastry, each sheet being 8 inches (20cm) square
cornflour
oil for deep-frying

FILLING
4oz (110g) lean leg of pork
2oz (50g) white crab meat
2oz (50g) brown crab meat
1 inch (2.5cm) cube galangale or ginger

6–8 red Thai baby cayenne chillies
some bean sprouts, finely chopped
2 tablespoons sesame oil
2 garlic gloves, crushed
2–3 spring onions, bulbs and leaves shredded
1 tablespoon chopped fresh basil
1 stalk fresh lemon grass
$\frac{1}{2}$ teaspoon nam pla fish sauce (chef's tip, page 172)

METHOD

1. Finely mince together the pork, crab meat, galangale, chillies and bean sprouts.

2. Heat the sesame oil in a wok over a high heat. Stir-fry the garlic for 30 seconds, add the spring onions and fresh basil and continue to stir-fry for 1–2 more minutes. Add the minced mixture, the lemon grass and the fish sauce and stir-fry for about 6 minutes.

3. Allow to cool.

4. To make the spring rolls, mix some cornflour with water to make a paste. Set aside.

5. Spring roll (or filo) pastry needs careful handling (see chef's tip). Open the packet and remove 1 sheet of pastry. Cover the packet with a clean, damp tea towel.

6. Lay the sheet flat on a clean work surface.

7. Place about 3 tablespoons filling on one corner of the sheet.

8. Spread it evenly over about 4 inches (10cm).

9. Roll the sheet over the filling once.

10. Fold the sides in and over the covered filling.

11. Roll up reasonably tightly until a small triangle remains.

12. Brush some cornflour paste on the triangle and finish rolling up. Repeat with the other 23 sheets.

13. Cook in a deep-fryer at 375°F/190°C for 8 minutes.

Note: Surplus spring rolls can be frozen before or after cooking.

Chef's Tip

SPRING ROLL OR FILO PASTRY

These are both thin pre-rolled pastries available in packets and containing several sheets. Using it requires some care. Once out of the packet the pastry will soon dry up, becoming brittle and unpliable. To keep the pastry moist, use a clean damp cold tea towel to cover the rest while you are working on one sheet.

Incidentally, spare pastry can be returned to its packet, wrapped in cling film and stored in the freezer.

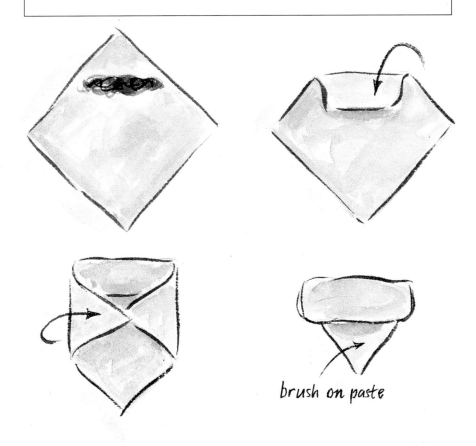

brush on paste

CHA GIO
—— *Crispy Crab Rolls* ——

VIETNAM

Vietnamese cooking is Chinese- and Thai-influenced. Called *nem ran* in North Vietnam and *cha gio* in the South, these spring rolls are smaller and crispier than those in the previous recipe. The principal difference is that these rolls use rice paper as their wrapper instead of pastry. Use the same filling, and the same wrapping technique, except that rice papers come in discs rather than squares.

SERVES 4

METHOD

1. Follow the method in the previous recipe but cook the spring rolls for only 5 minutes.

2. To serve, wrap the rolls in lettuce leaves and dip into *Nuoc Cham* sauce (page 290).

Q'ROOT
—— *Savoury Yoghurt* ——

AFGHANISTAN

Q'root (pronounced *Kroot*) is strained yoghurt which is pressed and dried into hard white marbles. These keep indefinitely and are reconstituted with water when required. A favourite way of eating *Q'root* is to combine it with salt, pepper, garlic and mint. In this recipe I am using yoghurt, cream cheese (or cottage cheese) and sour cream to create a thick and creamy texture, such as you would get by reconstituting the dried *Q'root*. Use *Q'root* as a starter, snack, dip or chutney.

SERVES 4

INGREDIENTS

5fl oz (150ml) Greek or strained yoghurt
5fl oz (150ml) cream cheese or cottage cheese
5fl oz (150ml) sour cream

1–2 garlic cloves, finely chopped
1 teaspoon ground black pepper
1/2 teaspoon aromatic salt (page 46)
chopped fresh or dried mint to garnish

METHOD

In a bowl mix together the yoghurt, the cream cheese or cottage cheese and sour cream, beating briskly. Add the garlic, pepper and salt. Chill in the refrigerator for a minimum of 2 hours before serving in individual bowls garnished with mint.

TEMPURA
—— *Fish and Vegetables in Batter* ——

JAPAN

For those who think Japanese food is all about raw fish, the next three recipes should be a pleasant surprise. *Tempura* is a great starter, involving a choice of the freshest ingredients dipped in the lightest batter and served at once, along with a dipping sauce (common to both *Tempura* and *Kuroke*, see next recipe). Chillies did not figure largely in traditional Japanese cooking until relatively recently. But the Japanese are now taking to chilli heat in a big way. Other hot flavourings, like wasabi, green horseradish and pepper, have always been popular in Japan.

I'll leave the choice of ingredients to you – but here are some suggestions. Allow about 6–8 different items per person. The batter makes enough to coat about 32 items.

INGREDIENTS

king prawns, raw, shelled and head off but tail left on
Dover sole, filleted and cut into 1 inch (2.5cm) squares
beaten rump steak or pork, cut into 1 inch (2.5cm) squares
chicken breast, cut into 1 inch (2.5cm) cubes
fresh button mushrooms
red and/or green bell pepper, cut into large pieces
red and/or green whole cayenne chillies
celery sticks, cut into pieces
white radish (daikon or mooli), cut into cubes

courgettes, sliced
fresh horseradish, cut into cubes
spring onion bulbs with a few leaves attached
fresh ginger, sliced
fresh red or green chillies, any type
oil for deep-frying

BATTER
8oz (225g) plain white flour
$1/2$ pint (300ml) cold water
1 egg
$1/2$ teaspoon salt
$1/8$ teaspoon baking powder

METHOD

1. Mix the **batter** ingredients together in a large bowl, whisking until smooth. You'll almost certainly need to add a little more cold water to achieve a smooth, easily pourable, thinnish batter.

2. Use the batter at once. Dip each item into the batter (use chopsticks or a fork), knock off excess batter and place the item in a deep-fryer with the oil preheated to 375°F/190°C (chip-frying temperature).

3. Cooking times will vary between 3 and 8 minutes, depending on the size, density and wetness of the item, so watch for crispness and a pale golden colour.

4. Make the dipping sauce (see next recipe) and serve at once.

KUROKE

—— *Spicy Japanese Fish Balls or Fingers* ——

JAPAN

The Japanese have a way with fish. Eaten cold, these fish fingers transform your view of Captain Bird's Eye! I've used Japanese ultra-hot red santaka chillies. They are a cayenne derivative so you can use those as a substitute. The dipping sauce has its own heat source too – wasabi (hot green horseradish powder) for which there is no substitute. Nor should you omit the sake (Japanese rice wine, pronounced sar-kay), which should also be served hot in liqueur glasses to accompany this starter. In fact it accompanies the cooking rather well too!

Bonito (dried fish) flakes, sake and wasabi powder are all available at Japanese food shops.

MAKES 16

INGREDIENTS

14oz (400g) cod or haddock
  steaks, filleted
1 medium-sized carrot, finely
  grated
2–3 spring onions, bulbs and leaves
  finely shredded
2–3 red santaka chillies, chopped
1 tablespoon cornflour
1 egg
1/2 teaspoon salt
oil for deep-frying

DIPPING SAUCE
4fl oz (120ml) Japanese rice wine
  (sake)
2 tablespoons tomato ketchup
1 teaspoon soy sauce
2–4 teaspoons wasabi powder
1/2 teaspoon black pepper

GARNISH
spring onion leaves, shredded
bonito (dried fish) flakes

METHOD

1. Combine all the ingredients, except the oil, **garnish** and **dipping sauce**, into a mouldable mash, using a little water as needed.

2. Divide the mash into four, then four again, to create 16 equal portions.

3. Shape each portion into a finger or ball.

4. Heat the oil to 375°F/190°C (chip-frying temperature) in a deep-fryer. Cook the *kurokes* for 8–10 minutes.

5. During stage 4, combine the **dipping sauce** ingredients. Heat in a small saucepan for 1–2 minutes.

6. Serve the *kurokes* and the sauce hot or cold. Garnish with the spring onion leaves and bonito (dried fish) flakes.

YAKITORI

—— *Skewered Grilled Chicken* ——

JAPAN

This is the Japanese version of the kebab, using marinated chicken breast, heart or liver and fresh vegetables of your choice. See the *Tempura* recipe (page 73) for vegetable ideas. Marinate the chicken for 1–2 hours but not the vegetables.

MAKES 8

INGREDIENTS

12oz (350g) skinned and filleted chicken breast and chicken hearts, livers, kidneys (see chef's tip, page 250)
8×8 inch (20cm) bamboo skewers
vegetables of your choice
2 tablespoons sesame oil

MARINADE
6fl oz (175ml) Japanese rice wine (sake)

2 tablespoons tomato ketchup
2 tablespoons soy sauce
1 teaspoon brown sugar
2–4 teaspoons wasabi powder
1 teaspoon red chilli mash (pages 286–7)
2 garlic cloves, crushed
2–3 spring onions, bulbs and leaves shredded

METHOD

1. Cut the chicken breast into bite-sized cubes.

2. Mix the **marinade** ingredients together in a large bowl. Put in the chicken breast pieces, heart, liver and kidney, cover and refrigerate for 1–2 hours (see page 42).

3. Soak the skewers in warm water for 1 hour to prevent them burning during cooking.

4. Preheat the grill to medium heat. Thread the chicken pieces interspersed with vegetables on to the skewers, leaving small gaps between each item. Put the skewers on the grill rack over the grill pan and place at the midway position.

5. Cook for about 4 minutes. Remove and baste with excess marinade. Turn over and return to the heat for 3 more minutes.

6. Repeat for a final 2–3 minutes.

7. During stage 6, heat the sesame oil in a pan. Carefully add the spare marinade (there should be at least half left) and stir-fry it for less than a minute. Serve it with the skewers as a warm dip.

IMOJO

—— *Fish and Shrimp Salad* ——

SIERRA LEONE

In Sierra Leone, they cook, then strain and cool the ingredients to make this salad. Here, for convenience, I've used pre-cooked fish and shrimps. The resulting creamy salad, spiked with chillies, makes a tasty starter served alongside other delicacies.

SERVES 4 as part of a starter

INGREDIENTS

7oz (200g) cod steaks, cooked
8oz (225g) shrimps, peeled and cooked
2–3 garlic cloves, finely chopped
1 teaspoon green peppercorns in brine
1 tablespoon chopped sun-dried tomatoes in oil (chef's tip)
2–3 spring onions, bulbs and leaves chopped

2 tablespoons chopped red bell pepper
2–3 green African snub or jalapeno chillies, sliced
1 teaspoon Hungarian paprika
2 tablespoons fresh lime juice
2 tablespoons olive oil
3fl oz (75ml) sour cream
aromatic salt (page 46)

METHOD

1. Using a fork, carefully flake the cod into small pieces.

2. In a large bowl, mix all the remaining ingredients together with the fish, adding aromatic salt to taste.

3. Cover and refrigerate for 2–3 hours to marinate (see page 42). Serve chilled.

Chef's Tip

SUN-DRIED TOMATOES

These are one of Italy's great flavouring secrets. Exceptionally tasty egg-shaped plum tomatoes called *pomodoro* (or 'apple of gold') are skinned, sliced, seeded and dried in the Mediterranean sun. You can purchase them dried or suspended in olive oil. The former are cheaper and can be ground to make a powder which you can add to spice mixtures. Alternatively, they can be reconstituted overnight by soaking in water, or they can be bottled in oil for indefinite storage.

You will notice that I often call for them, even in non-Italian recipes. Their intensity of flavour is unmatchable.

INGELEGDE VIS
—— *Pickled Fish* ——

SOUTH AFRICA The Portuguese had the opportunity to colonise the southern extremity of Africa but they chose not to bother. This left the way open for the Dutch to use these lush lands in the mid-1600s as their supply base halfway between Holland and their East Indies colonies. They soon brought Indonesian and Malaysian slaves to South Africa and with them came this pickled fish dish. It became popular with Dutch mariners as an onboard delicacy.

The traditional choice of fish is pike (*snoek*). However, as pike is not usually available, I've chosen a common freshwater brown trout instead. But you can go and catch a pike if you wish! Frying the filleted fish first is essential to dry it and prepare it for pickling.

SERVES 4

INGREDIENTS

6 tablespoons ground nut oil
1 teaspoon ground turmeric
2–3 brown trout, skinned and
  filleted
1 inch (2.5cm) cube ginger, sliced
2–3 bay leaves

1 tablespoon black peppercorns
4oz (110g) sliced onion
2–3 red cayenne chillies, sliced
2 teaspoons aromatic salt (page 46)
distilled malt vinegar

METHOD

1. Put the oil in a flat pan over a high heat. Add the turmeric and briskly stir-fry it for 10–15 seconds. Add the fish fillets. Lower the heat and fry the fish for about 10 minutes, turning once halfway through.

2. Remove the fish and put it in a large sterilised jar or 2–3 smaller ones (see page 286).

3. Retaining the oil in the pan, increase the heat and add the ginger, bay leaves and peppercorns. After 10 seconds, add the onion, chillies and salt and stir-fry for about 10 minutes.

4. When cool, put this mixture in the jar(s) with the fish. Top up with the vinegar.

5. After 1–2 days shake the jar(s) to release any trapped air and, if necessary, top up with extra vinegar.

6. Store for 2–3 weeks before using. It can be served at once, or kept until it matures into a chutney.

SOUPS

Soups are a subject in themselves and they are to be found all over the world. We can treat them as starters if we wish, or they can be offered as part of a main course, in the way that most Asian countries would serve them.

In Japan, for example, soup is not served before the rest of the meal, but with it. Most soups, but particularly the more substantial ones like *Caldo Tlapeno* from Mexico or *Shorba Sultani* from India, can be served simply and deliciously as a meal in themselves, with some bread to help mop up. See the chapter on Breads for some ideas on what to serve with your soup.

OPPOSITE *Clockwise from back: A glass of Sangritta (page 284), a bottle of Hornitos, Mexico's favourite brand of tequila, fresh soft Tortillas (page 262), Chicken Soup with Mexican Vegetables (page 81), Mexican Marinated Fish (page 56) and Chicken Soup with Lime (page 80) served with strips of fresh Tortilla*

SOPADE LIMA
—— *Chicken Soup with Lime* ——

MEXICO

A light consommé with plenty of flavour – the lime juice should be tart but not dominant.

SERVES 4

INGREDIENTS

3–4 bay leaves
$^1/_2$ teaspoon green peppercorns (in brine or freeze-dried)
2 chicken legs and/or carcass remains from a roast chicken
3 tablespoons corn oil
2–4 garlic cloves, chopped
4–6 spring onions, leaves and bulbs chopped
2–4 African snub or jalapeno chillies, chopped

1 tablespoon chopped fresh coriander
2 tablespoons sun-dried tomatoes in oil, chopped (chef's tip, page 76)
salt
juice of 6 limes
whole fresh coriander leaves
4 lime wedges
4 freshly cooked Tortillas (page 262)

METHOD

1. Bring $1^1/_2$ pints (900ml) water to the boil with the bay leaves, peppercorns, chicken legs and/or carcass remains, but no skin or fat. Simmer for about 30 minutes, then strain and reserve the stock and, when cool enough, remove any edible meat.

2. During stage 1 heat the oil in a frying pan. Stir-fry the garlic for 30 seconds, then the spring onions and chillies for 2–3 minutes.

3. Bring the stock back to the simmer and add the stir-fry items, chicken, the fresh coriander and the sun-dried tomatoes. Add salt to taste.

4. Ladle into four bowls, equally distributing the lime juice and whole fresh coriander leaves. Place a lime wedge on the rim of each bowl. Cut the tortillas into strips and serve alongside the soup.

CALDO TLAPENO
——— *Chicken Soup with Mexican Vegetables* ———

MEXICO

This popular Mexican soup should be quite chunky and taste hot and sour.

SERVES 4

INGREDIENTS

2–3 tablespoons corn oil
2–4 garlic cloves, sliced
4oz (110g) onion, chopped
2–4 green chillies, chopped
$^1/_2$ red bell pepper, chopped
1$^1/_2$ pints (900ml) water or chicken
  stock
2 tablespoons uncooked rice
6–8oz (175–225g) fresh or cooked
  chicken pieces on the bone or
  off, but skinned

$^1/_2$ avocado, chopped
2–3 tablespoons vinegar, any type
3 tablespoons tinned or frozen
  sweetcorn
salt
1 lemon or lime

GARNISH
whole fresh coriander leaves
4 lemon or lime wedges

METHOD

1. Heat the oil in a 4–5 pint (2.25–2.75 litre) saucepan and stir-fry the garlic for 30 seconds. Add the onion, chillies and red pepper and stir-fry these for 5–8 minutes.

2. Add the water or stock, the rice, and the chicken and simmer for 20–30 minutes.

3. Add the avocado, vinegar and sweetcorn, and salt to taste, and simmer for about 5 more minutes.

4. Add a squeeze of lemon or lime juice and ladle into four bowls.

5. Garnish with the whole coriander leaves and a lemon or lime wedge on the rim of each bowl.

SOTO AYAM
—— *Malaysian Chicken Soup* ——

MALAYSIA

This soup is to be found everywhere in Malaysia and in neighbouring Indonesia. It's virtually a national dish. The basis is chicken. There they would use the best part of a whole chicken. Here I use the carcass of a roasted chicken with a reasonable amount of flesh on it.

SERVES 4

INGREDIENTS

1 leftover roasted chicken carcass with some cooked flesh remaining, jointed
1 teaspoon nam pla *fish sauce (chef's tip, page 172)*
1 stalk fresh lemon grass
2 tablespoons ground nut oil
2–4 garlic cloves, crushed
1 inch (2.5cm) cube ginger, grated
1 teaspoon blachan *shrimp paste (chef's tip, page 172)*
4–5 spring onions, bulbs and leaves chopped
6oz (175g) raw chicken breast, skinned, filleted and cut into thin slices

1 tablespoon chopped fresh coriander
1 tablespoon ketjap manis *(chef's tip, page 192)*
aromatic salt *(page 46)*

SPICES
1 teaspoon coriander seeds, crushed
1 teaspoon black peppercorns
5–6 curry leaves
$^{1}/_{2}$ teaspoon ground turmeric *(chef's tip, page 183)*

GARNISH
a few feathery fronds of fresh dill

METHOD

1. Put the jointed chicken carcass, the fish sauce, the lemon grass and 2 pints (1.2 litres) water in a 5–6 pint (2.75–3.5 litre) saucepan, and bring to a simmer.

2. Simmer for about 45 minutes. About halfway through, extract the carcass pieces and pull the flesh off the bones. Return the flesh to the pan and discard the bones.

3. Strain the soup, pressing the meat hard against the strainer to extract all the liquid. Discard the solids.

4. Bring the soup back to a simmer.

5. Heat the oil in a wok or karahi over a high heat. Add the garlic and ginger and stir-fry for 30 seconds. Add the **spices**, the shrimp paste and the spring onions and stir-fry for a further 3–4 minutes.

6. Add the sliced raw chicken breast pieces and stir-fry these in the mixture for another 3–4 minutes.

7. Add this mixture to the simmering liquid. Add the fresh coriander, *ketjap manis* and aromatic salt to taste. Simmer for a few more minutes.

8. Garnish with the fresh dill and serve very hot.

SOPA DE AJO
—— *Garlic Soup* ——

SPAIN

This popular soup is to be found wherever the Spanish and Portuguese created their empires. Curiously, the further from home the soup went, the more chillies it seemed to require. Although there is so much garlic in the recipe its flavour does not overpower the soup. Try it and see!

SERVES 4

INGREDIENTS

1 teaspoon olive oil
2 tablespoons corn oil
20 garlic cloves, chopped
4oz (110g) onion, chopped
1¹/₂ pints (900ml) water or
  vegetable stock
1–4 fresh red chillies, any type,
  chopped
1 tablespoon chopped fresh parsley

1 tablespoon chopped fresh basil
salt
4 eggs

GARNISH
fried bread croûtons
a few sprigs of fresh parsley
freshly milled black pepper

METHOD

1. Heat the oils in a saucepan over a high heat, then stir-fry the garlic for 30 seconds.

2. Add the onion and reduce the heat. Stir-fry for 10 minutes, until the onion becomes translucent and begins to brown.

3. Add the water or stock and chillies. Simmer for 30–45 minutes.

4. Add the fresh herbs, salt to taste and, one at a time, the eggs.

5. When these are poached (about 4 minutes), serve the soup in four bowls with one egg per portion. Serve, garnished with the croûtons, parsley and some generous twists of black pepper.

AJI GAZPACHO
—— Chilli Cold Soup ——

COLOMBIA

One of Spain's main claims to fame is its wonderful gazpacho, that cold puréed soup which turns sweltering summer days into savoury dreams. This Colombian version gets its fire from habanero chillies.

SERVES 4

INGREDIENTS

6–8 plum tomatoes, chopped
1 tablespoon chopped sun-dried tomatoes in oil (chef's tip, page 76)
4oz (110g) onion, chopped
6–8 garlic cloves, chopped
1 green bell pepper, chopped
4 inch (10cm) piece cucumber, peeled and chopped

1–3 fresh red habanero chillies, chopped
1 tablespoon olive oil
7fl oz (200ml) dry white wine
1 teaspoon aromatic salt (page 46)

GARNISH
tortilla chips
fresh chives

METHOD

1. Put all the ingredients into a blender or food processor and, using just enough water, pulse down to a thick, pourable purée.

2. Chill in the fridge. Then serve in four soup bowls, garnished with tortilla chips and some fresh chives.

GOHAN ZOSHUI
—— Japanese Soup Rice ——

JAPAN

This recipe includes a selection of tasty treasures from the Japanese kitchen: shoba (buckwheat noodles), wakame (dry seaweed strands), wasabi (green horseradish powder), santaka (red chillies) and mirin (sweet wine) or sake (dry wine). You should be able to obtain them from Chinese or Japanese shops.

SERVES 4

INGREDIENTS

2oz (50g) short-grain rice
2oz (50g) shoba (buckwheat noodles)
2 tablespoons wakame seaweed, shredded
2 teaspoons wasabi (green horseradish powder)
1 teaspoon light soy sauce

4fl oz (120ml) mirin (sweet wine) or sake (dry wine)
1–2 santaka or cayenne red chillies, chopped
salt

GARNISH
a few feathery fronds of fresh dill

METHOD

1. Rinse the rice several times to remove the starch.

2. Bring 1³/₄ pints (1 litre) water to the boil in a 4 pint (2.25 litre) saucepan.

3. Add the rice and simmer for 10 minutes, stirring occasionally to prevent sticking.

4. Add all the remaining ingredients, including salt to taste.

5. Serve garnished with the fresh dill.

MISO SHIRU
—— *Asparagus and Red Soy Soup* ——

*J*APAN

Like all Japanese dishes, this simple consommé should look tempting and fresh. Miso (red bean paste), available from Japanese shops and health food stores, gives a pinky-brown look and the briefly simmered vegetables retain their contrasting colours and flavours.

SERVES 4

INGREDIENTS

1³/₄ pints (1 litre) vegetable stock
3¹/₂oz (100g) miso (red bean paste)
2 garlic cloves, thinly sliced
8–12 fresh asparagus tips
2–4 red cayenne chillies, stalks on,
  cut into tassels (chef's tip, page
  211)

2 tablespoons grated carrot
soy sauce

GARNISH
2 tablespoons chopped chives

METHOD

1. Put the stock in a 4 pint (2.25 litre) saucepan and bring to a simmer.

2. Sieve the bean paste into the stock. Mash the paste against the sieve and discard the remains.

3. Add the garlic, asparagus tips, chillies and carrot. Then add soy sauce (like salt) to taste. Simmer for 3–5 minutes until the asparagus is just cooked.

4. Serve hot, distributing the asparagus tips equally between the four bowls. Garnish with the chopped chives.

SHORBA SULTANI
—— Cream of Cashew and Asparagus Soup ——

INDIA

Literally 'the King's broth', this creamy North Indian soup would have been served alongside curries in the palaces of the rich monarchs of Lucknow. I have retained the traditional thick creamy cashew nut and spice base, but I've added some intriguing extras which would not have appeared at court, such as asparagus and coconut milk powder. Serve piping hot as a nourishing thick soup, with Dominique's Naan Bread Rolls (see page 267).

SERVES 4

INGREDIENTS

6–8 young, fresh asparagus stalks
2¹/₂fl oz (70ml) double cream
2 tablespoons coconut milk
  powder (page 44)
1³/₄ pints (1 litre) water or akhni
  stock (page 44)
2 tablespoons walnut or pistachio
  nut oil
2–4 garlic cloves, crushed
aromatic salt (page 46)

PURÉE
7oz (200g) cashew nuts

2 tablespoons chopped fresh
  coriander
1 tablespoon chopped fresh mint
1 teaspoon cummin seeds, roasted
1 teaspoon coriander seeds
1 teaspoon garam masala (page 47)

GARNISH
chopped pistachio nuts
whole fresh coriander leaves
4 asparagus tips, cooked (optional)

METHOD

1. Steam or microwave the asparagus tips and soft stems until tender.

2. Mulch them down in a blender with the cream and coconut milk powder and enough water to create a pourable paste. Pour this into a 4–5 pint (2.25–2.75 litre) saucepan, washing out the blender jug with about half the measured water or stock and pouring this into the saucepan.

3. Bring the soup to a gentle simmer.

4. Mulch the **purée** ingredients down in the blender, using enough water to make an easily pourable purée.

5. Heat the oil in a karahi or wok. Stir-fry the garlic for 1 minute, add the purée and stir-fry for about 5 more minutes, adding a little water as needed.

6. During stage 5, wash out the blender jug with the remaining measured water or stock and pour this into the saucepan, allowing it to return to the simmer.

7. Add the stir-fried ingredients to the saucepan, and stir occasionally during a final 5-minute simmer. Add aromatic salt to taste.

8. Ladle into four bowls, garnish with the chopped pistachio nuts, whole fresh coriander leaves and asparagus tips, and serve.

BELOW *Cream of Cashew and Asparagus Soup (opposite) served with Dominque's Naan Bread Rolls (page 267)*

MIRCHI RASAM
—— *Pepper Soup* ——

INDIA

A *rasam* is a thin consommé from South India where most people like it hot! When I recently invited some Bangalore friends to lunch, I served this *rasam*, much to their delight. I therefore dedicate this recipe to Balan and Raji, and commend it to all heat-lovers. And yes, fresh green peppercorns do turn up in vegetable markets sometimes.

SERVES 4

INGREDIENTS

1 tablespoon mustard oil
1 tablespoon sesame oil
1 tablespoon sunflower oil
2–3 garlic cloves, chopped
2 tablespoons green moong lentils, split, skin on
2 tablespoons fresh grated coconut (page 44)
4oz (110g) finely chopped onion
1 tablespoon tamarind purée (page 44)
1 teaspoon fresh green peppercorns (chef's tip) or green peppercorns in brine
1–2 fresh green cayenne chillies, chopped

6–8 fresh or dried curry leaves
aromatic salt to taste

SPICES
1 teaspoon mustard seeds
1 teaspoon sesame seeds
1 teaspoon ground turmeric (chef's tip, page 183)
$^{1}/_{2}$ teaspoon cummin seeds
1–3 teaspoons chopped dried red chillies

GARNISH
chilli powder or crushed roasted dried red chillies

METHOD

1. Heat the oils in a wok or karahi and stir-fry the **spices** for about 20 seconds. Add the garlic and continue to stir-fry for a further 30 seconds.

2. Add the moong lentils and coconut and, 10 seconds later, the onion. Stir-fry for about 5 more minutes.

3. During stage 2 bring 1$^{3}/_{4}$ pints (1 litre) water to the boil in a 4–5 pint (2.25–2.75 litre) saucepan.

4. Add the stir-fry and all the other ingredients. Simmer gently for a minimum of 40 minutes – longer won't hurt.

5. Serve hot, sieved for clear soup, or as it comes, or puréed. Garnish with a sprinkling of chilli powder or crushed roasted dried chillies.

Chef's Tip

FRESH PEPPERCORNS

Fresh peppercorns are very pretty indeed and a gorgeous green colour. They turn up in our vegetable markets from time to time (when they are in season). There is nothing on earth like fresh green peppercorns. If ever you see them my advice is to buy all you can (blow the expense) and freeze them on oven trays (so that each corn is separate, like frozen peas). Then you can always use them as required.

CHILLI JAL JEERA
—— *Hot Cummin Consommé* ——

<u>I*NDIA*</u>

A simple tasty tangy Gujerati consommé which takes only a few minutes to prepare.

SERVES 4

INGREDIENTS

2 tablespoons soy or sunflower oil
1–3 fresh green cayenne chillies,
    sliced lengthways
1³/₄ pints (1 litre) water or akhni
    stock (page 44)
2 tablespoons finely grated carrot
2 teaspoons tamarind purée
    (page 44)
1 teaspoon Worcester sauce
1 teaspoon brown Muscovado
    sugar

1 tablespoon chopped fresh
    coriander
1 tablespoon chopped fresh mint
aromatic salt to taste (page 46)

SPICES
1 teaspoon cummin seeds
2 teaspoons ground cummin
1 teaspoon garam masala (page 47)

GARNISH
a few feathery fronds of fresh dill

METHOD

1. Heat the oil in a karahi or wok. Stir-fry the **spices** for about 1 minute, add the chillies and continue to stir-fry, briskly, for a further minute.

2. Add the water or stock and the other ingredients, and simmer for 10–15 minutes.

3. Serve in four bowls, garnished with the fresh dill.

Note: This can also be served cold. In fact it's almost better, placed on a bed of crushed ice, on a hot summer's afternoon.

TOM YAM KAENG
—— *Spicy Thai Prawn Soup* ——

THAILAND

This is one of Thailand's most popular dishes. It is a coconut-flavoured king prawn soup, with those delicious Thai fragrances of lemon grass and lime leaves.

SERVES 4

INGREDIENTS

2 tablespoons soy oil
2–4 garlic cloves, finely chopped
4oz (110g) onion, finely chopped
2 inch (5cm) cube galingale or
   ginger, grated
1–4 fresh green or red cayenne
   chillies, chopped
8 king prawns
4–6 dried lime leaves
2 stalks fresh or 2 tablespoons
   dried ground lemon grass

2oz (50g) mooli (white radish),
   grated
1 teaspoon nam pla *fish sauce*
   (chef's tip, page 172)
2oz (50g) coconut milk powder
   (page 44)
6–8 fresh basil leaves, chopped

GARNISH
a few sprigs of fresh coriander

METHOD

1. Heat the oil in a karahi or wok. Stir-fry the garlic, onion and galingale or ginger for 5 minutes. Add the chillies and the prawns and continue to stir-fry for 5 more minutes.

2. Transfer the stir-fry to a 5 pint (2.75 litre) saucepan. Add 1³/₄ pints (1 litre) water and bring to the boil, then reduce the heat to a simmer. Add the lime leaves, lemon grass, mooli and fish sauce. Simmer for 8–10 minutes.

3. Mix the coconut milk powder with enough water to make a runny paste. Add it to the soup with the basil at the end of stage 2 and simmer for a few more minutes.

4. Garnish with the sprigs of fresh coriander and serve, ensuring that the prawns are evenly distributed between the four bowls.

CHIN-HIN
—— *Burmese Sour Fish Soup* ——

BURMA

This Burmese soup is enjoyed for its chilli-hot, tamarind-sour and spicy savoury tastes. I've taken a short cut here by using canned pilchards in tomato sauce. The liquid should be clear and thin like a consommé, with chunks of fish, and the green herbs retaining their colour.

SERVES 4

INGREDIENTS

2 tablespoons vegetable oil
2–4 garlic cloves, crushed
5–6 spring onions, bulbs and leaves chopped
$1/2$ teaspoon ground turmeric (chef's tip, page 183)
$1^3/_4$ pints (1 litre) water or fish or vegetable stock
1 tablespoon tomato purée
3–4 red cayenne chillies, chopped
7oz (200g) can pilchards or herrings in tomato sauce

1 tablespoon tamarind purée (page 44) or lemon juice
2 teaspoons ketjap manis (page 192)
$1/2$ teaspoon ground black pepper aromatic salt (page 46) or sea salt to taste
1 bunch watercress leaves
2 tablespoons whole fresh coriander leaves

METHOD

1. Heat the oil in a karahi or wok. Stir-fry the garlic, spring onions and turmeric for about 5 minutes.

2. Transfer this mixture to a 4 pint (2.25 litre) saucepan. Add the water or stock and tomato purée and chillies. Bring to the boil, then reduce the heat and simmer for 10–15 minutes.

3. Bone the pilchards or herrings and carefully fork into small chunks. Put the fish and sauce into the saucepan.

4. Add the tamarind purée or lemon juice, *ketjap manis*, black pepper and salt to taste. Bring back to a simmer.

5. Just before serving, add the watercress and whole fresh coriander leaves. Once the soup comes to a simmer again, serve immediately in four bowls.

YU CHITANG FAN CHIEW
—— Shark's Fin Chilli Soup ——

CHINA

It's probably because the shark is so menacing that this soup is so popular in China. It represents man's ultimate control over nature and has been in the Chinese repertoire for thousands of years.

Shark's fin itself is rather tasteless and has a soft, fleshy texture. It is available dried or canned from Chinese shops. The former requires lengthy simmering to reconstitute it, while the latter just needs draining and rinsing thoroughly. The liquid from the can may be added to the stock, but taste it first to see if you like it.

For those, like Dominique, who don't like the idea of shark, I've offered an alternative . . . cod steak.

SERVES 4

INGREDIENTS

1¾ pints (1 litre) chicken stock or water
4 whole garlic cloves
1 inch (2.5cm) cube ginger, grated
3–4 spring onions, bulbs and leaves chopped
7–8oz (200–225g) canned shark's fin, drained then rinsed thoroughly, or cod steak
4 dried Chinese mushrooms, reconstituted (page 93)
2oz (50g) carrot, grated
2–4 red chillies, chopped into fine strips

1 tablespoon cornflour
1 tablespoon Chinese white rice vinegar or white wine vinegar
1 tablespoon light soy sauce
1 teaspoon brown sugar
1 teaspoon Chinese five-spice powder (page 46)
salt
2 tablespoons Chinese yellow rice wine or sweet sherry

GARNISH
1 tablespoon finely chopped fresh coriander

METHOD

1. Bring the stock or water to the boil in a 5 pint (2.75 litre) saucepan, together with the garlic, ginger and spring onions, and the liquid from the canned shark's fin, if you like the taste.

2. Add the shark's fin or cod steak, mushrooms, carrots and chillies and simmer for 10 minutes.

3. Mix the cornflour with the vinegar and add to the stock, together with the soy sauce and sugar. Add the five-spice powder and salt to taste. Bring back to a simmer.

4. Add the rice wine or sweet sherry and serve piping hot, garnished with the chopped fresh coriander.

SICHUAN LA TANG
—— *Sichuan Hot and Sour Soup* ——

CHINA

China's western province of Sichuan shares a border with Burma. This Burmese-influenced hot and spicy soup can be served with prawn crackers, or as part of the main course with rice and other Chinese dishes. If the stock is not concentrated enough add 1–2 chicken stock cubes at stage 1 to give a more intense flavour.

SERVES 4

INGREDIENTS

2 tablespoons sesame oil
2 teaspoons white sesame seeds
1 teaspoon Sichuan peppercorns, crushed
2–3 garlic cloves, grated
1 inch (2.5cm) cube ginger, grated
2–3 slices rindless, smoked streaky bacon, chopped
2oz (50g) skinless chicken breast, shredded
2oz (50g) lean ham, chopped
2–6 fresh or dried Sichuan chillies
1³/₄ pints (1 litre) chicken stock
3–4 Chinese dried mushrooms (chef's tip, below)

3–4 spring onions, bulbs and leaves chopped
1oz (25g) bean sprouts
2 tablespoons Chinese red rice vinegar or red wine vinegar
1 teaspoon dark soy sauce
1 teaspoon brown sugar
3 tablespoons Chinese yellow rice wine or sweetish table wine
2 eggs, beaten
salt

GARNISH
4 spring onion tassels (chef's tip, page 211)

METHOD

1. Heat the oil in a wok. Stir-fry the sesame seeds, peppercorns, garlic and ginger for 30 seconds. Add the bacon, chicken, ham and chillies, and stir-fry for 3–4 minutes until the bacon is crispy.

2. Bring the stock to the boil in a 5 pint (2.75 litre) saucepan. Add the mushrooms and spring onions and simmer for 3–4 minutes.

3. Add the stir-fry, bean sprouts, vinegar, soy sauce, sugar and wine. While simmering, trickle in the beaten egg and the salt to taste. Pour into four bowls, garnish and serve piping hot.

Chef's Tip

USING DRIED CHINESE MUSHROOMS
You can put these directly into soups and stews without reconstituting them providing cooking time is at least 30 minutes. Otherwise, reconstitute by placing in a large bowl and pouring over boiling water to fill the bowl. Soak for about 30 minutes, then drain, and use in your cooking.

MEAT
DISHES

Meat remains the number one choice for most of the world's population, and my selection of 25 dishes for this chapter was no easy matter, as so many fabulous recipes had to be left out. I hope you'll find many of your tasty spicy favourites amongst those that are here.

From the world's tables I've chosen the widest selection of cooking methods – amongst which are stews, casseroles, pot roasts, oven roasts, stir-fries, marinated stews, slow-cooks and deep-fries. I have also tried to cover the widest range of ingredients.

I've tended to use the traditional meat where appropriate, for example: pork in Portugal, Latin America and Goa; lamb in India and Greece; beef in Mexico, Thailand and for the great Chili Con Carne of the USA; and veal for Hungary. However, you could substitute different meats for most of the recipes. But why not be adventurous and try all these exquisite treats with my suggested main ingredient? For those who are really brave, there's alligator from Louisiana, cooked Cajun style.

OPPOSITE *Clockwise from top: Ham and Pork Hotpot (page 106), Peruvian Roast Pork (page 107) served with Brazilian Rice Cake (page 253), Peruvian Potatoes (page 206) and Mexican Red Hot Chutney (page 290)*

CHILI CON CARNE
—— *Chilli Meat* ——

USA

'Make no mistake about it y'all,' drawled a deep Texan voice. 'No one makes good chili but the Texicans.' Was it John Wayne, or Jim Bowie or General Custer? No it was Willie, our Dallas taxi driver. Texicans, it seems, are Texans who adore their version of Mexican food. I was impressed. Then I visited Arizona and found that the Arizonans make the best chili. Soon I was to find that only Californians or New Mexicans can cook chili. Three things were abundantly clear – they don't make chili in Mexico, they don't put beans in and they use chopped meat not minced meat. That put paid to all my preconceptions.

In fact cooking chili is taken very seriously in south-west USA. Chili contests are held all over the place, with hundreds of entrants cooking their favourite (and of course highly secret) recipe for a panel of nose-twitching, tongue-trilling 'expert' judges. If ever you're in the area and there's one of these chili cook-offs being held – do go. The smells, the crowds, the atmosphere, the hype and the bullshit – it's all unmissable. You'll even get to taste the chili if you're lucky.

Meanwhile, to keep you going, here are a few different chilis, starting (sacrilegiously) with a simple but outstandingly effective (in my view anyway) mince version, complete with red kidney beans.

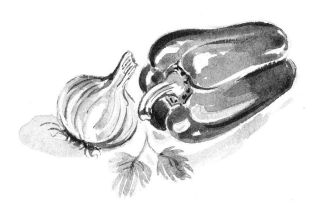

CHILI CON CARNE
—— *Chilli Meat* ——

USA

This is perhaps the least 'authentic' chili because it uses minced meat and kidney beans. It's superb nonetheless, and well worth defending against the versions which follow. Great with French bread, Indian Fry Bread (see page 258), rice or baked potatoes.

SERVES 4

INGREDIENTS

3 tablespoons ghee (page 43) or vegetable oil
1 teaspoon ground cummin
3–6 garlic cloves, chopped
8oz (225g) onion, finely chopped
7oz (200g) canned chopped tomatoes
1 tablespoon chopped red bell pepper
1–2 tablespoons red chilli mash (pages 286–7)

1½lb (675g) lean minced beef
1 tablespoon tomato purée
2 tablespoons tomato ketchup
½ teaspoon Worcester sauce
1 tablespoon chopped fresh basil
1 tablespoon chopped fresh coriander
8oz (225g) canned red kidney beans
salt

METHOD

1. Heat the ghee or oil in a karahi, wok or frying pan over a high heat, then stir-fry the cummin for 20 seconds. Add the garlic and continue stir-frying for a further 30 seconds.

2. Add the onion and reduce the heat. Stir-fry for 10 minutes, until the onion becomes translucent and begins to brown.

3. Using a suitable size lidded casserole dish, combine the fried ingredients with the tomatoes, bell pepper and chilli. Put the casserole in an oven preheated to 375°F/190°C/Gas 5.

4. Put the mince in the karahi, wok or frying pan and cook it for about 10 minutes to 'seal' or brown it and reduce any liquid.

5. Stir in the tomato purée, ketchup and Worcester sauce.

6. Transfer the meat to the casserole, mixing well.

7. Leave to cook in the oven for about 30 minutes. Then inspect, add the fresh herbs and the canned red kidney beans with their liquid, and return to the oven for a final 15 minutes. Add salt to taste and serve.

CHILI CON CARNE CALIFORNIAN STYLE
—— *Chilli Meat Californian-Style* ——

USA

This Californian recipe took some extracting from its inventor. The secret lies both in the 'grinding' (mincing) of the meat and in the marinade, the contents of which may surprise you! Serve with The Ultimate Garlic Bread (see page 268) and baked potatoes.

SERVES 4

INGREDIENTS

1¹/₂lb (675g) stewing steak, all fat
  and gristle removed
2–3 tablespoons butter
8oz (225g) onions, finely chopped
2 tablespoons sun-dried tomatoes,
  chopped (chef's tip, page 76)
12 cherry tomatoes, chopped
1 tablespoon green peppercorns in
  brine
1 tablespoon chopped fresh
  coriander
salt

MARINADE
2–4 garlic cloves, crushed
1 dry poblano chilli, chopped
1 dry pasilla chilli, chopped
1–3 teaspoons cayenne pepper
1 teaspoon ground cummin
¹/₂ pint (300ml) Guinness or other
  dark beer
4fl oz (120ml) Coke or Pepsi Cola
¹/₂ teaspoon aromatic salt (page 46)

METHOD

1. Cut the meat into cubes, then pass it through a mincer.

2. Place the minced meat in a non-metallic bowl with the **marinade** ingredients. Mix well, cover and refrigerate for up to 60 hours (see page 42).

3. Heat the butter in a frying pan. Stir-fry the onion for 5 minutes. Drain the marinade liquid and add it to the frying pan. Stir-fry for a further 10 minutes, reducing the liquid a little.

4. Using a 4–5 pint (2.25–2.75 litre) lidded casserole, combine the fried ingredients and the meat and place in an oven preheated to 375°F/190°C/Gas 5. After 20 minutes, inspect and stir, adding a little water or stock if it is becoming too dry. Repeat 20 minutes later, adding the remaining ingredients. Add salt to taste. Cook for a further 20 minutes or until cooked to your liking.

CHILI CON CARNE TEXICAN STYLE
—— *Chilli Meat Texican-Style* ——

USA

In this authentic Texan version of chili, called the 'bowl of red', the meat is finely diced not minced, and there are no beans. You can use cheaper cuts of beef, of course, but this is a prize-winning recipe.

SERVES 4

INGREDIENTS

3 tablespoons ghee (page 43) or corn oil
2–4 garlic cloves, chopped
8oz (225g) onions, finely chopped
1¹/₂lb (675g) lean rump steak, any fat and gristle removed, chopped into ¹/₄ inch (6mm) pieces
1–4 fresh red cayenne chillies, chopped
1–4 canned green jalapeno chillies, chopped

2 tablespoons vinegar, any type
10oz (300g) canned cream of tomato soup
salt

SPICES
1 teaspoon white cummin seeds
1 teaspoon green peppercorns in brine
¹/₂ teaspoon coriander seeds, crushed

METHOD

1. Heat the ghee or oil in a frying pan over a high heat. Then stir-fry the **spices** for 20 seconds. Add the garlic and continue stir-frying for a further 30 seconds.

2. Add the onion and reduce the heat. Stir-fry for 10 minutes, until the onion becomes translucent and begins to brown.

3. Add the meat and stir-fry for a few minutes to 'seal' it.

4. Using a 4–5 pint (2.25–2.75 litre) lidded casserole, combine the fried ingredients, meat, chillies, vinegar and soup, and place in an oven preheated to 375°F/190°C/Gas 5. After 20 minutes, inspect and stir, adding a little water or stock if it is becoming too dry. Repeat 20 minutes later. Add salt to taste. Cook for a further 20 minutes or until cooked to your liking.

SPAGHETTI WESTERN

I came across this absolutely delightful title for a spaghetti dish in a number of restaurants in south-west America, and of course I just had to tell you about it. My version is to serve any of the preceding chili con carne dishes over spaghetti. Hey presto you've created your own Spaghetti Western.

ALLIGATOR SAUSAGE

USA

'OK y'all jus must have gaydor sausage,' said the persuasive waitress at Chef John Fosse's restaurant in Louisiana. 'What's that?' we asked. 'Why it's minced alligator meat grilled on a stick.' 'It's delicious,' chorused the six elderly Cajun locals at the table next to us. 'Y'all must eat it and tell all those folks in lil ole England about it.' We did and I am.

You can buy frozen alligator meat in specialist butchers in many Western countries. It's fresh in bayou country, and alligators (sorry 'gaydors') over 15 feet (4.5m) in length are quite common. In fact there is a carefully regulated annual cull to prevent the alligator population exceeding that of New Orleans. The meat (best from the tail) is quite distinctive – sweetish, white like chicken and quite tender.

Turtle meat is equally popular in the Cajun swamplands. Turtles are as common as chickens and their meat is equally white and tender. Should you find yourself with some turtle meat to use up, substitute it for the alligator and grill it on sticks.

More seriously, chicken would make an acceptable substitute.

MAKES 8

INGREDIENTS

1¹/₂lb (675g) alligator tail steak
6 garlic cloves
2 tablespoons dried onion flakes (chef's tip, page 65)
2 tablespoons chopped fresh parsley

1 tablespoon chopped red cayenne chillies
1 teaspoon aromatic salt (page 46)
8×8 inch (20cm) bamboo skewers

METHOD

1. Chop the flesh into cubes and pulse all the ingredients in a food processor to achieve a mouldable texture.

2. Soak the bamboo skewers in water for 1 hour. This gives them a greater resistance to burning during cooking.

3. Divide the mixture into eight and mould into sausage shapes on the bamboo skewers.

4. Put them on a baking tray in an oven preheated to 375°F/190°C/Gas **5.** Cook for about 15 minutes and serve with a mixed salad.

CHILIS RELLENOS CON CARNE
——— *Chillies Stuffed with Meat* ———

USA

Large chillies, stuffed with spicily enhanced meat, are dipped in batter and deep-fried. Sounds like hard work, but it isn't really. These are great at parties – and you can vary the filling (see pages 156 and 251).

SERVES 4

INGREDIENTS

8 large green chillies or bell
  peppers
oil for deep-frying

STUFFING
1lb (450g) leg of veal, off the bone,
  all skin, fat and gristle removed
2–4 garlic cloves, chopped
2 tablespoons dried onion flakes
  (chef's tip, page 65)
1–2 tablespoons red chilli mash
  (pages 286–7)

1 tablespoon chopped fresh
  coriander
1 teaspoon cummin seed
$^1/_2$ teaspoon aromatic salt (page 46)

BATTER
4oz (110g) strong white flour
4oz (110g) cornmeal
2 egg yolks
5fl oz (150ml) milk
$^1/_2$ teaspoon aromatic salt (page 46)
whites of 2 eggs, beaten stiffly

METHOD

1. Pulse all the **stuffing** ingredients in a food processor or use a mincer to achieve a well-mixed cohesive paste.

2. For the **batter**, put the flour and cornmeal in a bowl, and fold in the egg yolks, milk and salt. Beat, then gently fold in the egg whites to achieve a thick batter. Adjust the quantity of milk as necessary.

3. Roast the chillies or bell peppers (see pages 41–2) and, whilst they are warm and soft, peel them and slit them carefully, leaving the stalk on, to create a pocket. Remove the seeds and pith but don't make holes other than the slit if possible.

4. Carefully insert the stuffing. Don't worry if there is some left over (it depends on the size of your chillies/peppers). We'll use it later.

5. Dip the stuffed chillies/peppers into the batter, ensuring that they are thickly coated.

6. Heat the oil in a deep-fryer to 375°F/190°C (chip-frying temperature) and cook them for about 10 minutes.

7. To serve, place two chillies/peppers per person on each plate. Serve with rice and salsas (see pages 232–3 and 290–2).

ABOVE *Alligator Sausage (page 100) accompanied by Heather's Chilli Bread (page 268)*

CHILE EN NOGADA
—— *Pork and Walnut-Stuffed Chillies* ——

MEXICO

This is a splendid stuffed chilli recipe from the Puebla district of Mexico.

A large poblano chilli or, in its absence, a green bell pepper is the vehicle. Traditionally served on feast days, the stuffing includes spicy, chilli-laced, minced pork with pinenuts. It is served with a white sauce of sour cream, green peppercorns and walnuts topped with translucent red pomegranate seeds, the green, white and red symbolising the colours of the Mexican flag.

SERVES 4

INGREDIENTS

3 tablespoons corn oil
2–4 garlic cloves, chopped
4oz (110g) Spanish onion, chopped
1lb (450g) lean leg of pork, minced
1 tablespoon red chilli mash
    (pages 286–7)
1 tablespoon pinenuts
1 tablespoon tomato purée
1 tablespoon chopped fresh
    coriander
1 teaspoon sugar
salt
8 large green chillies or bell peppers

SAUCE
^{1}/$_2$oz (15g) butter
1 tablespoon cornflour
^{1}/$_2$ pint (300ml) milk
5fl oz (150ml) sour cream
1 tablespoon freeze-dried green
    peppercorns (chef's tip, page
    109)
2 tablespoons walnuts, chopped

GARNISH
fresh pomegranate seeds
fresh whole coriander leaves

METHOD

1. Heat the oil in a large pan and stir-fry the garlic for 30 seconds. Add the onion, reduce the heat and cook for a further 10 minutes or so until golden.

2. Add the minced pork and chilli mash. Cook for at least 45 minutes. (I find it easier to casserole the mixture in the oven at 375°F/190°C/Gas 5 for the same length of time.)

3. Add the pine nuts, tomato purée, fresh coriander, sugar, and salt to taste. Stir and cook for a further 10–15 minutes.

4. During stage 3 'roast' the chillies or bell peppers (see page 00). Whilst they are warm and soft, peel them and slit them carefully, leaving the stalk on, to create a pocket. Remove the seeds and pith but don't make holes other than the slit if possible.

5. Carefully insert the mince stuffing. Don't worry if you have some left over (it depends on the size of your chillies/peppers).

6. Put the stuffed chillies or peppers on a flat baking tray in an oven preheated to 375°F/190°C/Gas 5.

7. Bake for 10 minutes.

8. For the **sauce**, melt the butter in a pan and stir in the cornflour to make a roux. Gradually add the milk on a lowish heat, stirring continuously until the sauce thickens.

9. Add the sour cream, green peppercorns and walnuts.

10. To serve, place two chillies per person on each plate, and any spare mince alongside or over the chillies. Pour the sauce over the chillies, dividing it equally. Then garnish with the pomegranate seeds and coriander leaves. Serve cold or hot with fresh Tortillas (see page 262).

FAJITAS
—— *Mexican Stir-Fry Beef* ——

MEXICO

Fajitas (pronounced far-hee-tarce) are one of Mexico's most popular dishes. Best steak is beaten and flattened, cut into strips, marinated, and stir-fried with other ingredients (not unlike the Chinese method). This recipe is offered as a tribute to the best *fajita* maker in Mexico, Raymundo Espinosa, whose taco bar I visited in Mexico.

SERVES 4

INGREDIENTS

1¹/₂lb (675g) lean steak
3 tablespoons corn oil
4–6 garlic cloves, crushed
8oz (225g) onions, finely chopped
¹/₂ red bell pepper, sliced
2–4 green snub chillies, sliced
8 freshly made Tortillas (page 262)
4fl oz (120ml) sour cream

MARINADE
4fl oz (120ml) tequila (optional)
8fl oz (250ml) red wine
4–6 garlic cloves, crushed
1 teaspoon chilli powder
¹/₂ teaspoon salt

METHOD

1. With a meat mallet, beat the beef steaks until they are as thin as you want them. Cut them into strips about 2 inches×¹/₂ inch (5×1.25cm).

2. Mix the **marinade** ingredients together in a large non-metallic bowl. Add the meat, mix well, cover and refrigerate for 6–8 hours.

3. Heat the oil in a large frying pan or wok. Stir-fry the garlic for 30 seconds, then add the onions and stir-fry for about 5 minutes.

4. Add the bell pepper, chillies, the meat and the marinade and stir-fry for a few minutes until cooked.

5. To serve, put some *fajita* in the centre of a home-made tortilla and put a dollop of sour cream on top. Serve with hot salsas such as *Pico de Gallo* and *Manzano Salsa* (see page 292).

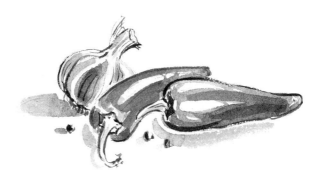

CHORIZO/CHOURIÇO
—— *Spicy Sausage* ——

MEXICO

This Hispano-Portuguese sausage is to be found in Mexico, Brazil, Africa, Goa and the East Indies in various guises. Away from home it acquires more and more chillies and spices. I particularly like this Mexican version reeking with chilli, garlic and spices. Don't bother with hard-to-get casings – just make them minced kebab style. Serve them as sandwich/tortilla fillings or as an ingredient in recipes (see Index) or in their own right as a main dish with vegetables.

MAKES 4

INGREDIENTS

1¹/₂ tablespoons distilled malt vinegar
1 large dried poblano chilli
4 fresh red habanero chillies or 1–3 teaspoons chilli powder
1¹/₂lb (675g) lean pork, coarsely chopped
1 tablespoon chopped fresh coriander

4–8 garlic cloves, chopped

SPICES
1 tablespoon Hungarian paprika
2 teaspoons ground cinnamon
1 teaspoon ground cummin
¹/₂ teaspoon ground cloves

METHOD

1. Mix the **spices** with the vinegar to make a runny paste.

2. Destalk the chillies, and soak them in the spice paste.

3. Mulch down the pork, fresh coriander, garlic and chilli spice mixture in a food processor or mincer until you achieve a cohesive texture. (Finish off by mixing well by hand to ensure that all the flavourings are equally distributed.)

4. Form the mixture into four sausage shapes. Place them on a flat oven tray in an oven preheated to 375°F/190°C/Gas 5.

5. Cook for 20 minutes. Inspect by cutting a sausage in half. It should be perfectly cooked right through (not pink). If not, cook for a few minutes more.

6. Serve hot or cold, chopped or whole.

PUCHERO
—— Ham and Pork Hot Pot ——

ARGENTINA

In Latin America *puchero* means both 'a slow-cooked stew' and the pot it is cooked in. Here, for this Argentinian stew, I use a casserole pot and ham with pork and *chorizo* sausage.

SERVES 4

INGREDIENTS

8oz (225g) lean gammon steak
8oz (225g) lean leg of pork
2 tablespoons corn oil
1 tablespoon olive oil
2–4 whole garlic cloves, peeled
6–8 small whole onions, peeled
1 large carrot, sliced
1 parsnip, sliced

2–4 fresh red cayenne chillies
2–3 bay leaves
8oz (225g) uncooked chorizo
  sausagemeat (page 105)
1 tablespoon chopped fresh
  coriander
1 tablespoon honey
aromatic salt (page 46)

METHOD

1. Cut the gammon and pork into cubes about 1¹/₂ inches (4cm) in size, remembering that they will shrink during cooking as the liquids come out.

2. Heat the oils in a karahi or wok. Stir-fry the garlic and the onions for 5 minutes.

3. Using a 4–5 pint (2.25–2.75 litre) lidded casserole, combine the garlic, onions, meat, carrot, parsnip, chillies, bay leaves and, as needed, about 8fl oz (225ml) water and place in an oven preheated to 375°F/190°C/Gas 5.

4. After 20 minutes, inspect and stir, adding water as needed, and return the casserole to the oven. At this stage shape the *chorizo* into 1 inch (2.5cm) balls. Place them on a flat oven tray and bake in the oven for 20 minutes.

5. Add the balls to the casserole, along with the fresh coriander and honey. Add aromatic salt to taste. Cook for a further 20 minutes or until cooked to your liking. Serve with rice.

LECHON ASADO
—— *Peruvian Roast Pork* ——

PERU

This Peruvian dish normally uses a marinated and slowly barbecued suckling pig. I've modified it to a leg of pork cooked in the oven. Serve it with freshly made Tortillas (see page 262) and/or *Chilis Rellenos con Arroz* (see page 251) or *Moros y Cristianos* (see page 252).

SERVES 4

INGREDIENTS

$3^1/_2$–4lb (1.5–1.8kg) leg of pork, on the bone

MARINADE
2 tablespoons red chilli mash (pages 286–7)
6 garlic cloves, crushed
1 teaspoon yellow mustard powder

4fl oz (120ml) corn oil
6 green olives, finely chopped
2 ripe bananas, mashed
1 ripe avocado, mashed
8fl oz (250ml) red wine
1 teaspoon aromatic salt (page 46)

METHOD

1. Mix the **marinade** ingredients together in a bowl.

2. Remove all fat, skin and membrane from the meat. Stab it all over with a small knife and coat thoroughly with the marinade in a large non-metallic dish. Cover and refrigerate for at least 24 hours and no more than 60 hours.

3. Preheat the oven to 350°F/180°C/Gas 4. Transfer the pork and marinade to a roasting dish and slow-roast for about 3 hours. When really tender the flesh should literally fall off the bone. Before serving, let it rest for 30 minutes or so in a low oven. Use the cooking juices as gravy.

Note: During the cooking, cover the pork with foil after about 30 minutes and remove the foil after about 2 hours.

COCHITA PIBIL
—— *Marinated Roast Pork* ——

VENEZUELA

In this Venezuelan dish a small suckling piglet is marinated in a chilli, spice, citrus and garlic mixture. It is then wrapped in banana leaves and slowly cooked in a barbecue pit. This delicious modification achieves a similar result using leg of pork, tin foil and the oven. Try it with Red Indian Fry Bread (see page 258) and/or Spanish Saffron Rice (see page 236).

SERVES 4

INGREDIENTS

$3^1/_2$–4lb (1.5–1.8kg) leg of pork, on the bone

MARINADE
$^1/_2$ pint (300ml) fresh or bottled orange juice
juice of 4 lemons

6–8 garlic cloves, crushed
1–4 tablespoons red chilli mash (pages 286–7)
1 teaspoon salt
$^1/_2$ teaspoon ground cinnamon
$^1/_4$ teaspoon ground cloves

METHOD

1. Mix the **marinade** ingredients together in a bowl.

2. Remove all fat, skin and membrane from the meat. Stab it all over with a small knife and coat thoroughly with the marinade in a non-metallic dish. Cover and refrigerate for at least 24 hours (see page 42).

3. Preheat the oven to 350°F/180°C/Gas 4 maximum. Transfer the pork and marinade to a roasting dish and slow-roast for about 3 hours. When really tender the flesh should literally fall off the bone. Before serving, let it rest for 30 minutes or so in a low oven.

Note: During the cooking, cover the pork with foil after about 30 minutes and remove the foil after about 2 hours.

LEITÃO RECHEADO
—— *Brazilian Roast Pork* ——

BRAZIL

In Brazilian (Portuguese) *leitão* means 'suckling pig' and *recheado* means 'stuffed'. Indeed, you'll find *recheado* (stuffed) dishes in Goa in India. The Brazilian version of this dish is marinated in red wine, vinegar, garlic, bay leaves, cloves and chilli. This marinade derives from the Portuguese version which uses white wine, garlic, bay leaves and pepper. The Brazilian piglet is stuffed with bread, ham, bacon and spices and is roasted. In Brazil this would be on the spit.

SERVES 4–6

INGREDIENTS

1 small suckling pig

MARINADE
8fl oz (250ml) red wine
2fl oz (50ml) red chilli vinegar (page 286)
6 garlic cloves, crushed
4 bay leaves
6 cloves, crushed
1 tablespoon red chilli mash (pages 286–7)
1 teaspoon aromatic salt (page 46)

STUFFING
breadcrumbs made from 6 or more slices white bread, including crusts
2oz (50g) cooked ham, chopped
2oz (50g) cooked bacon, chopped
2 bay leaves
6 cloves
1 teaspoon black peppercorns
1 tablespoon chopped fresh basil leaves

METHOD

1. Mix the **marinade** ingredients together in a bowl.

2. Remove all fat, skin and membrane from the meat. Stab it all over with a small knife and coat thoroughly with the marinade in a large non-metallic dish. Cover and refrigerate for at least 24 hours and no more than 60 hours.

3. Mix the stuffing ingredients together and use to stuff the cavity of the marinated piglet.

4. Preheat the oven to 350°F/180°C/Gas 4. Transfer the piglet and marinade to a roasting dish and slow-roast for about 3 hours. When really tender the flesh should literally fall off the bone. Before serving, let it rest for 30 minutes or so in a low oven. Use the cooking juices as gravy.

Chef's Tip

PEPPERCORNS
Everyone has a peppermill filled with black peppercorns. Why not buy another mill and fill it with green peppercorns? Try them in an acrylic transparent mill. You could even buy a further mill and fill it with pink peppercorns. These colourful peppercorns look good and taste wonderful. Green peppercorns are now available freeze-dried.

SHASHLIK KEBABS
—— *Skewered Spicy Grilled Meat* ——

ARMENIA

The shashlik originates from Armenia and is found all over the Middle East and Turkey. Chunky meat cubes are marinated, then grilled or barbecued. Serve on a bed of salad topped with fresh herbs, accompanied by lemon wedges, Harissa (see page 293), rice and Pitta Bread (see page 257).

SERVES 4

INGREDIENTS

1¹/₂lb (675g) topside of beef or
  1 inch (2.5cm) thick fillet or
  sirloin steak
1 red bell pepper
1 green bell pepper
1 Spanish or large onion
4 whole garlic cloves, peeled
  (optional)
4 green chillies (optional)

MARINADE
4fl oz (120ml) olive oil
1 teaspoon ground cummin
¹/₂ teaspoon powdered cassia bark
  or cinnamon
4fl oz (120ml) red wine
1 tablespoon lemon juice
2 teaspoons tomato purée
¹/₂ teaspoon finely chopped garlic

METHOD

1. Thoroughly mix together all the **marinade** ingredients in a bowl.

2. Remove any gristle, fat and skin from the meat and cut into 20 cubes at least 1 inch (2.5cm) each.

3. Mix the meat with the marinade in a non-metallic bowl, then cover and refrigerate for at least 24 hours (see page 42).

4. After the meat has marinated, cut the red pepper into 8×1 inch (2.5cm) diamonds or squares. Then do the same with the green pepper. Separate the layers of the onion and cut 20 pieces to the same shape.

5. Preheat the oven to 350°F/180°C/Gas 4, and meanwhile thread the items on to four skewers: onion, meat, green pepper, meat, onion, red pepper, meat, onion, green pepper, meat, onion, red pepper, meat, onion. Put a clove of garlic and/or a green chilli on to each skewer if you wish. Ensure that all the items are close together but not squashed.

6. Place the skewers on a wire rack and the rack on a foil-lined oven tray. Baste the skewers with the excess marinade.

7. Cook in the oven for 8–10 minutes for rare meat, 10–15 minutes for medium and 15 or more minutes if you like your meat well done. Alternatively, cook under the grill at medium heat with the rack at the lowest level for the same times, or cook over a barbecue.

PORCO COM VINHO E ALHOS
—— *Pork with Vinegar and Garlic* ——

PORTUGAL

I simply could not omit this dish from this book. Its basis is a long marinade in wine, vinegar (*vinho*), spices and garlic (*alhos*). The same marinade appears in a number of traditional Portuguese dishes.

As conquistadors, the Portuguese introduced their religion, their pigs and their cuisine into Goa in 1508. The Indians took Portuguese cooking to heart and made it their own. It was not long before *Vinho e Alhos* evolved into India's most famous dish – vindaloo. Compare the two (see recipe on page 116) and note the subtle change from paprika in Portugal to chilli in India.

Serve with plain boiled rice.

SERVES 4

INGREDIENTS

1¹/₂lb (675g) lean leg of pork, off the bone, any fat, gristle and skin removed
1¹/₂oz (40g) butter
1 tablespoon olive oil
4–6 garlic cloves, chopped
8oz (225g) onions, finely chopped
salt

MARINADE
7fl oz (200ml) vinho verdhe white wine
2 tablespoons red wine vinegar
2–4 garlic cloves, crushed
4–6 cloves
4 bay leaves
2 tablespoons Hungarian paprika

METHOD

1. Cut the meat into cubes about 1¹/₂ inches (4cm) in size, remembering that they will shrink during cooking as the liquids come out.

2. Pulse the **marinade** ingredients down to a thin purée in a blender or food processor.

3. In a large non-metallic bowl, mix the meat and the marinade. Cover and refrigerate for up to 60 hours (see page 42).

4. Put the butter and oil in a pan over a high heat. Add the garlic and stir-fry for 30 seconds. Add the onions, reduce the heat and stir-fry for about 10 minutes, until they are golden.

5. Using a 4–5 pint (2.25–2.75 litre) lidded casserole, combine the fried ingredients and the meat with its marinade and place in an oven preheated to 375°F/190°C/Gas 5.

6. After 20 minutes, inspect and stir, adding a little water or vegetable stock if it is becoming too dry. Repeat 20 minutes later. Add salt to taste. Cook for a further 20 minutes or until tender.

MOUSSAKA

GREECE

Moussaka is the classic Greek dish using finely chopped mutton or goat meat (I'm using home-minced lamb), cooked with a topping of sliced fried aubergines. In fact the dish is made up of layers of aubergines and mince. Above the top layer I like a thick creamy further layer of white sauce (to which I add a mustardy piquance) and cheese. You can omit this layer if you wish, but I think it's worth the effort. It's rich and yummy served with plain rice and/or Pitta Bread (see page 257) with Vinegared Chillies or Pickled Vegetables with Chilli (see pages 294–5).

SERVES 4

INGREDIENTS

1lb (450g) lean leg of lamb, off the bone
2 tablespoons ghee (page 43)
1 tablespoon olive oil
2–4 garlic cloves, crushed
8oz (225g) onions, chopped
1 tablespoon chopped sun-dried tomato in oil (chef's tip, page 76)
6oz (175g) mushrooms, sliced
1 tablespoon chopped fresh coriander
1 tablespoon chopped fresh parsley
aromatic salt (page 46)

3 1/2 oz (100g) butter
3–4 medium size aubergines, cut lengthways into 1/8 inch (3mm) thick slices, salted, and rinsed (chef's tip, opposite)
2 heaped tablespoons plain white flour
1 pint (600ml) full cream milk
1 teaspoon yellow English mustard powder
2–3 tablespoons breadcrumbs
8oz (225g) Cheddar, grated, or Mozzarella cheese, chopped

METHOD

1. Chop the lamb into suitable chunks for putting through the mincer and mince coarsely.

2. Heat the ghee and oil in a karahi or frying pan over a high heat, then stir-fry the garlic for 30 seconds.

3. Add the onions and reduce the heat. Stir-fry for 5 minutes. Add the mince and brown it for about 10 more minutes. Add the sun-dried tomato, mushrooms, coriander and parsley and mix well. Add aromatic salt to taste.

4. During stage 3 heat half the butter and fry the aubergine (about 1 minute per side).

5. Choose an oiled oven dish about 8×10×4 inches (20×25×10cm) in size. Put a layer of aubergine on the dish base, overlapping as needed so that you can't see the dish itself. Spread half the mince mixture on this. Put a second layer of aubergine on top of the mince and a second and final layer of mince on this. Now put the third and final layer of aubergine on top of the mince.

6. Put the dish, uncovered, into an oven preheated to 375°F/190°C/Gas 5.

7. Now make the white sauce as follows. Heat the remaining butter in a smallish saucepan over a lowish heat. Add the flour and stir continuously for 1–2 minutes, just until it starts to change colour. Take off the heat, add a little milk and mix to a cream. Repeat with a little more milk to achieve a thinner cream, and repeat this until you have used all the milk. This should give you a lump-free runny mixture. Add the mustard. Return to a medium heat and keep stirring until it will not thicken any further (depending on the heat, this should take no more than 5 minutes).

8. After about 15 minutes (enough time to make the white sauce) remove the moussaka from the oven. Pour all the white sauce evenly over the top. Return it to the oven.

9. After a further 15 minutes remove it again. This time, sprinkle over the breadcrumbs, then the cheese and return to the oven for a final 15–20 minutes. Serve straight from the oven dish.

Chef's Tip

SALTING AUBERGINES

Aubergines can have a bitter flavour. To avoid this, soak the aubergine (whole, sliced or chopped, depending on the recipe) in a bowl of well salted water (several tablespoons will be needed per pint/600ml) for 1–2 hours. This should leech out any bitter flavours. Rinse in fresh water and dry before use.

ARABIATA
—— *Italian Chilli Sauce* ——

ITALY

The use of Italian smoky bacon is what makes this chilli and tomato sauce really distinctive. Use *Arabiata* as a sauce with any pasta and sprinkle freshly grated Pecorino Romano cheese on top.

SERVES 4

INGREDIENTS

4 tablespoons olive oil
2–3 garlic cloves, crushed
3–4 thin slices Italian rindless smoky bacon, finely chopped
4 tablespoons sun-dried tomatoes in oil (chef's tip, page 76), finely chopped

1 tablespoon capers
14oz (400g) canned tomatoes
3 tablespoons red chilli mash (pages 286–7)
1 tablespoon chopped fresh parsley
salt
your choice of cooked pasta

METHOD

1. Heat the oil in a wok or frying pan over a high heat. Stir-fry the garlic for 20 seconds. Add the bacon and stir-fry for another minute.

2. Add the capers, tomatoes, chilli mash and parsley, keeping the pan on the heat just until the contents start to bubble. Salt to taste and serve with pasta.

SPAGHETTI ALLA SICILIANA
—— *Sicilian Spicy Mince* ——

SICILY

This is my spiced up version of Bolognese sauce and I eat it with spaghetti, rice or The Ultimate Garlic Bread (see page 268).

SERVES 4

INGREDIENTS

3 tablespoons vegetable oil
3–6 garlic cloves, chopped
8oz (225g) onions, finely chopped
14oz (400g) canned chopped
  tomatoes
2 tablespoons chopped red bell
  pepper
1–4 whole green chillies
1¹/₂lb (675g) lean minced beef
1 tablespoon tomato purée
2 teaspoons dried mixed herbs
1 tablespoon tomato ketchup
1 teaspoon Worcester sauce
2 teaspoons bought pesto sauce
1 tablespoon chopped fresh
  oregano

1 tablespoon chopped fresh
  coriander
aromatic salt (page 46)

SPICES
4–6 whole green cardamom
  pods
4–6 cloves
¹/₂ teaspoon cummin seeds
¹/₂ teaspoon coriander seeds
4 bay leaves
1–3 black peppercorns

GARNISH
grated Cheddar cheese
chopped fresh parsley

METHOD

1. Heat the oil in a karahi, wok or frying pan over a high heat, then add the garlic and stir-fry for 30 seconds.

2. Add the onions and reduce the heat. Stir-fry for 10 minutes, until the onions become translucent and begin to brown.

3. Place the garlic and onions in a suitable size lidded casserole dish, along with the tomatoes, bell peppers and chillies. Put the casserole into an oven preheated to 375°F/190°C/Gas 5.

4. Put the mince in the karahi, wok or frying pan and cook it for about 10 minutes to 'seal' or brown it and reduce the liquids.

5. Add the **spices**, tomato purée, dried herbs, ketchup, Worcester sauce and pesto. Add the spicy mince to the casserole, mixing well.

6. Leave to cook for 30 minutes, then add the fresh herbs, and return to the oven for 15 minutes. Add aromatic salt to taste, and serve, sprinkled with grated cheese and chopped parsley.

FACING PAGE *Left to right: Italian Chilli Sauce (opposite) and Sicilian Spicy Mince with spaghetti (above)*

PORK VINDALOO

INDIA

Compare this recipe with the one on page 111. The famous Goan pork Vindaloo evolved from Portugal's *Vinho e Alhos*. The long marinade is essential. This is the authentic centuries-old Goan Vindaloo which bears little resemblance to the popular Indian restaurant version. Readers who, like me, adore the latter will find recipes for it in my other curry cookbooks. Meanwhile, try this recipe – you'll probably like it as much or even more! Serve with plain rice, Chupattis (see page 264) and Raita (see page 296).

SERVES 4

INGREDIENTS

1¹/₂lb (675g) lean leg of pork, off the bone, any fat, gristle and skin removed
3 tablespoons ghee (page 43) or vegetable oil
4–6 garlic cloves, chopped
8oz (225g) onions, finely chopped
2 tablespoons mild curry paste (page 49)
2 tablespoons lemon juice
1 tablespoon garam masala (page 47)
1 tablespoon chopped fresh coriander
1–4 fresh red cayenne chillies, finely chopped

aromatic salt (page 46)

MARINADE
7fl oz (200ml) red wine
2 tablespoons red wine vinegar
4–6 garlic cloves, crushed
1–3 tablespoons red chilli mash (pages 286–7)
1 teaspoon aromatic salt (page 46)

SPICES
10 cloves
6 green cardamom pods
2 inch (5cm) piece cassia bark
1 teaspoon cummin seeds

METHOD

1. Cut the meat into cubes about 1¹/₂ inches (4cm) in size, remembering that they will shrink during cooking as the liquids come out.

2. In a large non-metallic bowl, mix the meat and the **marinade**. Cover and refrigerate for up to 60 hours (see page 42).

3. Heat the ghee or oil in a karahi or wok. Stir-fry the garlic and the **spices** for a minute, then add the onions and continue to stir-fry for 5 minutes. Add the curry paste and stir-fry for a further 3 minutes.

4. Using a 4–5 pint (2.25–2.75 litre) lidded casserole, combine the fried ingredients, the pork and its marinade and place in an oven preheated to 375°F/190°C/Gas 5.

5. After 20 minutes, inspect and stir, adding a little water or akhni stock (see page 00), if it is becoming too dry. Repeat 20 minutes later, adding the remaining ingredients. Add aromatic salt to taste. Cook for a further 20 minutes or until cooked to your liking.

LAL QILA KHURMA KI SHAH JEHAN
—— *Shah Jehan's Last Stew* ——

INDIA

It was Shah Jehan who, as the fourth Mogul Emperor, built the Taj Mahal in Agra. It was the privilege of the emperor to build the most opulent mosque imaginable, as a mausoleum to house his coffin. When his principal wife Mumtaz died in 1647, Shah Jehan, stricken with grief, announced that he would immediately order the building of a mosque, ultimately intended to house himself, but which would for now house Mumtaz.

In just 11 years the most talented artists and craftsmen in his empire had erected the Taj Mahal, the white marble wonder of the world. It cost the treasury dearly. But the result was exceptional – and it was fitting that the greatest Mogul should have the greatest mausoleum. Then Shah Jehan made a daring new announcement – the white Taj was to be used solely for Mumtaz. An identical one, sited on the opposite bank of the River Jumna, would be built for him. It would be made of black marble.

Work started on the second Taj, and the foundations can be clearly seen to this day. However, it was never to be completed. Shah Jehan's eldest son, Aurangzeb, realising that not even the mighty Mogul Empire had the funds to create a second Taj Mahal, had his father arrested and imprisoned. The Shah's prison was the Red Fort, which was within sight of the Taj Mahal.

Aurangzeb declared himself Emperor and his father insane. Work on the black Taj Mahal stopped.

The story has a sad end. Poor Shah Jehan was never allowed out of the Red Fort. He languished there for seven years, reportedly continuously grieving for Mumtaz. The story goes that he was allowed just one meal a day, containing whatever he wished. Shah Jehan interpreted this to mean that he could never vary his choice, and for seven years he always had the same dish until he died.

So we can say with authority that this dish was Shah Jehan's last stew. (The authority in this case is Manjit Gill, consultant chef to London's famous Red Fort Restaurant, where he put this dish on the menu.) But the saddest thing of all was the loss to the world of a black Taj Mahal.

This dish combines meat with vegetables, nuts and dried fruit (in Persian style) in a rich creamy sauce. It is very rich and nourishing and is perfect eaten with Naan Bread (see page 266).

SERVES 4

INGREDIENTS

1¹/₄lb (560g) lean leg of lamb, off
   the bone, any fat, skin and gristle
   removed
3 tablespoons ghee (page 43)
2 garlic cloves, crushed
8oz (225g) onions, finely chopped
2 medium parsnips, chopped
2 medium carrots, chopped
¹/₂ pint (300ml) water or akhni
   stock (page 44)
3–4 pieces cauliflower, broken into
   small florets
20 Kenyan green beans, topped
   and tailed
2 tablespoons green pistachio nuts
1 tablespoon chopped fresh
   coriander
6 stoned dates
4fl oz (120ml) double cream
20 saffron strands
aromatic salt (page 46)

PASTE
7oz (200g) blanched almonds

4fl oz (120ml) thick plain yoghurt
2 garlic cloves, crushed
1 inch (2.5cm) cube ginger,
   chopped
3 tablespoons coriander seeds,
   roasted and ground
1 teaspoon cummin seeds, roasted
   and ground
1 teaspoon ground cinnamon
¹/₂ teaspoon green cardamom seeds,
   crushed
¹/₂ teaspoon fennel seeds, crushed

WHOLE SPICES
2 teaspoons cummin seeds, roasted
4–5 brown cardamom pods
10–12 cloves
2×2 inch (5cm) pieces cassia
   bark
1 inch (2.5cm) piece mace

GARNISH
cooked onion tarka (page 44)
whole fresh coriander leaves

METHOD

1. Mulch the **paste** ingredients down in a food processor, using enough water to achieve a creamy, pourable purée.

2. Cut the meat into cubes about 1¹/₂ inches (4cm) in size, remembering that they will shrink during cooking as the liquids come out.

3. Heat the ghee in a karahi or wok. Stir-fry the garlic and the **whole spices** for a minute, then add the onions and continue to stir-fry for 5 minutes. Add the paste, and stir-fry for 3 more minutes.

4. Using a 4–5 pint (2.25–2.75 litre) lidded casserole, combine the fried ingredients, meat, parsnips and carrots and place in an oven pre-heated to 375°F/190°C/Gas 5.

5. After 20 minutes, inspect and stir, adding a little water or akhni stock if it is becoming too dry. Repeat 20 minutes later, adding the remaining ingredients, including aromatic salt to taste. Cook for a further 20 minutes or until cooked to your liking.

FACING PAGE *Shah Jehan's Last Stew (this page) served with Bombay Tomato Rice (page 244), Chupattis (page 264) and a selection of homemade and commercial chutneys*

6. Serve garnished with the onion tarka and whole fresh coriander leaves.

DHAI KAJU GOSHT
—— *Lamb and Cashew Curry* ——

NEPAL

In northern India and Nepal they enjoy hearty curries. They need them to fend off the bitterly cold mountain weather. They use yoghurt to tenderise the meat and cashew nuts to create a creamy sauce. Serve with Parathas (see page 265) or plain rice.

SERVES 4

INGREDIENTS

1½lb (675g) lean leg of lamb, off the bone, any fat, gristle and skin removed
4 tablespoons ghee or niter kebbeh (page 43)
4 garlic cloves, crushed
1 inch (2.5cm) cube fresh ginger, grated
8oz (225g) onions, finely chopped
1½ teaspoons mild curry paste (page 49)
5fl oz (150ml) yoghurt
aromatic salt (page 46)

PURÉE
7oz (200g) cashew nuts

2–4 green cayenne chillies, chopped
2 tablespoons chopped fresh coriander
1 tablespoon chopped fresh mint
1 tablespoon poppy seeds
2 tablespoons cummin seeds, roasted
2 tablespoons coriander seeds, roasted
1 tablespoon garam masala (page 47)

GARNISH
devilled chilli cashew nuts (page 65)
whole fresh coriander leaves
lemon wedges

METHOD

1. Mulch the **purée** ingredients down in a blender or food processor, using enough water to achieve an easily pourable purée.

2. Cut the meat into cubes about 1½ inches (4cm) in size, remembering that they will shrink during cooking as the liquids come out.

3. Heat the ghee or *niter kebbeh* in a karahi or wok. Stir-fry the garlic and the ginger for a minute, then add the onions and continue to stir-fry for 5 minutes. Add the curry paste, and stir-fry for 3 more minutes. Add the **purée** and stir-fry for about 5 more minutes, adding a little water as needed.

4. Using a 4–5 pint (2.25–2.75 litre) lidded casserole, combine the fried ingredients, meat, and yoghurt and place it in an oven preheated to 375°F/190°C/Gas 5.

5. After 20 minutes, inspect and stir, adding a little water or akhni stock if it is becoming too dry. Repeat 20 minutes later. Add aromatic salt to taste. Cook for a further 20 minutes or until cooked to your liking.

6. Serve, garnished with the devilled cashew nuts, whole fresh coriander leaves and lemon wedges.

JERK VEAL

Jerk flavouring is a favourite in the Caribbean, especially in Jamaica. I have chosen veal but any meat or poultry can be cooked in this way.

The jerk flavouring is actually a sweet, hot and salty marinade, invented, some say, by escaped Jamaican slaves who preserved meat by rubbing it with chilli-based jerk sauce, then drying it. In fact its true origins go back much further. For as long as anyone can remember, Red Indian tribes used 'jerky' to preserve buffalo meat before sun-drying it. Cowboys and drifters also used beef jerky as a staple. In that great movie *The Outlaw Josie Wales* Clint Eastwood orders 'ten pounds of beef jerky' whilst on the run from the bluecoats.

You can buy packets of jerk-dried meat in the Caribbean and USA. This recipe captures the flavour in a casserole version. You should find grenadine syrup at an off-licence.

SERVES 4

INGREDIENTS

$1^1/_2$lb (675g) lean veal
chilli powder

MARINADE
6fl oz (175ml) orange juice
6fl oz (175ml) pineapple juice
1 tablespoon red chilli mash
   (pages 286–7)

2 tablespoons grenadine syrup
4fl oz (120ml) red wine vinegar
2 teaspoons garlic powder
1 teaspoon brown sugar
1 teaspoon dark soy sauce
$^1/_2$ teaspoon salt

METHOD

1. Cut the meat into cubes about $1^1/_2$ inches (4cm) in size, remembering that they will shrink during cooking as the liquids come out.

2. In a large non-metallic bowl mix the **marinade** ingredients together. Add the meat, cover and refrigerate for up to 60 hours (see page 42).

3. Put the meat in a 4–5 pint (2.25–2.75 litre) lidded casserole and place in an oven preheated to 375°F/190°C/Gas 5.

4. After 20 minutes, inspect and stir, adding a little water or akhni stock if it is becoming too dry. Repeat 20 minutes later. Add chilli powder to taste. Cook for a further 20 minutes or until cooked to your liking. Serve with Rice and Peas (see page 239).

BEEF CASSEROLE WITH HORSERADISH AND MUSTARD

GREAT BRITAIN

There is nothing more British than the traditional roast beef served with horseradish and mustard. When accompanied by Yorkshire pudding – that stupendous, unique, savoury, crispy, chewy batter 'pastry' which mops up the rich brown gravy – and green vegetables and roast potatoes, let anyone dare to say that British cooking is the worst in the world.

Here is a casserole version, using the favourite British hot spices of horseradish and mustard, enhanced with brown sauce and Worcestershire Sauce.

Serve it with roast potatoes and two vegetables, or it goes very well with plain boiled rice (page 232). The best accompaniment of all is Chilli Toad in the Hole (page 225).

SERVES 4

INGREDIENTS

3 tablespoons vegetable oil
8oz (225g) onions, sliced
4¹/₂oz (125g) plain flour
salt and pepper to taste
1¹/₂lb (675g) trimmed lean steak
1 pint (600ml) stock, any kind
2 teaspoons bottled yellow mustard
　paste

1¹/₂oz (40g) fresh horseradish,
　finely chopped (chef's tip
　opposite) **or** 2 tablespoons
　bottled hot horseradish sauce
2 teaspoons bottled brown sauce
1 teaspoon Worcestershire Sauce

METHOD

1. Heat the oil in a karahi or wok and stir-fry the onions over a medium heat for about 10 minutes.

2. In a bowl, mix together the flour, salt and pepper. Toss pieces of meat in the seasoned flour then add to the onions in the karahi or wok.

3. Stir-fry the meat until all the pieces are 'sealed' on all sides (ie: they no longer look raw).

4. Preheat the oven to 375°F/190°C/Gas 5. Transfer the onions and meat to a 4–5 pint (2.25–2.75 litre) lidded casserole. Add the stock, mustard, horseradish, brown sauce and Worcestershire Sauce, stir well, cover and place in the oven.

5. Check it after 30 minutes, giving it a good stir. Return to the oven, still covered.

6. It should be ready after a further 50–60 minutes, but test it for tenderness, and add salt to taste. You should have a thick dark brown sauce.

ABOVE *Left to right: Beef Casserole with Horseradish and Mustard (opposite), Chilli in the Hole (page 225) and Peruvian Hot Potatoes (page 205)*

Chef's Tip

FRESH HORSERADISH

Horseradish is a root that has more affect on the eyes than chopping onions – you have been warned! Commercially bottled products aren't a patch on fresh horseradish for flavour or strength.

To prepare the fresh root, trim off any little rootlets and wash off all the earth. Either grate by hand or use a food processor. Mix with whipped cream or yoghurt to make horseradish sauce.

STOBA
—— *Spicy Curaçaoan Meat* ——

CURAÇAO

From Curaçao, the former Dutch colony in the West Indies, comes the celebrated liqueur of the same name. Less well known is this spicy goat recipe, *stoba*. It's a variation on a Jamaican recipe for goat curry. (Lamb can be substituted if you wish.) My recipe 'enhances' the flavours with the addition of some orange curaçao. The chef is at liberty to 'enhance' herself or himself with as many tots as necessary during the cooking of this dish! Serve with rice or bread.

SERVES 4

INGREDIENTS

1¹/₂lb (675g) lean leg of kid or goat, off the bone, any fat, gristle and skin removed
4 tablespoons corn oil
4–6 garlic cloves, chopped
2 inch (5cm) piece ginger, chopped
8oz (225g) onions, chopped
2–3 bay leaves
4oz (110g) chopped sun-dried tomatoes in oil (chef's tip, page 76)
8fl oz (225ml) concentrated orange juice
1–2 sticks celery, finely chopped

2–3 courgettes, chopped
aromatic salt (page 46)
2 teaspoons garam masala (page 47)
1 tablespoon chopped fresh coriander
3fl oz (75ml) orange curaçao

SPICES
1 teaspoon cummin seeds
1 teaspoon fennel seeds
¹/₂ teaspoon aniseed
¹/₂ teaspoon ground cloves
2 inch (5cm) piece cassia bark
6 green cardamom pods

METHOD

1. Cut the meat into cubes about 1¹/₂ inches (4cm) in size, remembering that they will shrink during cooking as the liquids come out.

2. Heat the oil in a karahi or wok. Stir-fry the garlic for 30 seconds. Add the ginger and **spices** and stir-fry for a minute, then add the onions and continue to stir-fry for 5 minutes. Add the bay leaves, sun-dried tomatoes and orange juice and stir-fry for 3 more minutes.

3. Using a 4–5 pint (2.25–2.75 litre) lidded casserole, combine the fried ingredients and the meat, and place in an oven preheated to 375°F/190°C/Gas 5.

4. After 20 minutes, inspect and stir, adding water or akhni stock if it is becoming too dry. Repeat 20 minutes later, adding the celery and courgettes and aromatic salt to taste. Cook for a further 20 minutes or until cooked to your liking.

5. Finally add the garam masala, fresh coriander and the curaçao. Mix in well, and serve at once.

PIRI-PIRI CURRY
—— *Hot Red Chilli Curry* ——

One African word for chilli is *piri-piri* and one of the very hottest chillies is a small pequin type called the bird chilli. Chillies were introduced to Africa by the Portuguese who stumbled across them in Brazil. They were planted in Portuguese African territory and the wild birds, who adored eating the small red pods, helped to spread them around the continent.

I serve this with rice or Ethiopian Millet Bread (see page 261).

SERVES 4

INGREDIENTS

$1^1/_2$lb (675g) lean beef, off the bone, any fat, gristle and skin removed
4 tablespoons ghee (page 43) or vegetable oil
2 garlic cloves, chopped
2 inch (5cm) piece ginger, chopped
8oz (225g) onions, chopped
$^1/_2$ each of red, green and yellow bell peppers, chopped
2–3 tablespoons piri-piri *sauce* (page 293)
2 teaspoons garam masala (page 47)

2 teaspoons ground fenugreek
2 tablespoons chopped fresh coriander
2 fresh tomatoes, chopped
aromatic salt (page 46)

SPICES
2 teaspoons chilli powder
1 teaspoon mild curry paste (page 49)
1 teaspoon ground cummin
$^1/_2$ teaspoon ground coriander
$^1/_2$ teaspoon ground black pepper

METHOD

1. Cut the meat into cubes about $1^1/_2$ inches (4cm) in size, remembering that they will shrink during cooking as the liquids come out.

2. Heat the ghee or vegetable oil in a karahi or wok. Stir-fry the garlic for 30 seconds. Add the ginger and **spices** and stir-fry for 1 minute, then add the onions and continue to stir-fry for 5 minutes. Add the bell peppers and *piri-piri* sauce and stir-fry for 3 more minutes.

3. Using a 4–5 pint (2.25–2.75 litre) lidded casserole, combine the fried ingredients and the meat, and place in the oven preheated to 375°F/190°C/Gas 5.

4. After 20 minutes, inspect and stir, adding a little water or akhni stock if it is becoming too dry. Repeat 20 minutes later.

5. Finally, add the garam masala, fenugreek, fresh coriander, tomatoes and aromatic salt to taste. Mix in well, and serve.

GAENG PED NUA
—— *Thai Red Beef Curry* ——

THAILAND

Red curry is hot and flavourful and traditional to Thailand. You'll notice that this recipe has two applications of red chilli. Those who don't like it so hot should reduce the quantities of chilli. Serve with plain rice or Malaysian Fried Rice (see page 240).

SERVES 4

INGREDIENTS

2 tablespoons corn oil
4 garlic cloves, chopped
2 inch (5cm) cube galingale or ginger, chopped
8oz (225g) onions, chopped
2 tablespoons mild curry paste (page 49)
1 tablespoon red chilli mash (pages 286–7)
1¹/₂lb (675g) lean stewing steak, chopped into bite-size cubes
2 stalks fresh lemon grass
6–7 lime leaves, fresh or dried

14fl oz (400ml) canned coconut milk (page 44)
1 tablespoon fresh whole baby Thai cayenne chillies
2 tablespoons nam pla *fish sauce (page 172)*
8–9 fresh basil leaves, coarsely chopped
1 tablespoon chopped fresh coriander
aromatic salt (page 46)

GARNISH
4 chilli tassels (chef's tip, page 211)

METHOD

1. Heat the oil in a karahi or wok. Stir-fry the garlic and galingale or ginger for 1 minute. Add the onions and stir-fry for 5 more minutes.

2. Add the curry paste and chilli mash and stir-fry for 3 more minutes.

3. Using a 4–5 pint (2.25–2.75 litre) lidded casserole, combine the fried ingredients, the meat, lemon grass, lime leaves and coconut milk and place in an oven preheated to 375°F/190°C/Gas 5.

4. After 20 minutes, inspect and stir, adding water or akhni stock if it is becoming too dry. Repeat 20 minutes later, adding the remaining ingredients. Add aromatic salt to taste. Cook for a further 20 minutes or until cooked to your liking.

5. Serve each portion garnished with a chilli tassel.

FACING PAGE *Thai Red Beef Curry (above) served with Thai Hot Chilli Sauce (page 289) and surrounded by Thai vegetables, including, from left to right, pea aubergines, galingale, knobbly limes and garden aubergines*

GOULASH
—— *Hungarian Paprika Stew* ——

HUNGARY

The national dish of Hungary has become internationally known as Goulash. In Hungary it is called *Gylyas*. It is a meat stew flavoured with and coloured by Hungarian paprika. I use veal because its subtle taste and pale colouring are enhanced by the red of the paprika.

We rarely come across fresh paprika at the greengrocer's, which incidentally can come hot or mild, so I'm using a combination of paprika powder and fresh red chillies which you can omit if you don't want the heat. But if ever you do find fresh paprika, remember this dish and use them in it for a memorable experience. Serve it with rice, potatoes or The Ultimate Garlic Bread (see page 268).

SERVES 4

INGREDIENTS

1¹/₂lb (675g) lean leg of veal, off the bone, any fat, gristle and skin removed
6oz (175g) fresh hot Hungarian red paprika chilli, chopped, or 3 tablespoons Hungarian paprika powder and 1–3 fresh red cayenne chillies, chopped
4 tablespoons vegetable oil
2–4 garlic cloves, chopped

8oz (225g) onions, chopped
1 can chopped Italian plum tomatoes, with their juice
1 large stick celery, finely chopped
5fl oz (150ml) soured cream
salt

SPICES
1 teaspoon celery seeds
¹/₂ teaspoon caraway seeds
¹/₄ teaspoon aniseed

METHOD

1. Cut the meat into cubes about 1¹/₂ inches (4cm) in size, remembering that they will shrink during cooking as the liquids come out.

2. Mix the paprika powder with enough water to make a runny paste. (If using fresh paprika omit this stage and stage 4 and add the paprika at stage 5.)

3. Heat the oil in a karahi or wok. Stir-fry the garlic and the **spices** for a minute, then add the onions and continue to stir-fry for 5 minutes.

4. Add the paprika paste, and stir-fry for 3 more minutes.

5. Using a 4–5 pint (2.25–2.75 litre) lidded casserole, combine the fried ingredients, the meat, chillies, tomatoes and celery and place in an oven preheated to 375°F/190°C/Gas 5.

6. After 20 minutes, inspect and stir, adding a little water if it is becoming too dry. Repeat 20 minutes later, adding the soured cream. Salt to taste. Cook for a further 20 minutes or until to your liking.

COUSCOUS MEAT STEW

MOROCCO

Couscous is described as the national dish of Morocco. It is certainly one of their most well-known dishes. To cook the stew, with couscous, the Moroccans use a *couscousière*, a special double boiler, and if you want to cook couscous a lot, it is worth obtaining one. Otherwise use a deep lidded saucepan of about 8 inches (20cm) in diameter, and a sieve of the same diameter which fits well without its bottom touching the liquid inside the saucepan.

There are many brands of couscous on the market. These have been pre-cooked and dried, leaving you the relatively easy task of finishing off. Timings vary depending on the manufacturer and invariably it requires less time than the packet says.

SERVES 4

INGREDIENTS

1¹/₂lb (675g) stewing steak
4 tablespoons ghee (page 43) or
*   vegetable oil*
8oz (225g) onions, chopped
1 teaspoon ground cummin

4–6 canned tomatoes
1 red bell pepper, chopped
8oz (225g) couscous
black pepper and salt
1 recipe harissa (page 293)

METHOD

1. Remove all fat, gristle and skin from the meat, then cut it into 1¹/₂ inch (4cm) cubes.

2. Heat the ghee or oil, and stir-fry the onion and ground cummin for 5 minutes. Add the meat and stir-fry for 10 minutes to 'seal' it.

3. Transfer these ingredients and the tomatoes and red pepper to a saucepan as described above, adding approximately the same volume of boiling water, and bring it to the boil on the stove. Simmer for 30 minutes, stirring occasionally.

4. Put the couscous into a muslin-lined sieve which fits on to the meat saucepan. Put the lid on the sieve and continue to simmer the stew for 20 minutes more. The steam cooks and flavours the couscous. Keep fluffing it up with a fork about every 5 minutes.

5. When the couscous is cooked to your liking, remove it from the muslin liner and carefully pile it up into a cone shape in a serving dish. Put it in a warmer until you are ready to serve.

6. Meanwhile season the stew with pepper and salt to taste, then strain it, putting the liquid into a gravy boat.

7. Make a depression in the couscous and nestle the dry stew inside it. To serve, place the dish on the table allowing the diners to help themselves and add gravy and harissa to their liking.

POULTRY DISHES

A round the spicy world, there is a special adoration of poultry, with a proliferation of outstanding dishes. My choice brings together some of the best of those from Latin America, Mexico, Portugal, Austria, Africa, Iran, India and the Indian Ocean, Malaysia, Thailand and the USA. Ingredients include chicken, guinea fowl, quail, duck and turkey.

There are currys, roasts, rissoles, hot pots and stir-fries to choose from. Notable amongst several curries are Thai Jungle Fowl Curry and the gorgeously presented *Karamba Kulkul Issu* – chicken and prawn curry in a coconut shell, appropriately from the Indian Ocean islands of the Seychelles. For a remarkable party piece from India's Lucknow, serve Duck-Stuffed Quails en Croute. Be sure to try all the recipes in this chapter, but above all do not miss the Mexico Aztec national dish, Guajolote Molé Poblano – turkey in a chilli and chocolate sauce.

OPPOSITE *Top to bottom: Chicken and Prawns in Coconut Shells (page 153), Maldavian Chicken Rissoles (page 133) sitting on pandana leaves, and Creamy Coconut Lentils (page 181). Notice the fresh peppercorn vines (bottom left) the coiled long beans, and the banana leaf*

AJI DE GALLINA
—— *Chilli Chicken Hotpot* ——

PERU

All over Latin America you'll find variations of this dish. *Aji* (the Inca word for 'chilli') is popular everywhere. Of course you can change the timings and substitute shellfish, vegetables or meat for the chicken. In fact a Peruvian favourite is *Aji de Cuy* (guinea pig)! Here we'll use the casserole to pot-roast the bird.

SERVES 4

INGREDIENTS

$1\times3^1/_2$–4lb (1.5–1.8kg) roasting
  chicken with giblets
8oz (225g) onions, sliced
6 whole garlic cloves
1 carrot, sliced
2–3 whole red cayenne chillies
3–4 bay leaves
1 teaspoon black peppercorns
4 tablespoons corn oil
$1^1/_2$ teaspoons ground turmeric
4–6 garlic cloves, finely chopped
2 inch (5cm) cube ginger, grated
8oz (225g) onions, finely chopped
2 dry guajillo or mirasol chillies,
  soaked (page 42) and chopped

1oz (30g) butter
1 tablespoon cornflour
$^1/_2$ pint (300ml) milk
4 slices crustless white bread,
  crumbled
6–8 walnuts, quartered
4oz (110g) Cheddar cheese, grated
1 tablespoon chopped fresh
  coriander
6 tablespoons fresh lime juice
1 teaspoon aromatic salt (page 46)

GARNISH
a few whole fresh coriander leaves
toasted pinenuts

METHOD

1. Quarter the chicken, skin and clean it. Put it and the liver, neck and giblets into a large casserole dish (of at least 6 pint/3.4 litre capacity), along with the onion slices, whole garlic cloves, carrot, cayenne, chillies, bay leaves and peppercorns. Add 1 pint (600ml) boiling water and place in an oven preheated to 375°F/190°C/Gas 5.

2. During this stage heat the oil in a frying pan. Stir-fry the turmeric for 30 seconds. Add the chopped garlic and continue stir-frying for a further 30 seconds. Then add the ginger, chopped onion and guajillo or mirasol chillies and stir-fry for about 10 minutes.

3. After an hour in the oven take out the casserole dish and remove the chicken pieces. When cool, remove the meat from the bones. Strain the liquid and return it and the fried items to the casserole dish. Chop the chicken, add it to the casserole and return to the oven for at least 15 minutes.

4. In the frying pan heat the butter. Mix the cornflour and milk together, then add to the hot butter, stirring constantly until it thickens into a white sauce. Add the bread, walnuts, cheese and fresh coriander.

5. Add this sauce to the casserole, stir in the fresh lime juice and add the aromatic salt.

6. Garnish with the whole fresh coriander leaves and pinenuts, and serve with rice or Tortillas (see page 262).

MURGH CUTLISS
—— *Chicken Rissoles* ——

THE MALDIVES

These rissoles require a little effort for their three-stage preparation – the cooking of the minced chicken, making mashed potato to enrobe the chicken (unless you happen to have some leftover mashed potato) and frying the finished rissole. This recipe from the Maldive Islands, just off the south Indian coast, makes a fine snack, or main course when served with curried vegetables and rice.

SERVES 4

INGREDIENTS

12oz (350g) chicken breast, off the
   bone, skinned
2–3 garlic cloves, crushed
1 inch (2.5cm) cube ginger, grated
1 tablespoon chopped fresh mint
2–4 fresh green chillies, chopped
4 tablespoons ghee (page 43)

1lb (450g) mashed potato
2 eggs
a pinch of aromatic salt (page 46)
4oz (110g) fresh breadcrumbs or
   5oz (150g) packet breadcrumbs
oil for deep-frying

METHOD

1. Pulse the chicken, garlic, ginger, mint and chillies in a food processor or put through a mincer to create a mouldable texture.

2. Divide the mixture into 16 and mould into egg shapes.

3. Heat the ghee in a flat frying pan and fry the 16 pieces for about 6 minutes, turning each one to ensure even cooking.

4. Set aside to cool.

5. Coat each piece all over in mashed potato.

6. Whisk the eggs with the aromatic salt, dip each rissole in the beaten egg, then roll in the breadcrumbs until well coated.

7. Heat the oil in a deep-fryer to 375°F/190°C (chip-frying temperature) and fry until golden (about 6 minutes).

POLO CON MOLÉ POBLANO
—— *Chicken with Chilli and Chocolate* ——

MEXICO

The *molé*, meaning 'mixture of ingredients', is arguably one of the most important elements in Mexican cooking. Of the many *molé* sauces, this one with chocolate and chilli is probably the most interesting. The *molé* story is told on page 22. Making a *molé* is as easy as making a curry paste.

It is traditional to use the three Mexican chilli types stated. They are 'black' in colour and high in flavour. Ordinary chilli powder can be substituted but the colour and taste will be different.

SERVES 4

INGREDIENTS

4 tablespoons corn oil
2–4 garlic cloves, chopped
8oz (225g) Spanish onion, chopped
1¹/₂lb (675g) chicken breast, off the bone
2oz (50g) dark or bitter chocolate (chef's tip opposite), melted
1 tablespoon tomato purée
7oz (200g) canned tomatoes
1 tablespoon chopped fresh coriander
salt

SPICES
1 teaspoon ground black pepper
1 teaspoon sesame seeds
¹/₂ teaspoon coriander seeds
¹/₂ teaspoon aniseed

¹/₂ teaspoon cummin seeds
2 inch (5cm) piece cinnamon quill
6 cloves

MOLÉ POBLANO PASTE
1 tablespoon finely chopped mulato chilli
1 tablespoon finely chopped pasilla chilli
1 tablespoon finely chopped ancho chilli
6–8 tortilla chips, crumbled
1 tablespoon golden sultanas
1 tablespoon brown sugar
1 tablespoon pumpkin seeds
1 tablespoon pinenuts
20 hazelnuts
20 almonds

METHOD

1. Heat a dry wok or frying pan on the stove, add the **spices** and 'roast' them for about 30 seconds, then allow them to cool and grind to a fine powder (see page 45).

2. Put the **paste** ingredients in the same hot pan and 'roast' them for 30 seconds.

3. Transfer the ground spices and roasted ingredients to a food processor or blender. Add water and pulse down to a paste of pouring consistency. Leave this in the container until stage 5.

4. Heat half the oil in your pan over a high heat, then stir-fry the garlic for 30 seconds. Add the onion and reduce the heat. Stir-fry for 10 minutes, until the onion becomes translucent and begins to turn brown.

5. Allow this to cool, then purée in the food processor with the paste ingredients.

6. Heat the remaining oil in the pan and add the purée, stir-frying for about 5 minutes. You'll notice that it goes darker as it cooks. When the oil 'floats' the purée is ready.

7. Add the chicken meat and cook for about 5 minutes, stirring from time to time. Add a little water or chicken stock if it is becoming too dry.

8. Add the remaining ingredients, and salt to taste, and stir-fry for about 10 more minutes or until the chicken is fully cooked. Serve with Tortillas (see page 262).

Chef's Tip

CHOCOLATE

Use plain or 'bitter' chocolate. It must contain as high a proportion of cocoa solids as possible. Most of the popular chocolate bars contain around 35 per cent cocoa. The best contains 70 per cent. This sort of chocolate is more expensive, but will give you the best results. Read the packaging labels carefully or ask at your local deli.

To melt the chocolate, bring a pan of water to a simmer. Break the chocolate up into squares and place in a heatproof glass bowl which fits over the pan. Ensure that the base of the bowl does not touch the water. The chocolate will melt fast, so keep stirring.

GUAJOLOTE MOLÉ POBLANO
—— *Turkey in Chilli and Chocolate Sauce* ——

MEXICO

Turkey was indigenous to Mexico (the chicken arrived with the Spanish invaders) and this dish was Montezuma's favourite. Use the chicken recipe opposite, but allow slightly longer for the turkey to cook. A photo of this dish appears on page 22.

PIPIAN MOLÉ VERDE
—— *Chicken in a Green Hot Molé Sauce* ——

MEXICO

This *molé* has a dark natural green colour. It should not be lurid so please do not be tempted to use food colouring.

SERVES 4

INGREDIENTS

4 tablespoons corn oil
2–4 garlic cloves, chopped
8oz (225g) Spanish onions, chopped
1¹/₂lb (675g) chicken breast, off the bone
4oz (110g) Kenyan green beans, chopped
1 tablespoon chopped fresh coriander
salt

PASTE
4–6 green cayenne chillies

1 green bell pepper
6oz (175g) marrow
6oz (175g) green peas
2–3 green tomatoes
2 ripe bananas
2 tablespoons ground almonds

SPICES
1 tablespoon pumpkin seeds
1 tablespoon sesame seeds
2 teaspoons green peppercorns (in brine or freeze-dried)
1 teaspoon coriander seeds

METHOD

1. Chop the **paste** ingredients where necessary, then pulse them in a blender or food processor with enough water to make a pourable paste.

2. Heat a dry wok or frying pan on the stove, add the **spices** and 'roast' them for about 30 seconds, then allow them to cool and grind to a fine powder (see page 45). Add this to the blender or food processor.

3. Follow stages 4–8 of the recipe on pages 134–5 and serve with Tortillas (see page 262).

POLLO DEL MOLÉ DEL COLORADO
——— *Minced Chicken in Red Molé Sauce* ———

MEXICO

In this attractive red *molé* sauce (enhanced with red wine) I've used minced chicken breast for a change.

SERVES 4

INGREDIENTS

4 tablespoons corn oil
2–4 garlic cloves, chopped
8oz (225g) Spanish onions, chopped
1¹/₂lb (675g) chicken breast, off the bone, minced
8fl oz (250ml) red wine
1 tablespoon chopped fresh coriander
1 tablespoon chopped fresh oregano
salt

PASTE

4–6 red habanero chillies
1 red bell pepper
4oz (110g) carrot, grated
14oz (400g) canned red tomatoes with their juice
1 tablespoon tomato purée
2 tablespoons ground almonds
1 teaspoon ground coriander
1 teaspoon ground white pepper

METHOD

1. Chop the paste ingredients where necessary, then pulse them in a blender or food processor to make a pourable paste.

2. Follow stages 4–8 of the recipe for *Polo Con Molé Poblano* (see page 134) and serve with Tortillas (see page 262).

GUMBO CREOLE

USA

According to Chef John Fosse at his Louisiana restaurant, Laffitte's Landing, Gumbo is derived from the French Bouillabaisse (or, as he says it, 'Boo-yar-bayees'). Gumbo is a thick gelatinous dark-coloured soup-like stew from Louisiana. The word derives from *gambo*, the African for 'okra', and the dish came to the area with the slaves. It was the sap from the okra which created the thick texture. Nowadays okra is often omitted and in its place people use a seasoning called filé (pronounced fee-lay), an ancient Red Indian (Choctaw Tribe) powder made from sassafras leaves. This is available from specialist shops but can be omitted. Either way there is an endless list of Gumbo recipes using chicken, seafood, meat, game and vegetables.

Indeed, as with most things Cajun and Creole, it seems that anything goes: I've even seen a recipe for Squirrel Gumbo. ('Take one fine squirrel and cut it up as for fricasee.' Or, as they say, 'frik-eeairssay'!) It could be worse, I've also got recipes for racoon, armadillo and, heaven forbid, skunk!

Before you turn over, I should say that I've played safe here, with a combination of turkey, chicken, shrimp and ham. You can use some or all of these, or any other items in your Gumbo. But I have retained okra, deliberately allowing it to go sappy to thicken the stew. Serve on top of plain boiled rice.

SERVES 4

INGREDIENTS

1oz (30g) butter
2–3 garlic cloves, chopped
4oz (110g) onion, chopped
2–3 red cayenne chillies, chopped
2 green bell peppers, chopped
6oz (175g) raw turkey breast, skinned and chopped
6oz (175g) raw chicken breast, skinned and chopped
6oz (175g) uncooked shrimps, any type, shell off

6oz (175g) uncooked ham, chopped
4fl oz (120ml) vegetable oil
2oz (50g) plain white flour
1 tablespoon chopped fresh thyme
salt

GARNISH
chopped fresh parsley
chopped fresh oregano
filé powder (optional)

METHOD

1. Heat the butter in a 5 pint (2.75 litre) lidded flameproof casserole. Stir-fry the garlic, onion, chillies and bell peppers for about 3 minutes. Add the turkey, chicken, shrimps and ham and stir-fry for a further 5–6 minutes.

2. In a karahi or wok, heat the oil until it is just smoking. Add the flour little by little, stir-frying with a wire whisk until it is all in and mixed. Continue cooking until it becomes brown (not too dark). Then, bit by bit, add 2 pints (1.2 litres) water, whisking until it is fully combined.

3. Put this sauce into the casserole along with all the stir-fried ingredients.

4. Place in an oven preheated to 375°F/190°C/Gas 5 and cook for about 45 minutes with the lid on.

5. Add the thyme, and salt to taste, and serve garnished with the parsley, oregano and, if you can get it, filé.

BELOW *Left to right: Gumbo Creole (opposite) and Dirty Rice (page 250) garnished with a Chilli Tassel (page 211)*

BATTERED FRIED FROG'S LEGS

USA

This recipe works perfectly well with chicken drumsticks but in France and the bayou swamps of Louisiana frog's legs are regarded as a great delicacy. We were offered this dish at Laffitte's Landing restaurant in Donaldsonville, Louisiana. Dominique, who was shocked at the idea of edible frog, said, 'Poor little frogs.' The Cajun waitress immediately replied, 'They ain't small honey,' and they weren't!

This recipe involves a 24–60 hour marinade followed by deep-frying the batter-dipped legs. Only the hind legs are used. They resemble long thin chicken drumsticks and the texture is midway between fish and chicken but there is no fishy taste.

SERVES 4

INGREDIENTS

*4 pairs frog's legs or 4 chicken
    drumsticks, skinned*
*oil for deep-frying
drumsticks, skinned*
*4oz (110g) fresh breadcrumbs or
    5oz (150g) packet breadcrumbs*

MARINADE
*8fl oz (250ml) olive oil or red chilli
    oil (page 286)*
2 garlic cloves, crushed
1 teaspoon salt

BATTER
4 eggs
4 tablespoons double cream
*1–2 teaspoons red chilli mash
    (pages 286–7)*
1 tablespoon cornflour
1 teaspoon salt

GARNISH
lettuce and radiccio
fresh dill
lemon wedges

METHOD

1. Blanch the legs in boiling water for about 5 minutes. Plunge into cold water to cool. Dry them well with kitchen paper.

2. Mix the **marinade** ingredients together in a non-metallic bowl. Add the legs, cover and refrigerate for a minimum of 24 hours and a maximum of 60 hours.

3. Next day, beat the **batter** ingredients in a bowl until creamy.

4. Heat the oil in a deep-fryer to 375°F/190°C (chip-frying temperature).

5. Put the breadcrumbs on a flat dish. Then dip the legs in the batter until thoroughly coated and roll in the breadcrumbs.

6. Put them in the deep-fryer and cook for about 6–8 minutes (it depends on the size of the legs).

7. Serve on a bed of lettuce, radiccio and fresh dill, with wedges of lemon and a chilli sauce or relish of your choice (see pages 286–96).

JOCON
—— *Guatemalan Herbal Chicken* ——

GUATEMALA

This chicken hotpot from Guatemala should be fragrant and green in colour, due to the herbs, spices and green chillies. Serve with Jollof rice (see page 247) or Tortillas (see page 262).

SERVES 4

INGREDIENTS

1×3¹/₂–4lb (1.5–1.8kg) chicken
4 tablespoons corn oil
2–4 garlic cloves, chopped
6–8 spring onions, bulbs and leaves
    chopped
4–6 leaves spinach, chopped
¹/₂ bulb fennel, chopped
2 sticks celery, chopped
1 green bell pepper, finely chopped
2–3 green tomatoes, chopped
2 tablespoons chopped fresh
    coriander

2–4 fresh green cayenne chillies
salt

SPICES (roasted and ground, page 45)
8 green cardamom pods
1 teaspoon coriander seeds
1 teaspoon seeds from any chillies

GARNISH
whole fresh coriander leaves
whole chives
chilli powder

METHOD

1. Quarter the chicken, skin and clean it. Put it and the liver, neck and giblets into a large casserole dish (of at least 6 pint/3.4 litre capacity). Add 1 pint (600ml) boiling water and place in an oven preheated to 375°F/190°C/Gas 5.

2. During this stage heat the oil in a frying pan. Stir-fry the **spices** for 30 seconds. Add the garlic and stir-fry for a further 30 seconds, then add the spring onions and stir-fry for about 10 minutes.

3. As soon as this mixture is ready pulse it in a blender or food processor along with the other ingredients, using enough water to achieve a runny paste.

4. Stir-fry this paste for about 5 minutes. Then, when the casserole has cooked for about 20 minutes, add it to the casserole.

5. Return the casserole to the oven for a further 30 minutes, inspecting it about halfway through the cooking time and adding a little water if needed. Add salt to taste.

6. Serve the chicken on the bone, garnished with the whole fresh coriander leaves and chives and a sprinkling of chilli powder.

FRANGO PIRI-PIRI
—— *Chilli Roast Chicken* ——

PORTUGAL

It was the Portuguese who first transported the chilli from its native America to Africa, India and the Orient. Ironically the Portuguese themselves never really took to chillies. This is one of the few Portuguese chilli recipes and it hails from the northern state of Minho, also the home of the fabulous *vinho verde* ('green wine'). *Piri-Piri* chilli sauce is smeared over a chicken which is spit-roasted over coals (or it can just be oven-roasted). Serve with potatoes and a selection of vegetables.

SERVES 4

INGREDIENTS

1×3¹/₂lb (1.5kg) roasting chicken

MARINADE
3–4 tablespoons piri-piri *sauce*
  (page 293)

2–4 garlic cloves, crushed
3 tablespoons corn oil

METHOD

1. Check that the cavity inside the chicken is empty. Place the chicken on a baking tray.

2. Mix the marinade ingredients together, then rub all over the chicken. Refrigerate for 2 hours minimum and 24 hours maximum (see page 42). Baste from time to time if possible.

3. Preheat the oven to 375°F/190°C/Gas 5. Put the chicken on a rack over the oven tray, basting with the marinade. Pour off any excess marinade and keep for later.

4. Roast for 20 minutes per lb (450g). Baste every 15 minutes with the spare marinade.

5. On the hour, for a 3¹/₂lb (1.5kg) bird, increase the heat to 425°F/220°C/Gas 7, and give it a final 10 minutes at that heat.

6. Remove the chicken from the oven, and let it rest for 15 minutes in a warmer.

Chef's Tip

CHECKING POULTRY IS COOKED
To check that chopped poultry is cooked right through, simply halve a large piece: breast meat should be white, leg meat brown or pink (but not raw pink). Both should be an even colour right through.

Roasts and cooked whole birds require a different technique. When the cooking time is up, check first a thigh and then a breast by poking a thin sharp skewer into the thickest part. Withdraw the skewer. Clear fluid will run out of the holes in a cooked bird, but coloured fluid indicates a bird which needs a little more cooking.

FACING PAGE *Portuguese Chilli Roast Chicken (above), served with plain rice*

DUM KI BATAR KARSHA
—— *Duck-Stuffed Quails en Croute* ——

INDIA

Inspired by the cooking of the Nawabs of Lucknow, this dish is a real party piece. A whole boned quail is stuffed with mince and part-baked. It is then cooled and wrapped in puff pastry and the baking is completed. Boned quails do not yield much flesh, so serve this with another curry main dish, as well as rice, vegetables and chutneys, but arrange the servings so that the quail is the centrepiece.

SERVES 4

INGREDIENTS

4 boned quails
10oz (300g) duck breast, skinned
4 garlic cloves, crushed
1 inch (2.5cm) cube ginger
1–3 red chillies, chopped
20 fresh mint leaves, chopped
1 tablespoon baharat (page 48)

1 teaspoon aromatic salt (page 46)
8oz (225g) ready-made puff pastry, thawed if frozen
3 eggs
1 tablespoon garam masala paste (page 49)
fresh whole coriander leaves

METHOD

1. Buy the quails already boned from your butcher. You'll need to cut off the tiny wing bone (which is usually left on).

2. Pulse the duck breast in a food processor with the garlic, ginger, chillies, mint, baharat and aromatic salt or put through a mincer to achieve a mouldable texture.

3. Take a golf ball-size piece of duck stuffing and wrap each quail around it to re-create the shape of a plump, round quail.

4. Divide the remaining mince into four portions, flatten and place under each quail.

5. Place the quails on a rack over an oven tray and place in an oven preheated to 375°F/190°C/Gas 5. Bake for about 12 minutes.

6. Remove and leave until cool enough to handle.

7. Turn up the oven to 425°F/220°C/Gas 7.

8. Roll out the pastry until very thin. Wrap a piece of pastry around each quail and its base. Beat the eggs with the garam masala paste and brush the pastry with it.

9. Put the quails on the oven tray and return to the oven. Bake for 20 more minutes until golden, brushing again with the remaining egg mixture about halfway through the cooking time.

10. Serve as described, garnished with fresh whole coriander leaves.

SHIKARA MURGH BHARVARA KA KEEMA
—— *Spicy Chicken Stuffed with Curry Mince* ——

INDIA

This fabulous combination of tastes and textures is a real winner. A whole chicken is marinated, then stuffed with raw minced curry and roasted.

A boned chicken (ask your butcher to bone it) is a great idea for this recipe. Use the mince to shape the chicken to its pre-boned shape. When it is sliced, the appearance is delightful. It's a bit pricey, so save it for a special occasion.

SERVES 4–6

INGREDIENTS

1×2¹/₂lb (1.1kg) roasting chicken, fully boned and skinned

STUFFING
1lb (450g) lean fillet steak, chopped into small pieces
4 garlic cloves, crushed
4 tablespoons dried onion flakes (chef's tip, page 65)
2–4 red cayenne chillies, chopped
2 tablespoons garam masala (page 47)

2 tablespoons chopped fresh coriander
¹/₂ teaspoon aromatic salt (page 46)

MARINADE
12fl oz (350ml) freshly squeezed lemon juice
¹/₂–2 tablespoons red chilli mash (pages 286–7)
4–6 garlic cloves, crushed
1 teaspoon salt

METHOD

1. Pulse the **stuffing** ingredients in a food processor or put through a mincer, to form a well mixed and mouldable coarse paste.

2. Check that the cavity inside the chicken is empty. Fill it with the mince stuffing. Place the chicken on an oven tray.

3. Mix the **marinade** ingredients together, then rub all over the chicken. Refrigerate for 2 hours minimum and 24 maximum (see page 42). Baste from time to time if possible.

4. Preheat the oven to 375°F/190°C/Gas 5. Put the chicken on a rack over the oven tray and baste with the marinade. Pour off any excess marinade and keep for later.

5. Roast for 20 minutes per lb/450g (remember to add the weight of the mince to that of the bird). Baste every 15 minutes with the spare marinade.

6. On the hour, for a 2¹/₂lb (1.1kg) bird plus 1lb (450g) stuffing, increase the heat to 425°F/220°C/Gas 7, and give it a final 10 minutes at that heat. Remove from the oven and rest for 15 minutes in a warmer.

GALINHA CAFREAL
—— *Casseroled Coconut Chicken* ——

MOZAMBIQUE

On my recent travels I kept on coming across a simple marinade of lime juice, garlic, chilli and salt. I found it in India, in Latin America, and in Africa. In my *250 Favourite Curries* I gave a recipe for *cafreal* from Goa. I was therefore pleasantly surprised to find this interesting version in Mozambique. As ever, the Portuguese provided the link. This is very good with Jollof rice (see page 247).

SERVES 4

INGREDIENTS

4 large chicken legs (thigh and
    drumstick), skinned
vinegar (any type)
1 pint (600ml) canned coconut
    milk (page 44)
4 teaspoons olive oil
1 teaspoon salt

MARINADE
7fl oz (200ml) fresh lemon juice

10–12 garlic cloves, crushed
1–3 habanero chillies, finely
    chopped
1 teaspoon aromatic salt (page 46)

GARNISH
devilled cashew nuts (page 65)
chopped fresh chives

METHOD

1. Mix the **marinade** ingredients together.

2. Cut small gashes in the chicken legs with a sharp knife, then rub the drumsticks with vinegar to de-grease the meat. Wipe dry.

3. Work the marinade on to the legs and into the gashes. Put into a suitably sized bowl, pouring over all the excess marinade. Cover and refrigerate for 24–60 hours (see page 42).

4. Put the chicken legs in a shallow roasting tin. Pour over the excess marinade and place in an oven preheated to 375°F/190°C/Gas 5. Cook for 10 minutes.

5. Mix together the coconut milk, oil and salt, use half the mixture to baste the chicken legs and cook for 10 more minutes.

6. Transfer the chicken and all its juices to a lidded casserole. Add the remaining coconut mixture and return to the oven for a final 10–20 minutes.

7. Serve, garnished with the cashew nuts and chopped chives.

GAENG SOM PET
—— *Orange Duck Curry* ——

THAILAND

The three main Thai curries are green curry, red curry and orange curry. The flavouring ingredients are common to all three. It is the accompanying ingredients which dictate the colour – in this case orange chillies, bell peppers, carrot, sweet potato and mango.

SERVES 4

INGREDIENTS

1 medium red sweet potato (American yam), scrubbed
1 ripe mango
2 tablespoons soy oil
1 teaspoon blachan *shrimp paste (chef's tip, page 172)*
1 tablespoon mild blend curry paste (page 49)
1 garlic clove, chopped
2 inch (5cm) cube galingale or ginger, sliced
2–3 orange habanero chillies, chopped
1/2 pint (300ml) akhni stock (page 44) or water
14fl oz (400ml) canned coconut milk (page 44)

2 lemon grass stalks
6–7 dried lime leaves
1 1/2lb (675g) duck, filleted and skinned
1 large carrot, grated
1 orange bell pepper, finely chopped
2 tablespoons coarsely chopped fresh basil
2 tablespoons coarsely chopped fresh coriander
1 teaspoon nam pla *fish sauce (chef's tip, page 172)*
aromatic salt (page 46)

METHOD

1. Peel and dice the sweet potato into 1×1/2 inch (2.5×1.25cm) cubes.

2. Halve and pit the mango, and scoop out the flesh.

3. Heat the oil, and stir-fry the shrimp paste and curry paste for 20 seconds. Add the garlic, galingale or ginger, and the chillies, and continue to stir-fry for a further 30 seconds.

4. Add the stock or water, coconut milk, lemon grass, lime leaves and, when simmering, add the sweet potato cubes and the duck slices.

5. Transfer this mixture to a 4–5 pint (2.25–2.75 litre) lidded casserole and place in an oven preheated to 375°F/190°C/Gas 5.

6. After 20 minutes, inspect and stir. Add the mango, carrot and bell pepper, as well as a little water if it is becoming too dry. Return to the oven for a further 10 minutes.

7. Remove again, this time, adding the fresh basil and coriander, and fish sauce, and aromatic salt to taste. Serve with rice.

KAENG PA GAI
—— *Thai Jungle Fowl Curry* ——

THAILAND

I have always believed that our domestic chickens were descended from the guinea fowl, and have stated as much in my previous books. I am delighted to be gently corrected by Richard Parsons of Bridgnorth, Shropshire, who tells me that the title of ancestry 'goes to the Red Jungle Fowl (*Gallus gallus*) found throughout Asia and Indo-China. Guinea Fowl (*Numida meleagris*) belong to a quite different family of birds. The latter come from the African continent and were probably not domesticated for several thousand years after the jungle fowl.'

This ancient Thai recipe no doubt uses jungle fowl, but as these are generally unavailable in the West, I've called for guinea fowl.

SERVES 4

INGREDIENTS

1×2½lb (1.1kg) guinea fowl, on the bone, cut into eight pieces and skinned
2 stalks fresh lemon grass
6–8 lime leaves, fresh or dried
2 tablespoons mild blend curry paste (page 49)
1 teaspoon soy sauce
1 teaspoon nam pla *fish sauce* (chef's tip, page 172)
2 tablespoons vinegar, any type
7fl oz (200ml) fresh lime juice
3 tablespoons ghee (page 43)
1 teaspoon blachan *fish paste* (chef's tip, page 172)
14fl oz (400ml) canned coconut milk (page 44)
4–5 spinach leaves, destalked and chopped

8–9 fresh holy basil leaves, coarsely chopped
2 tablespoons chopped fresh coriander
aromatic salt (page 46)

PURÉE
2–4 green cayenne chillies
6 garlic cloves
1 inch (2.5cm) cube galingale or ginger
4oz (110g) spring onions, bulbs and leaves
1 tablespoon whole fresh coriander leaves
½ teaspoon Chinese five-spice powder (page 46)

METHOD

1. Put the guinea fowl, lemon grass and lime leaves in a non-metallic bowl with the curry paste, soy sauce, fish sauce, vinegar and lime juice, cover and refrigerate for up to 60 hours (see page 42).

2. Put the **purée** ingredients in a food processor or blender with enough water to achieve a thick pourable purée.

3. Heat the ghee in a karahi or wok. Stir-fry the *blachan* for 1 minute. Add the purée and briskly stir-fry for about 5 minutes.

4. Add the lemon grass, lime leaves and guinea fowl with all its juices and stir-fry for another 10 minutes.

5. Add the coconut milk, spinach, basil, coriander, and aromatic salt to taste, and stir-fry for about 5 minutes more. Test the guinea fowl (see page 143) and serve with rice.

HÜHN BURGENLANDER
—— *Chicken Paprika* ——

AUSTRIA

There's a delightful Austrian restaurant in Haslemere, called The Tirol. It is run by a married couple, Shirley and Helmut. Helmut comes from Burgenland, that part of Austria which shares a border with Hungary and also a passion for Hungarian paprika. He talks lovingly of his occasional visits home, and of gathering hot long peppers and mild paprikas which he makes into *ristras* (long strings) and dries above the fireplace in the cosy restaurant.

SERVES 4

INGREDIENTS

1¼ pints (700ml) chicken stock or water
8–12 bite-size chicken breast pieces, skinned and filleted
1 teaspoon chopped fresh red chilli and 2 teaspoons chopped red bell pepper or 1 tablespoon finely chopped fresh red hot paprika pepper

8–12 bite-sized cubes boiled leg of ham
8oz (225g) canned sauerkraut with its liquid
7fl oz (200ml) single cream
salt

GARNISH
finely chopped chives
Hungarian paprika powder

METHOD

1. Put the stock or water in a saucepan and bring to a simmer. Add the chicken pieces and the chilli and the bell pepper, or the paprika. Simmer for 15–20 minutes.

2. Add the ham and sauerkraut and continue to simmer for another 10 minutes.

3. Mix in the cream, add salt to taste, garnish, and serve with potatoes or plain rice.

FAISINJAN KORESH
—— Duck in a Sweet and Sour Sauce ——

IRAN

At the time of the Shahs of Persia, peacock would have been the subject of this dish. At court the whole cooked peacock would be presented on a sea of bright red pomegranate seeds surrounded by saffron-yellow rice on a huge jewel-encrusted gold serving dish, adorned with peacock feathers.

Today *faisinjan* is still served at weddings and celebrations, and when a special guest visits the household. The main ingredient is usually pheasant or wild duck. The sourness of the dried pomegranate contrasts with game extremely well. I have modified this dish a little by using domestic duckling which I roast rather than casserole. This allows you to get rid of the vast amount of fat. If you can't get fresh pomegranate for the garnish you can substitute redcurrants.

SERVES 4

INGREDIENTS

1×3½–4lb (1.5–1.8kg) whole duckling or small duck, oven ready
4 tablespoons duck fat
2 garlic cloves, finely chopped
8oz (225g) onions, chopped
1 teaspoon ground cummin
1 teaspoon ground turmeric
1 teaspoon powdered cinnamon
4oz (110g) ground almonds

2–4 tablespoons dried pomegranate seeds
1–3 tablespoons brown sugar
lemon juice

GARNISH
4oz (110g) fresh pomegranate seeds or redcurrants
2 tablespoons chopped pistachio
2 tablespoons chopped fresh coriander

METHOD

1. Roasting the duckling takes 30 minutes per lb (450g), or a total of 2 hours for a 4lb (1.8kg) duckling. Preheat the oven to 425°F/220°C/ Gas 7. Check that the cavity inside the duckling is empty, put on an oven tray and place in the oven for 20 minutes. Then reduce the oven temperature to 350°F/180°C/Gas 4.

2. Remove the duckling, baste and pour off excess fat. Return to the oven for a further 20 minutes.

3. Repeat stage 2 three more times over the next hour.

4. During stage 3, make the sauce. Heat the duck fat in a frying pan and stir-fry the garlic and onion for 5 minutes. Add the cummin, turmeric and cinnamon and stir-fry for a further 2–3 minutes. Now cool and purée this mixture in a food processor or blender, adding enough water to get a creamy texture. Return it to the frying pan, and add the ground almonds and enough water to make a thick gravy.

5. In a separate small pan boil ¹/₂ pint (300ml) water and put the dried pomegranate seeds into it. Simmer for 5 minutes, cool, then strain, pushing the flesh through the strainer. Return the liquid to the pan. Add the brown sugar, and lemon juice to taste, if you want a tarter flavour. Add this to the gravy. You should now have about ³/₄ pint (450ml) thickish gravy.

6. Remove the duckling from the oven at the end of stage 3 and drain off all fat. Now use about one-third of the gravy to baste the duckling. Return it to the oven for a final 20–30 minutes (or until tender), during which you should baste it twice more, using all the gravy.

BELOW Duck in a Sweet and Sour Sauce (opposite) on a bed of Persian Rice (page 241)

7. To serve, use an attractive oval platter. Place the duckling in the centre and garnish with the fresh pomegranate seeds or redcurrants, pistachio nuts and fresh coriander. Serve with a rice dish such as Iranian *Pollou* (see page 241).

INCHE KABIN
—— *Crispy Malaysian Chicken* ——

MALAYSIA

This dish comes from the Strait of Malacca, between Sumatra and the Malay Peninsula. Chicken drumsticks are marinated in a thick curry paste, then deep-fried until crispy. Served with a thin soy-based sauce and prawn crackers, it is a typical example of the way Malaysians have combined the cuisines of India and China to make something unique.

SERVES 4

INGREDIENTS

8 chicken drumsticks, skin on
oil for deep-frying

MARINADE
4 garlic cloves, chopped
4oz (110g) onion, chopped
2 tablespoons garam masala paste (page 49)
4 tablespoons coconut milk powder (page 44)
1–3 teaspoons red chilli mash (pages 286–7)
1 teaspoon aromatic salt (page 46)

SAUCE
1/2 pint (300ml) water or akhni stock (page 44)

3–4 spring onions, leaves and bulbs finely chopped
1 tablespoon brown Muscovado sugar
1 tablespoon ketjap manis (page 192)
1 teaspoon nam pla fish sauce (chef's tip, page 172)
1 tablespoon tamarind purée (page 44)
1 tablespoon thin red chilli sauce (page 287–8)
1 stalk lemon grass

METHOD

1. Wash and dry the drumsticks. Slash them with little cuts.

2. Put all the **marinade** ingredients into a blender or food processor with enough water to make a pourable thick paste.

3. Rub this paste into the drumsticks, ensuring that they are well coated. Put them in a non-metallic bowl, cover and refrigerate for up to 60 hours (see page 42).

4. Make the **sauce** by boiling the water or stock and adding the other ingredients. Simmer until ready to serve.

5. Heat the oil in a deep-fryer to 375°F/190°C (chip-frying temperature). Put the drumsticks in, four at a time, and fry for 12–15 minutes. Set aside.

6. Just before serving, heat the drumsticks under the grill until they sizzle. Turn them over to sizzle on the other side. Serve with the hot sauce.

KARAMBA KULKUL ISSU
—— *Chicken and Prawns in Coconut Shells* ——

THE SEYCHELLES

The Seychelles, which lie in the Indian Ocean between Africa and India, are the original desert islands. The pace of life is slow and dreamy, tourists are rare, and nothing ever changes. This dish, as made in the Seychelles, requires large smooth green coconuts and the water from them, some of which is used to make a liqueur toddy, locally and appropriately known as *karamba*! I've substituted whisky for it and I've used our regular hairy brown coconuts.

SERVES 4

INGREDIENTS

4 coconuts, water extracted and
  tops cut off (see page 43 and
  below)
2 tablespoons corn oil
2–4 garlic cloves, crushed
$^1/_2$ teaspoon ground turmeric
$^1/_2$ teaspoon ground cloves
$^1/_2$ pint (300ml) coconut water
12oz (350g) chicken breast, minced
12oz (350g) cooked prawns, any
  type, shell off

2–4 fresh red chillies, chopped
4 tablespoons minced coconut flesh
1 tablespoon chopped fresh
  coriander
4 tablespoons whisky
aromatic salt (page 46)

GARNISH
onion tarka (page 44)
fresh grated coconut

METHOD

1. Prepare the coconuts. Extract all the water you can. If it is not enough to make $^1/_2$ pint (300ml) top up with water and coconut milk powder. Cut off the tops with a hack saw and smooth the bottoms, so that the shells stand up. Extract as much flesh as you can from the coconuts. Grate the flesh or mince it in a food processor, use the amount needed for this recipe and freeze any spare or make it into Coconut Chutney (see page 295).

2. Heat the oil in a karahi or wok. Stir-fry the garlic for 20 seconds. Add the turmeric and ground cloves and stir-fry for 20 seconds more. Add the coconut water and the minced chicken and simmer for about 8 minutes.

3. Add the prawns, chillies, coconut flesh and chopped coriander. Simmer for 8 more minutes, until it starts to thicken.

4. Add the whisky, and aromatic salt to taste.

5. Then put the mixture into the coconut shells, garnish with onion tarka and grated coconut, and serve with plain rice.

153

FISH
& SEAFOOD
DISHES

Because most of the ancient world lived by the sea or a river or lake, it is not surprising that there is a vast supply of delicious spicy recipes using a seemingly endless list of exotic species of underwater creatures.

I have chosen some of the world's best and most popular spicy fish dishes, modifying them to use fish and shellfish which are easily obtainable in our specialist stores and fishmongers. Nevertheless, my choice of ingredients is quite wide and includes Dover sole, halibut, cod steaks, haddock (fresh and smoked), fresh water and sea trout, salmon, tuna, mackerel, pomfret, shrimps and prawns of all sizes, crab, scallop, crawfish and lobster.

If the fish you want is not available on the day, then choose something which is as close to it as possible. Fresh fish can be stored in the freezer until you need it, and with the delicious spicy treatments here, you'll hardly be able to tell fresh produce from frozen.

OPPOSITE *Clockwise from top: Indonesian Vegetable Curry (page 193), Balinese Fish (page 176), Sweet and Sour Fish (page 175) and Sweet Chilli Purée (page 288). The vegetables at the front right of the picture are green radishes – a variety of mooli used to make Japanese horseradish* (wasabi)

CHILIES RELLENOS PESCADOS
—— *Chillies Stuffed with Fish* ——

MEXICO

Large chillies stuffed with spicily enhanced fish and shrimps, are dipped in batter and deep-fried. These are definitely worth the minimal effort required. They're great at parties and you can vary the fillings (see pages 102 and 218).

SERVES 4

INGREDIENTS

8 large green chillies or bell
   peppers
oil for deep-frying

STUFFING
5oz (150g) cod steak, filleted and
   skinned
3oz (75g) small cooked shrimps
2–4 garlic cloves, chopped
2 tablespoons yoghurt or sour
   cream
2 tablespoons dried onion flakes
   (chef's tip, page 65)
1–2 tablespoons red chilli mash
   (pages 286–7)

1 tablespoon chopped fresh
   coriander
1 teaspoon cummin seed
$^1/_2$ teaspoon aromatic salt (page 46)

BATTER
4oz (110g) strong white flour
4oz (110g) cornmeal
2 egg yolks
5fl oz (150ml) milk
$^1/_2$ teaspoon aromatic salt (page 46)
whites of 2 eggs, beaten stiffly

METHOD

1. Pulse all the **stuffing** ingredients in a food processor or use a mincer to achieve a well-mixed cohesive paste.

2. For the **batter**, put the flour and cornmeal in a bowl, fold in the yolks, then the milk and aromatic salt. Adjust the quantity of milk if necessary to achieve a thick batter. Then gently fold in the egg whites.

3. Roast the chillies or bell peppers (see pages 41–2) and, whilst they are warm and soft, peel them and slit them carefully, leaving the stalk on to create a pocket. Remove the seeds and pith but don't make holes other than the slit if possible.

4. Carefully insert the stuffing. Don't worry if there is some left over (it depends on the size of your chillies/peppers). We'll use it later.

5. Dip the stuffed chillies/peppers into the batter, ensuring that they are thickly coated. Heat the oil in a deep-fryer to 375°F/190°C (chip-frying temperature) and cook them for about 10 minutes.

6. To serve, place two chillies/peppers per person on each plate. Serve with rice and salsas (see pages 230–53 and 290–92).

Note: If there is any filling left, thicken it with flour, then divide it into four portions. Dip it in the batter and deep-fry it, as you did with the chillies.

AMBULTHIAL
—— *Tuna in Tamarind Sauce* ——

SRI LANKA

Tuna is a large fish, abundant in the Atlantic and Mediterranean. It is also popular in the Indian Ocean. This Sri Lankan recipe makes the most of dark red fleshy tuna (*balaya*) steaks. The use of tamarind (*goraka*) and lime juice creates a delicious sour taste.

SERVES 4

INGREDIENTS

1¹/₂lb (675g) filleted tuna steaks
3¹/₂fl oz (100 ml) fresh lime juice
2 tablespoons tamarind purée
  (page 44)
3 tablespoons soy or sunflower oil
2–4 garlic cloves, chopped

2 inch (5cm) cube ginger, chopped
¹/₂ teaspoon ground cloves
1–3 fresh green cayenne chillies,
  chopped
6–8 curry leaves, fresh or dry
aromatic salt (page 46)

METHOD

1. Cut the fish into bite-size chunks and wash them.

2. Mix the lime juice and tamarind purée in a non-metallic bowl. Add the fish chunks, cover and refrigerate for 2 hours (see page 42).

3. Using a flat frying pan, heat the oil and stir-fry the garlic, ginger, ground cloves, chillies and curry leaves for about 1 minute.

4. Add ¹/₂ pint (300ml) water and bring to a simmer. Stir in the tuna and its marinade and simmer for about 20 minutes. Add aromatic salt to taste, and serve with plain rice.

CHILLI TUNA

INDIA

This delightfully simple way to spice up canned tuna steaks is my mother's invention, inspired by her years in India.

SERVES 2

INGREDIENTS

$3^1/_2$oz (100g) canned tuna fish
  steak in oil
1 tablespoon finely chopped onion
1 teaspoon tomato ketchup

1 teaspoon vinegar, any type
$^1/_2$ teaspoon red chilli, finely
  chopped
salt

METHOD

1. Strain off and discard the oil from the tuna.

2. Mix with the remaining ingredients, adding salt to taste.

3. Serve cold as a sandwich filler, with cucumber slices, or as part of a salad dressed with Pat's Spicy Vinaigrette (see page 296).

Note: You can substitute canned pilchards or sardines for the tuna.

LOGOSTA ROSEA AFRIKANA
—— *Chilli Crawfish* ——

SOUTH AFRICA

In Portugal the crawfish is known as *logosta rosea*, rosy lobster. We also know it as the spiny lobster. It resembles the lobster proper except that it has no claws. It is called a crayfish by some, although it is quite a different creature from the small freshwater crayfish which are the crawfish so popular in Creole and Cajun cooking. These European crawfish lobsters grow to 20 inches (50cm) in length. The flesh is virtually indistinguishable from true lobster, and the price is about the same. So you can substitute one for the other.

You are unlikely to find the crawfish lobster in the USA, and you won't find the true lobster in Africa or India. This economical recipe from South Africa uses just one lobster to serve two people for a main course.

SERVES 2

INGREDIENTS

1³/₄lb (800g) cooked female
   crawfish, complete with coral
   (red eggs)
2 egg yolks
1 teaspoon red chilli mash
   (pages 286–7)
3 slices white crustless bread,
   crumbled, or 6 tablespoons
   cooked plain rice

2 garlic cloves, crushed
4 tablespoons dry white wine
4fl oz (120ml) double cream
1 tablespoon fresh mint leaves
1 ripe avocado, halved, pitted and
   skinned
aromatic salt (page 46)

GARNISH
any fresh herbs and lime leaves

METHOD

1. Extract all the crawfish flesh, liver and coral (see chef's tip), retaining the shell halves.

2. Chop all the flesh into small pieces (or mince it). Mix it together with the liver and coral along with the remaining ingredients, adding aromatic salt to taste. Pulse in a food processor or blender, adding enough water to achieve a glutinous adhesive texture.

3. Spoon this mixture into the two halves of the shell, heaping it up as required but using it all up.

4. Place the shells in an oven preheated to 375°F/190°C/Gas 5 and bake for 20 minutes. Garnish with fresh herbs and lime leaves, and serve.

Chef's Tip

PREPARING A LOBSTER

1. Though unappealing, it is easy to cook a live lobster. Place it in a saucepan of boiling water for a minimum of 3 minutes (for uncooked flesh) and 20 minutes (for cooked flesh).

2. Twist off the legs and pincers. Extract the flesh using pliers and a pick. Discard the cartilage.

3. If using the shell, halve it by cutting down the centre line. Keep the tail on. Wash the shell halves when the flesh has been removed.

4. Discard the hard and soft material in the head area. Cut the flesh away from the shell, and separate it. Spoon out the creamy white liver and the red eggs (coral) if present.

5. Cut up and mix all the meat, liver and coral.

Note: The yield of meat from a 1³/₄lb (800g) lobster is about 8oz (225g).

BREDIE
—— *Layered Fish and Pumpkin Stew* ——

SOUTH AFRICA

Bredie (pronounced bray-dee) is a well-spiced Malaysian-influenced layered casserole, which, cooked properly, provides a sensual combination of taste, fragrance, texture and colour. Pumpkin is a traditional ingredient so it's a good dish for Hallowe'en. At other times of the year use marrow or courgettes.

This recipe was given to me by a young South African chef called Christie who has worked with me at Curry Club functions.

SERVES 4

INGREDIENTS

4 tablespoons niter kebbeh *(page 43)* or ghee *(page 43)*
2–4 garlic cloves, chopped
2 inch (5cm) cube ginger, grated
2 Spanish onions, cut into thin rings
7fl oz (200ml) dry white wine
1lb (450g) Dover or lemon sole, skinned and filleted
aromatic salt *(page 46)*
2 tablespoons chopped fresh coriander
4 tablespoons fresh lime juice
2–4 whole fresh green cayenne chillies
2–3 celery sticks, cut into long thin strips
2–3 large carrots, cut into long thin strips
12–16 Kenyan green beans

12–16 mangetouts
3–4 large whole spinach leaves, destalked
2 teaspoons garam masala *(page 47)*
8oz (225g) pumpkin, thinly sliced
$\frac{1}{2}$ pint (300ml) stock, any type
1 tablespoon mild curry paste *(page 49)*
1 teaspoon soy sauce
1 teaspoon Worcestershire sauce
1 tablespoon tomato ketchup

SPICES
4 brown cardamom pods, halved
1 teaspoon cloves
2 inch (5cm) piece cassia bark

GARNISH
any fresh herbs

METHOD

1. Heat the *niter kebbeh* or ghee in a large flat frying pan. Stir-fry the **spices** for 10 seconds, add the garlic and ginger and continue stir-frying for about 40 seconds. Add the onion rings and carefully (so as not to break them) coat them with the oil, lower the heat and leave them to cook undisturbed until golden.

2. After about 10 minutes add the wine, remove from the heat and wait for a few minutes to loosen the onion rings.

3. Choose a lidded oven dish about 8×10×5 inches (16×25.5×12.5cm) in size. Transfer the onion rings and liquid to the oven dish, ensuring that they cover the base evenly.

4. Place the fish fillets on top of the onion, sprinkling some aromatic salt, chopped coriander and lime juice over them.

5. Next add the chillies, celery, carrots, Kenyan green beans and mangetouts, arranging them tidily. Top with the spinach leaves. Sprinkle over some more salt, coriander leaves, lime juice and the garam masala.

6. Arrange the pumpkin slices so that they cover the spinach. Put the lid on and place the dish in an oven preheated to 375°F/190°C/Gas 5.

7. After 15 minutes, put the stock, curry paste, soy sauce, Worcestershire sauce and tomato ketchup in a pan and bring to a simmer. Add to the casserole, and cook for a further 15–20 minutes. Serve, garnished with fresh herbs of your choice, with Clove Rice (see page 248).

MOOQUECA/MUQUECA
—— *Spicy Brazilian Fish* ——

BRAZIL

This dish is a speciality from the north-east corner of Brazil. The fish is stewed with fried condiments, and oil is added at the end.

SERVES 4

INGREDIENTS

4×6oz (175g) fillets of halibut, skinned

PASTE
3–6 garlic cloves
6oz (175g) onion, sliced
2–4 fresh green cayenne chillies, chopped
corn oil
4 tablespoons fresh lemon juice

14fl oz (400ml) canned coconut milk (page 44)
1/2 teaspoon salt
4 tablespoons olive oil
4fl oz (120ml) white wine
1 teaspoon yellow mustard powder
6 cherry tomatoes, quartered

GARNISH
fresh dill

METHOD

1. Pulse all the paste ingredients in a food processor or blender, using enough water to achieve a pourable paste. Preheat the oven to 375°F/190°C/Gas 5.

2. Put the fish in a lidded casserole and cover it with half the paste. Put the lid on and place the dish in the preheated oven.

3. Cook for about 20 minutes. Inspect and pour on the remaining paste. Cover and cook for a final 10 minutes. Garnish with fresh dill and serve.

VATAPA
—— *Coconut Shrimps* ——

BRAZIL

Another dish with African origins exported to Brazil by Portuguese mariners in the early days. Prawns and/or fish are cooked with spices in coconut milk thickened with ground peanuts. It was originally made using fresh river fish from the Amazon.

SERVES 4

INGREDIENTS

8oz (225g) dried shrimps
4 tablespoons corn oil
2–4 garlic cloves, crushed
2–4 fresh red chillies, chopped
6oz (175g) onion, chopped
4 tablespoons chopped fresh parsley
4 tablespoons chopped fresh chives
8 cherry tomatoes, chopped

1lb (450g) fresh shrimps, any size, cooked and thawed if frozen, shell off
14fl oz (400ml) canned coconut milk (page 44)
6oz (175g) pan-roasted peanuts (page 60), ground
1 teaspoon black pepper
salt

Note: Keep back some of the parsley and chives for garnish.

METHOD

1. Put the dried shrimps in a bowl with enough water to cover them and soak for 2 hours.

2. Heat the oil and stir-fry the garlic, chillies, onion, parsley, chives and tomatoes for about 10 minutes.

3. Add the dried shrimps with their water and stir-fry for 5 minutes.

4. Add the fresh shrimps and continue to stir-fry until they are hot and sizzling.

5. Add the remaining ingredients and stir-fry until the mixture has finished thickening. It should be almost porridge-like. Keep control over this by adding water bit by bit, as needed.

6. Garnish with a little chopped parsley and a few chopped chives, and serve with Brazilian Rice Cake (see page 253) or Spanish Saffron Rice (see page 236).

BLACKENED CRAWFISH
—— *Spicy Pan-Fried Crayfish* ——

USA

You can't go far in Louisiana without encountering crawfish. But let's get the nomenclature sorted out. What the Cajuns call crawfish are not the large spiny lobsters called crawfish elsewhere. These do not grow in America. The American crawfish is the crayfish of Europe! It is a freshwater miniature lobster complete with pincers, known as écrevisse in France, which grows to a length of about 6 inches (15cm). UK readers can substitute Dublin Bay prawns (scampi) or king prawns.

Blackened fish or shrimp is the creation of one of Louisiana's top chefs, Paul Prudhomme. Bearded, rotund and charismatic, Prudhomme is a major US television personality. He is chef proprietor at the celebrated K-Paul's Louisiana Kitchen in New Orleans.

'Blackening' involves coating the crawfish with melted butter and covering it in a mixture of spices. It is pan-fried, but beware the plumes of oily smoke which leave a greasy film over every surface in the kitchen. The answer is to do this outside on a barbecue or purchase (as Prudhomme has) a powerful extractor fan, not to mention a huge team of washers-up and cleaners!

SERVES 4

INGREDIENTS

*16 crayfish, shelled and deveined
  (chef's tip, page 169)*
melted butter

SPICES
2 teaspoons chilli powder

2 teaspoons white pepper
2 teaspoons mustard powder
2 teaspoons ground cummin
2 teaspoons dried oregano
2 teaspoons garlic powder

METHOD

1. Get the barbecue up to maximum heat.

2. Mix the **spices** together in a dish. Brush the crayfish liberally with melted butter, and immediately dab them in the spicy mixture (as if breadcrumbing).

3. To cook, apply maximum heat by placing the rack as near the coals as possible.

4. Cook for about 8 minutes, turning as necessary.

ÉCREVISSE ÉTOUFFÉE
—— *Stewed Crawfish (Crayfish)* ——

USA

This is a good example of Creole cooking using that favourite of favourites in New Orleans, crawfish (known as crayfish elsewhere, see previous recipe). *Étouffée* means 'slowly stewed' in French. This dish could be simple Cajun style, but the addition of the roux makes it positively Creole. Any shellfish or fish can be substituted for the traditional crawfish.

SERVES 4

INGREDIENTS

1oz (30g) butter
4 garlic cloves, chopped
8oz (225g) onions, chopped
1 red bell pepper, chopped
1½lb (675g) crayfish, shell off,
  deveined (chef's tip, page 169)
2 sticks celery, finely chopped

2–4 green chillies, chopped
1 tablespoon tomato purée
2½oz (65g) plain flour
1 tablespoon chopped fresh parsley
1 tablespoon chopped fresh basil
salt

METHOD

1. Heat the butter in a wok or karahi. Stir-fry the holy trinity – garlic, onion and bell pepper – for 5 minutes.

2. Add the crayfish, celery, chillies and tomato purée and stir-fry for a further 5 minutes, adding a little water as necessary.

3. Add the flour, bit by bit, whisking in enough water, to make a roux. Once it stabilises and stops thickening, transfer the mixture to a 4–5 pint (2.25–2.75 litre) lidded casserole and place in an oven preheated to 375°F/190°C/Gas 5. Cook, with the lid on, for about 20 minutes.

4. Inspect, add more water if needed, and the fresh herbs, and salt to taste.

5. Cook for about 10 more minutes. Serve with rice and chilli relishes.

ABAY WOT
—— *Fish Stew* ——

ETHIOPIA

What's *wot*? It's the national dish of Ethiopia, a stew in which a very hot red spicy sauce, *berebere* (almost as complex as curry) is the principal player. In fact there are many types of *wot* – *sik-sik* or *beg* (beef or mutton) *wot*, *doro* (chicken) *wot*, *shiro* (peanut and vegetable) *wot*. Fish *wot* is made in Ethiopia using fish from the Ethiopian source of the Blue Nile river (the Abay). Freshwater fish are plentiful there but seasonal, so they are salted to preserve them. In this interpretation of *abay wot*, I've used smoked haddock but you could substitute any white fish steaks. It's best served with *Inerja* (see page 261), a kind of Ethiopian millet bread, or Indian Chupattis (see page 264).

SERVES 4

INGREDIENTS

4 tablespoons groundnut oil
8oz (225g) onions, chopped
4 tablespoons berebere *(page 293)*
1lb (450g) skinned and filleted smoked haddock, cut into large pieces

15fl oz (500ml) milk
4 hard-boiled eggs, halved
1 tablespoon clear honey
aromatic salt (page 46)

METHOD

1. Heat the oil in a karahi or wok. Stir-fry the onion on a medium heat for about 10 minutes. Add the *berebere* and stir-fry it for 3–4 more minutes.

2. Add the fish and the milk. Increase the heat and bring it to a simmer. Continue to cook for about 15 minutes, adding water as needed.

3. Add the eggs, honey, and aromatic salt to taste. Simmer for at least 5 more minutes. To serve, line each diner's plate with *inerja* or chupatti and place the *wot* on top.

KILICH SHISH

—— *Skewered Swordfish* ——

TURKEY

Walk past any seaside café in Turkey and you will be tantalised by the aroma of fish sizzling over charcoal. Big, fat, skewered cubes of fish drip their oily herbal marinade on to the coals and in a few minutes they are served with a garlic and lemon dip inside pitta bread (see page 257) for a snack, or with rice for a more substantial meal.

Use a large fish with firm white flesh. Swordfish is traditional. Alternatives include shark, barracuda or halibut.

SERVES 4

INGREDIENTS

2lb (900g) swordfish
4 long metal skewers

MARINADE
6 tablespoons olive oil
2 tablespoons lemon juice
2oz (50g) onion, finely chopped
2 teaspoons paprika
1 teaspoon white pepper
1/2 teaspoon ground bay leaves
1/2 teaspoon aromatic salt (page 46)

**GARLIC, LEMON AND FRESH
CORIANDER DIP**
6 tablespoons hazelnut oil
2 tablespoons lemon juice
*2 tablespoons finely chopped fresh
   coriander*
*2–6 garlic cloves, very finely
   chopped*
*1 teaspoon coarsely ground black
   pepper*
1/2 teaspoon aromatic salt (page 46)

METHOD

1. To prepare the fish, remove the skin and fillet carefully. Cut into large cubes averaging 1¹/₂ inches (4cm). Aim to get at least 24 cubes. (Use any offcuts to make fish soup or stock.)

2. Mix the **marinade** ingredients together in a large non-metallic dish, then immerse the fish cubes, cover and refrigerate for up to 2 hours (see page 42).

3. Preheat the grill to medium, line the grill pan with foil, and place on the lowest level. Thread the fish cubes on to four skewers, and arrange on the grill rack. Ensure the cubes are well coated with marinade, pouring any excess over them.

4. Grill (or barbecue) for 10 minutes, turning once or twice.

5. During stage 4, mix the **dip** ingredients together. Serve, dipping the hot unskewered cubes of fish into the cold dip.

FACING PAGE *Skewered Swordfish (above) with its Garlic, Lemon and Fresh Coriander Dip*

CARURU
—— *Shrimps with Okra* ——

SUDAN

Dried shrimps, okra and nuts are the main players in this dish which the Portuguese took from Sudan to Brazil. Serve with Brazilian Rice Cake (see page 253).

SERVES 4

INGREDIENTS

12oz (350g) dried shrimps
3oz (75g) pan-roasted cashew nuts
  (page 60)
3oz (75g) pan-roasted peanuts
  (page 60)
12oz (350g) fresh okra
3 tablespoons corn oil
1¹/₂ tablespoons olive oil

2–4 garlic cloves, crushed
2–4 fresh red chillies, chopped
14fl oz (400ml) canned coconut
  milk (page 44)

SPICES
1 teaspoon coriander seeds
¹/₂ teaspoon green peppercorns (in
  brine or freeze-dried)

METHOD

1. Grind the dried shrimps, cashews and peanuts to a powder in a food processor or with a mortar and pestle. Add enough water to make a runny paste.

2. Just before cooking this dish, wash and destalk the okra and chop them into bite-size pieces. Don't do this any earlier or they will become sappy.

3. Heat the corn oil in a pan and stir-fry the paste until it is cooked (about 5 minutes).

4. In a clean pan heat the olive oil, and stir-fry the **spices** and garlic for 30 seconds. Add the okra and chillies and stir-fry for 5–8 minutes, by which time the okra should be firm and cooked but not gummy.

5. Mix in the paste and coconut milk. When simmering, serve.

PIRI-PIRI DIABOLE
—— *Mozambiquan Chilli Prawns* ——

MOZAMBIQUE

The former Portuguese coastal African nation of Mozambique is home to *piri-piri*. You'll find it elsewhere in Africa, and in Brazil. You'll even find it in Portugal (see pages 14 and 142). But nowhere will you find it as fiery as in Mozambique. Meat, chicken, fish and vegetables can all be the subjects of *piri-piri*. But in my view there is nothing to beat king prawns. Here I use a large '20 to the pound' size. They are good served with Paella (see page 236).

SERVES 4

INGREDIENTS

2lb (900g) or approximately 40 king prawns, heads and shells off
4 tablespoons ghee (page 43)
2–4 garlic cloves, crushed
7fl oz (200ml) fresh lime juice

6fl oz (175ml) piri-piri sauce (page 293)

GARNISH
4 or more lime wedges
finely chopped chives

METHOD

1. These prawns look most attractive if you leave the tails on. Devein them (see chef's tip below).

2. Heat the ghee in a karahi or wok over a high heat. Add the garlic and stir-fry for 30 seconds.

3. Add the lime juice and the *piri-piri* sauce and continue to stir-fry for 2–3 minutes.

4. Add the prawns and briskly stir-fry, ensuring that they are evenly coated in the red sauce.

5. Lower the heat and cook for about 8 minutes, adding splashes of water as needed.

6. Serve each portion garnished with a wedge of lime and a sprinkling of chives.

Chef's Tip

DEVEINING PRAWNS AND SHRIMPS
Prawns and shrimps of all sizes have a vein which runs down the back (the convex or outside of the curved prawn). Sometimes this can be dark coloured and dirty, and it can impart an unpleasant taste to the cooked prawn.

It is best to remove this vein. It's rather like stringing beans. Use a small, sharp paring knife and make an incision right down the vein. Then pull the vein away and discard it, washing the prawns after it is done. Deveining is impractical in the case of tiny prawns which are too fiddly, so pragmatism must prevail here (or a lot of hard work).

Incidentally, the shells of some small and most minute cooked prawns are soft enough to eat, indeed their slight crunchiness improves their taste texture. A little taste trial on each occasion, as to how much shell, head and tail to leave on may be needed.

BLEHAT SAMAK
—— *Arabic Fried Fish Balls* ——

SAUDI ARABIA

You'll find these all over the Arab world. They are small balls of ground fish, deep-fried and served as a main course with rice and vegetables or as a hot or cold starter. The Israeli gefilte fish is the same except that it does not include coriander and garlic.

SERVES 4

INGREDIENTS

1¹/₂lb (675g) skinned and filleted
 white fish such as cod or
 haddock
4oz (110g) onion, chopped
2 red cayenne chillies, chopped
2–4 garlic cloves, finely chopped
1 tablespoon chopped fresh
 coriander

¹/₂ teaspoon cummin seeds
¹/₂ teaspoon ground cinnamon
2 eggs
2oz (50g) fresh or packet
 breadcrumbs
salt and pepper
oil for deep-frying

METHOD

1. Cut the fish into pieces to fit the mincer.

2. Put all the ingredients except the oil through a fine mincer or blend in a food processor to achieve a sticky paste.

3. Divide the mixture into four, then sub-divide each quarter into four, six or eight balls, depending on the size you want.

4. Heat the oil in a deep-fryer to 375°F/190°C (chip-frying temperature). Put the balls into the oil, one by one, until half are in the fryer, then cook for 7–8 minutes. Remove and keep warm while you cook the second batch.

5. Serve cold as a snack, or hot with French fries and a twist of lemon.

SHABBAT KUWAITI
—— *Baked Curried Salmon or Sea Trout* ——

KUWAIT

This recipe comes from the sixty-chef kitchen of a new, very luxurious hotel, The Regency, in Kuwait, which is renowned for its cooking.

SERVES 4

INGREDIENTS

1×3lb (1.3kg) whole sea trout or 1 middle cut 2lb (900g) piece of salmon
6–8 garlic cloves
1 inch (2.5cm) cube ginger
8oz (225g) onions
6 tablespoons vegetable oil
6 canned plum tomatoes, chopped
aromatic salt (page 46)
olive oil

SPICES (all ground)
2 teaspoons cummin seeds

1 teaspoon cinnamon
1 teaspoon coriander seeds
1/2 teaspoon black mustard seeds
1/2 teaspoon green cardamom seeds
1/4 teaspoon fenugreek seeds

GARNISH
lemon wedges
fresh fennel leaves
fresh whole coriander leaves

METHOD

1. Wash the fish, dry and cut small diagonal slashes in the flesh to allow the coating to penetrate.

2. Mix the **ground spices** together, with enough water to make a pourable paste. Set aside to blend.

3. Put the garlic, ginger and onion into a food processor or blender and purée.

4. Heat the vegetable oil, and stir-fry the purée for 10 minutes. Add the spice paste and stir-fry for a further 5 minutes. Add the tomatoes, and aromatic salt to taste. Allow to cool.

5. To cook, preheat the grill to three-quarters heat and coat the fish with the paste. Line the grill pan with foil, put the fish on the grill rack and place in the midway position under the heat.

6. Sprinkle with olive oil and grill for about 8 minutes. Turn over, baste with a little more olive oil and finish off with a further 5–6 minutes. Serve with lemon wedges, rice or Pitta Bread (see page 257) or *Kavgir* (see page 258), a crispy bread from Turkey.

CHERMOULA SAMAK
—— Spicy Marinated Grilled Trout ——

MOROCCO

Chermoula is a spicy coating or marinating paste which is widely used with Moroccan meat dishes. In this recipe the paste is rubbed into fish steaks and the fish is left to marinate. Sea fish such as sea bass or bream would normally be used, but freshwater trout works perfectly.

SERVES 4

INGREDIENTS

4×12oz (350g) fresh trout

MARINADE
8oz (225g) onions, roughly chopped
4–6 garlic cloves, roughly chopped
2–6 red cayenne chillies, roughly chopped
1 tablespoon Hungarian paprika

1 tablespoon chopped fresh coriander leaves
1 teaspoon ground cinnamon
1 teaspoon ground saffron
1 teaspoon salt

GARNISH
whole fresh coriander leaves

METHOD

1. Pulse the **marinade** ingredients together in a blender or food processor, using enough water to achieve a thick pourable paste.

2. Gut the trout, keeping them whole. Carefully wash and dry them.

3. Cut each trout into four pieces, then mix with the marinade in a large non-metallic bowl.

4. Cover the bowl and refrigerate for a minimum of 6 and a maximum of 12 hours (see page 42).

5. To cook, preheat the grill to medium hot, line the grill pan with foil and place at its lowest level.

6. Put the fish on the grill rack and grill for 10–15 minutes, turning twice.

7. Garnish with whole fresh coriander leaves and serve with *Filfil Pilav* (see page 243), a chilli fried rice dish from Cyprus.

Chef's Tip

BLACHAN, NAM PLA AND NUOC MAM
Certain Thai, Vietnamese, Burmese and Indonesian recipes require *blachan* (shrimp paste) and *nam pla* or *nuoc mam* (fish sauce), available in some Oriental shops. If you can't obtain this use a teaspoon of anchovy paste from a tube. It won't taste quite the same, but it is not far off.

KARI NUOC PHNOM PENH
—— *Scallop Curry* ——

CAMBODIA

It probably does not occur to many people to visit Cambodia, Thailand's southern neighbour. One day I hope that will change and we'll have access once more to a stunningly beautiful country and to Cambodian curry. This is a cross between Thai curry and Chinese Sichuan (chilli-orientated) dishes. Here I've used queen scallops, for a change, but the recipe is suitable for any type of shellfish. Serve it with rice and *Nuoc Cham* sauce (see page 290).

SERVES 4

INGREDIENTS

4–5 dried Chinese mushrooms
7oz (200g) canned water chestnuts
   and their liquid
1 stalk lemon grass, bruised
2 teaspoons nam pla *fish sauce*
   (chef's tip, opposite)
1 tablespoon ketjap manis
   (page 192)
1/2 pint (300ml) akhni stock (page
   44) or water
2 tablespoons soy or sunflower oil
1 teaspoon ground turmeric
2 teaspoons ground coriander
4 garlic cloves, crushed
1 inch (2.5cm) cube galingale or
   ginger, grated

4–5 spring onions, bulbs and leaves
   chopped
1lb (450g) shelled scallops,
   weighed after thawing if frozen
1 tablespoon brown sugar
2 teaspoons red chilli mash
   (pages 286–7)
7fl oz (200ml) canned coconut
   milk (page 44)
aromatic salt (page 46)

GARNISH
chives
Chinese five-spice powder
   (page 46)

METHOD

1. Put the mushrooms in a cup, cover with warm water and leave to reconstitute for 10 minutes. Drain, quarter them and discard the water.

2. In a saucepan combine the mushrooms, water chestnuts and juice, lemon grass, fish sauce and *ketjap manis* with the stock or water and bring to a simmer. Continue to simmer for 10 minutes.

3. Heat the oil in a wok. Stir-fry the ground turmeric and coriander for a few seconds. Add the garlic and continue to stir-fry for 20 seconds. Add the galingale or ginger, and spring onions, and continue stir-frying for 3–4 minutes.

4. Transfer the stir-fry to a saucepan and add the scallops, sugar, chilli mash and coconut milk.

5. Simmer for about 10 minutes, and add aromatic salt to taste. Garnish with chives and five-spice powder, and serve.

ABOVE *Grilled Garlic Fish (below) with a dish of extra marinade*

FIHUNU MAS LEBAI
—— *Grilled Garlic Fish* ——

THE ANDAMAN
ISLANDS

The Andamans are a group of islands in the Indian Ocean, off Burma. Fish is abundant and this typical garlic and chilli coating is ideal for the barbecue. I've adapted the recipe for the grill which also works well, though it does make the house smell garlicky. Serve with plain rice and salad.

SERVES 4

INGREDIENTS

4×8oz (225g) whole red mullet,
  gutted, washed and dried
7fl oz (200ml) fresh lime juice
1 teaspoon aromatic salt (page 46)
2 teaspoons red chilli mash
  (pages 286–7)

PASTE
8 garlic cloves, crushed

6oz (175g) cashew nuts, chopped
1 tablespoon chopped fresh
  coriander
2–3 fresh green chillies, chopped
1 tablespoon sesame oil

GARNISH
4 lime wedges

174

METHOD

1. Make several slashes in the side of each fish with a sharp knife.

2. Mix the lime juice, salt and chilli mash together. Coat the fish, inside and out, cover and refrigerate for about 1 hour.

3. Meanwhile, pulse the **paste** ingredients in a food processor or blender, using enough water to achieve a smooth pourable paste. Rub the paste on both sides of the fish, keeping any excess for later.

4. Preheat the grill to medium and line the grill pan with foil. Put the fish on the grill rack and grill for 8–10 minutes.

5. Turn over and grill for a further 5–8 minutes. Baste with any remaining marinade. Serve, garnished with lime wedges.

MALACCA IKAN MANIS
—— *Sweet and Sour Fish* ——

INDONESIA

From the original home of the clove, mace and nutmeg comes this fish dish in an aromatic sweet and sour sauce.

SERVES 4

INGREDIENTS

4×12oz (350g) fresh mackerel, cleaned
2–4 whole fresh green chillies
1–2 stalks fresh lemon grass
14fl oz (400ml) milk
1 tablespoon tamarind purée (page 44)
1 tablespoon brown sugar
2 teaspoons ketjap manis *(page 192)*
2 teaspoons sambal manis *(page 288)*
7fl oz (200ml) canned coconut milk (page 44)

1 tablespoon chopped fresh mint
aromatic salt (page 46)

SPICES
$1/2$ teaspoon freshly grated nutmeg
6–8 whole cloves
1 teaspoon whole mace, crushed
4 inch (10cm) cinnamon quill

GARNISH (Optional)
2 tablespoons Macadamia or cashew nuts, chopped
whole fresh coriander leaves

METHOD

1. Put the fish, chillies and lemon grass in a lidded casserole dish.

2. Mix the milk, tamarind, brown sugar, *ketjap* and *sambal manis* and **spices** together. Pour over the fish, put the lid on the casserole, and place in an oven preheated to 375°F/190°C/Gas 5.

3. Cook for 30 minutes. Add the coconut milk and fresh mint. Cook for about 15 minutes more. Add aromatic salt to taste.

4. Garnish with the chopped nuts and whole coriander leaves if liked, and serve with Clove Rice (see page 248).

BOEMBOE BALI IKAN
—— *Balinese Fish* ——

INDONESIA

I once spent an unscheduled 48 hours in Bali while on my way to Sydney, Australia. Amongst the many delights on this island I discovered the wonderful food of Indonesia, including this Balinese fish dish. The recipe calls for filleted and skinned fish, but you could use a whole fish, as I sometimes do.

SERVES 4

INGREDIENTS

1½lb (675g) filleted and skinned pomfret
3½fl oz (100ml) lemon juice
1–3 tablespoons sambal oelek (page 288) or red chilli mash (pages 286–7)
4½oz (125g) plain white flour
4 tablespoons soy or sunflower oil
2–4 garlic cloves, chopped

2 inch (5cm) cube galingale or ginger, chopped
4oz (110g) onion, chopped
2 teaspoons brown sugar
1 tablespoon ketjap manis (page 192)
1 tablespoon coconut milk powder (page 44)
1 tablespoon tomato ketchup

METHOD

1. Cut the fish fillets into large bite-size pieces. Mix the lemon juice and sambal or chilli mash in a non-metallic bowl, add the fish pieces, cover and refrigerate for 2 hours.

2. To cook, remove the fish pieces from the juice (which we'll use later). Dab them in the flour and fry them in 3 tablespoons oil preheated in a large flat frying pan. Turn them over after 2–3 minutes and remove after a further 2 minutes. Set aside.

3. Using the same frying pan, top up with a further tablespoon of oil, add the garlic, galingale or ginger, and onion and stir-fry for about 3 minutes.

4. Mix in the sugar, marinade liquid, *ketjap manis*, coconut milk powder and tomato ketchup and, when sizzling well, add 6fl oz (175ml) water.

5. When simmering and reduced a little (after about 3 minutes), add the fish and stir-fry for 5–6 more minutes or until the fish is cooked through. Serve with *Sambal Manis* (see page 288) and rice or egg noodles.

KAKULUO

—— *Crab Curry* ——

MAURITIUS

The most common crab in the Indian Ocean is the long-clawed blue crab (*ketam biru*). The huge green crab is also popular. There are numerous other crabs, in various parts of the world, all yielding tasty flesh. This Mauritian recipe combines crab flesh with a spicy, creamy paste to create a delicious curry.

SERVES 4

INGREDIENTS

4×1lb (450g) cooked crabs (chef's tip)
1 tablespoon mustard oil (page 298)
2 tablespoons sesame oil
1 tablespoon chopped fresh coriander
aromatic salt (page 46)

PASTE
2–4 garlic cloves, crushed
4–5 spring onions, bulbs and leaves chopped
1–3 fresh red chillies, chopped
3oz (75g) fresh coconut flesh (page 43)

14fl oz (400ml) coconut milk (page 44)
3oz (75g) cooked plain rice

SPICES
mustard seeds
sesame seeds
fresh curry leaves

GARNISH
onion tarka (page 44)
fresh curry leaves
lime wedges

METHOD

1. Put the **paste** ingredients in a food processor or blender and mulch down, using just enough water to achieve a pourable paste.

2. Extract all the flesh you can from the pincers, claws and legs of each crab as well as the body.

3. Heat the oils in a karahi or wok. Stir-fry the **spices** for 20 seconds. Add the paste and stir-fry for 4–5 minutes.

4. Add the crab meat and fresh coriander and sufficient water to prevent it sticking. Add aromatic salt to taste.

5. Garnish with onion tarka, fresh curry leaves and lime wedges, and serve with rice.

VEGETABLE &
PULSE DISHES

I was surprised by recent research from India (by Dr Achaya, author of *Indian food, a Historical Companion*) which shows that in that great country of 850 million people, contrary to previously published beliefs, only 25–30 per cent are vegetarian. In Gujarat, the most prolifically vegetarian state, it is 69 per cent. In three coastal states (Kerela, Orissa and Bengal) the figure is 6 per cent, where, of course, seafood is important in the diet.

It is the same elsewhere in the world – vegetarianism is lower than widely believed, and in the West, where there are less financial constraints, it is closer to 5 per cent vegetarian with perhaps another 10 per cent who can be described as non-meat eaters (ie: they enjoy chicken occasionally and fish regularly).

Spices and chillies do wonders to vegetable cooking, as a graze through this chapter will show. And, whether you or your family or guests are vegetarians or not, it is perfectly feasible to create meals – dinner parties even – using as your main course a dish or a selection of dishes from this chapter, perhaps combining them with chutneys, rice and/or breads.

OPPOSITE *Clockwise from top: West African Rice (page 247), Regina's Selfridges Banana Beans (page 202) and Spinach and Sweet Potato Stir-fry (page 201)*

THAMBAPU KADALA
—— *Chickpea Curry* ——

SRI LANKA

From 'the resplendent isle', Sri Lanka, comes this typically spiced chickpea recipe which I encountered at the correspondingly resplendent Taj Samundra Hotel, Colombo.

SERVES 4

INGREDIENTS

8oz (225g) chickpeas
2 tablespoons mustard oil
  (page 298)
2–4 garlic cloves, chopped
8oz (225g) onions, chopped
2 tablespoons ghee (page 43)
3oz (75g) fresh grated coconut
  (page 43)
2–4 fresh red chillies, sliced
14fl oz (400ml) canned coconut
  milk (page 44)

1 tablespoon chopped fresh
  coriander
aromatic salt (page 46)

SPICES
1¹/₂ teaspoons mustard seeds
6–10 curry leaves, fresh or dried
1 teaspoon sesame seeds
¹/₂ teaspoon caraway seeds

GARNISH
onion tarka (page 44)

METHOD

1. Check that the chickpeas are free of grit, then rinse and soak them in twice their volume of water for 6–24 hours.

2. Strain the chickpeas, rinse with cold water, then simmer them in ample water for 40–45 minutes until tender.

3. About 5 minutes before they are ready, heat the oil in a karahi. Stir-fry the **spices** for 30 seconds, then add the garlic and stir-fry for 30 seconds more. Add the onion and stir-fry for about 10 minutes until the onion and garlic are golden.

4. Transfer this mixture to the saucepan.

5. Heat the ghee in a pan and stir-fry the grated coconut for 2 minutes. Add the chillies and, when simmering, the coconut milk and fresh coriander.

6. Add this mixture to the chickpeas and return the saucepan to the stove to heat up, stirring continuously to prevent sticking. Add aromatic salt to taste.

7. Garnish with the onion tarka and serve with plain rice.

PARIPPU

—— Creamy Coconut Lentils ——

THE MALDIVES

When I was in the RAF one of the most dreaded postings was to Gan, the most southerly of the Maldive Islands and positioned on the equator. It consisted of a runway, a lot of sea birds, rocks and hot, hot sun. The mess served typical British food and never, as far as I know, any of the absolutely delicious Indian/Maldivian dishes such as this one.

SERVES 4

INGREDIENTS

8oz (225g) yellow split peas (chana dhal)
4oz (110g) yellow oily lentils (toovar), split and polished
2 tablespoons sesame oil
4oz (110g) onion, finely chopped
14fl oz (400ml) canned coconut milk (page 44)
2oz (50g) creamed coconut block (page 44), chopped/grated
aromatic salt (page 46)

SPICES
1 teaspoon coriander seeds, crushed

1 tablespoon garam masala (page 47)
1 teaspoon mustard seeds
1 teaspoon sesame seeds

GARNISH
2 tablespoons ghee (page 43)
1 teaspoon mustard seeds
1 teaspoon cummin seeds
2–4 green chillies, chopped
2 tablespoons sun-dried tomatoes in oil (chef's tip, page 76)

METHOD

1. Pick through the lentils to remove any grit or impurities, combine them and rinse them several times. Then drain and soak in ample water for 24 hours.

2. Drain and rinse the lentils, then boil in twice their volume of water. Simmer until soft (about 45 minutes).

3. Towards the end of stage 2, heat the oil in a karahi and stir-fry the **spices** for 1 minute. Add the onion and fry for 5 minutes until brown.

4. Combine this stir-fried mixture with the lentils, adding the coconut milk and creamed coconut. Simmer for a few more minutes until the lentils are lovely and creamy. Add aromatic salt to taste.

5. In a clean karahi, heat the ghee and stir-fry the mustard seeds, cummin seeds, chillies and sun-dried tomatoes over a high heat for about 2 minutes (just long enough to singe them). Use this mixture to garnish the lentils, and serve with plain rice and/or Parathas (see page 265).

SINDHI LUKI MASALE DAR
—— *Pumpkin Curry* ——

PAKISTAN

This curry works perfectly well with any type of large fleshy gourd, such as a marrow, but there is no better subject than the gorgeous golden autumn pumpkin.

SERVES 4

INGREDIENTS

2lb (900g) pumpkin, yielding at least 1lb (450g) flesh
3 tablespoons ghee (page 43) or corn oil
2–4 garlic cloves, crushed
8oz (225g) onions, chopped
1/2 pint (300ml) akhni stock (page 44) or water
4fl oz (120ml) plain yoghurt
1lb (450g) chopped fresh spinach leaves
1 tablespoon chopped fresh mint
1 tablespoon chopped fresh coriander

4–5 plum tomatoes, chopped
aromatic salt (page 46)

SPICES
2 teaspoons coriander
1 teaspoon cummin
1 teaspoon paprika
1/2 teaspoon chilli powder
1/2 teaspoon ground turmeric
1/2 teaspoon panch phoran (page 48)

GARNISH
whole fresh coriander leaves
onion tarka (page 44)

METHOD

1. Cut the pumpkin into segments and chop the flesh into bite-size cubes. Alternatively, if you wish to use the empty pumpkin as a casing in which to serve the curry, cut off the top and carefully cut out the flesh, without puncturing the pumpkin case.

2. Heat the ghee or oil in a karahi over a high heat, then stir-fry the **spices** for 20 seconds. Add the garlic and continue stir-frying for a further 30 seconds.

3. Add the onion and reduce the heat. Stir-fry for 10 minutes, until the onion becomes translucent and begins to brown.

4. Add the stock or water and the yoghurt, spinach, mint, coriander and tomatoes.

5. Bring to a simmer, add the pumpkin pieces and simmer until they are tender enough to serve (about 10 minutes). Add aromatic salt to taste. Garnish with whole coriander leaves and onion tarka, and serve with other curries, rice and chutneys.

ABOVE *Gourds and corn cobs make a colourful display at a New Orleans' market*

Chef's Tip

FRESH TURMERIC

Fresh turmeric resembles ginger in appearance. Being a root (a rhizome actually), it will keep for a long time. It is gradually becoming more readily available in ethnic stores, and even larger supermarkets, in the West. A 1 inch (2.5cm) piece is really excellent in soups and stews, chopped or grated, in place of $1/2$ teaspoon ground turmeric.

FALAVDA

—— *Spicy Vegetable Fritters* ——

INDIA

These vegetable fritters are from the state of Gujarat in the most western part of India. It was the home of Mahatma Gandhi and is still the only place in India where wild lions are found.

Gujarat has an ancient history, being home 1000 years ago to the Parsees, a religious sect who escaped persecution in Persia. They brought new food concepts to India, and now live mainly in Bombay. This unusual combination of gram flour and semolina, spicy and sweet flavours, is typical of the Persian influence which now characterises Gujarati food.

SERVES 4

INGREDIENTS

2 tablespoons semolina
8oz (225g) gram flour (besan)
4 tablespoons ghee (page 43)
4 garlic cloves, crushed
4oz (110g) onion, chopped
1–4 red chillies, chopped
8oz (225g) white cabbage, shredded
8oz (225g) broccoli florets, as small as possible
2–3 spinach leaves, shredded
2 tablespoons chopped fresh coriander

2 tablespoons chopped cashew nuts
1 tablespoon chopped mango chutney
1 teaspoon aromatic salt (page 46)
oil for deep-frying

SPICES
1 tablespoon garam masala (page 47)
1 teaspoon ground turmeric
1 teaspoon black peppercorns
1 teaspoon caraway seeds

METHOD

1. Put the semolina and gram flour together in a bowl and mix together with enough water to make a pourable paste.

2. Heat the ghee in a karahi over a high heat, then stir-fry the **spices** for 20 seconds. Add the garlic and continue stir-frying for a further 30 seconds.

3. Add the onion and chillies and reduce the heat. Stir-fry for 10 minutes, until the onion becomes translucent and begins to brown.

4. Add the semolina and gram flour paste and stir-fry until it won't thicken any more. You'll need to add water bit by bit, little and often, but it must be quite a thick paste.

5. During stage 4, steam or boil the cabbage and broccoli, ensuring that they remain crisp. Drain thoroughly.

6. Add the paste, cabbage, broccoli, spinach, coriander, nuts, chutney and aromatic salt to the mixture in the pan. Mix well.

7. Heat the oil in a deep-fryer to 375°F/190°C (chip-frying temperature).

8. Scoop out 1 tablespoonful of mixture and carefully ease it into the deep-fryer.

9. Repeat until there are just enough fritters in the fryer to prevent congestion and fry for about 8 minutes. Remove with a slotted spoon and drain on kitchen paper.

10. When all the fritters are done, serve hot or cold as a snack with chutneys, or as a main course with curry and rice.

HARYALI ALOO
—— *Green Herbal Potatoes* ——

INDIA

India has such simple ways to spice up bland vegetables. Take this recipe, for example. Simply boil some potatoes, smother them with a herbal paste, and serve as a starter or an accompaniment to other curries and rice.

SERVES 4

INGREDIENTS

1¹/₂lb (675g) baby new potatoes, washed
3 tablespoons roughly chopped fresh coriander leaves
2 tablespoons roughly chopped fresh mint leaves
2–3 fresh green chillies, roughly chopped

1 teaspoon aromatic salt (page 46)
3fl oz (75ml) plain yoghurt
¹/₂ teaspoon mango powder
¹/₂ teaspoon lovage seeds
4 tablespoons fresh lime juice

METHOD

1. Boil the potatoes until tender – no need to remove the skins.

2. While they are cooking, put the coriander, mint, chillies, aromatic salt, yoghurt, mango powder, lovage seeds and lime juice into a blender or food processor and pulse down to a creamy purée.

3. When the potatoes are ready put them in a buttered casserole dish. Pour the purée over them, and mix well. Cover and keep warm for 15 minutes, to allow the flavours to be absorbed, then serve.

185

MIRCHI KA SALAN
—— *Green Chilli Curry* ——

INDIA

My very good friend Karan Bilimoria chose this as a star dish at his wedding feast in Secunderabad, India. It is deliciously tasty – I know because I was there. It is a famous Moghul dish from the area. I was so taken with it that the family gave me their recipe.

SERVES 4

INGREDIENTS

1lb (450g) green cayenne chillies
4 tablespoons corn oil
8oz (225g) onions, finely chopped
1 tablespoon chopped fresh
  coriander
3 tablespoons lemon juice
salt

SPICES (roasted and ground, see page 45)
4 tablespoons desiccated coconut
1 teaspoon mustard seeds
2 teaspoons sesame seeds
1 1/2 teaspoons cummin seeds
2 teaspoons coriander seeds

METHOD

1. Destalk and halve the chillies and discard the seeds.

2. Heat the oil in a karahi or wok and stir-fry the chillies for a few minutes until they soften. Strain the chillies, setting them aside for now, and return the oil to the pan.

3. Now stir-fry the onions until golden (about 10 minutes).

4. Add the **spices** and stir-fry these for 1 minute. Then add the chillies, fresh coriander and the lemon juice. Simmer for 10–15 more minutes. Add salt to taste, and serve with Curried Potato and Chickpea Rice (see page 244), Parathas (see page 265) and a chicken or meat curry.

KARELA DAHI
—— *Bitter Gourd in Yoghurt* ——

INDIA

Karela is a knobbly green gourd about the size of a large banana, available from Asian grocers. It is very bitter, so it is an acquired taste. I was given this recipe by Brian George, a Curry Club member and schoolteacher, who has visited India on a teaching exchange. Of karela he says, 'As with fine malt whisky, the first taste often repels, but equally like malt one grows to love it. Certainly, I developed a taste for it and would always recommend it be given a try.'

Gourds and tomatoes on sale in Mysore Market, South India

SERVES 4

INGREDIENTS

2 tablespoons soy oil
1 teaspoon mustard seeds
4–6 fresh curry leaves
8oz (225g) onions, chopped
1lb (450g) karela

$^{1}/_{2}$ teaspoon ground cummin
$^{1}/_{2}$ teaspoon ground coriander
10fl oz (300ml) plain thick yoghurt
aromatic salt (page 46)

METHOD

1. Heat the oil in a karahi. Add the mustard seeds and curry leaves. After 10 seconds add the onion and stir-fry for about 10 minutes.

2. During stage 1, wash the karela, trim off any hard skin and chop into bite-size slices. Boil in hot water until tender (usually for at least 10 minutes, sometimes longer). Drain.

3. Add the cummin and coriander to the pan. When mixed and sizzling, add the yoghurt.

4. Add the drained karela to the yoghurt. Add aromatic salt to taste, and serve hot or cold with rice or Parathas (see page 265).

BHINDI KARHI
—— *Punjabi Okra Curry* ——

INDIA

Yoghurt thickened with gram flour and spiced with aromatic spices is the creamy base to which stir-fried okra is added. Remember to keep the okra crisp, otherwise they go sappy.

SERVES 4

INGREDIENTS

2 tablespoons gram flour (besan)
1lb (450g) okra
2 tablespoons sesame oil
4oz (110g) onion, chopped
4 garlic cloves, chopped
1 tablespoon mild curry paste
  (page 49)
7fl oz (200ml) milk
10fl oz (300ml) plain thick yoghurt
2 tablespoons ghee (page 43)
aromatic salt (page 46)

SPICES
1 tablespoon garam masala
  (page 47)
1 teaspoon cummin seeds
1 teaspoon ground turmeric
1 teaspoon chilli powder

GARNISH
onion tarka (page 44)
whole fresh coriander leaves

METHOD

1. Put the gram flour in a bowl and mix with enough water to make an easily pourable paste.

2. Wash the okra, leaving them whole until stage 3.

3. Heat the oil in a karahi or wok. Stir-fry the onion and garlic for 2–3 minutes. Add the **spices**, gram flour paste and curry paste and continue to stir-fry for a further 2–3 minutes, until it thickens.

4. Little by little, add the milk, being careful not to let the mixture go lumpy. Add the yoghurt and continue simmering.

5. Destalk the okra, then cut into pieces about 1 inch (2.5cm) long.

6. In a flat frying pan heat the ghee. Place the okra in the pan and stir-fry for between 5 and 8 minutes, depending on the crispness you want. Sprinkle a little water into the karahi as needed to prevent sticking.

7. When the okra are ready, add them to the yoghurt curry sauce. Add aromatic salt to taste.

8. Garnish with the onion tarka and whole fresh coriander leaves and serve at once with plain rice, Puris (see page 266), a raita (see page 296) and Trevor Pack's Chilli Chutney (see page 295).

TANDOORI ALOO PESHWARI
—— *Stuffed Tandoori Potatoes* ——

INDIA

The normal tandoori subjects are meat and chicken. However, potatoes can also be stuffed and marinated for a few hours, then oven-cooked or barbecued.

SERVES 4

INGREDIENTS

4 large baking potatoes
juice of 1 lemon

STUFFING
6 tablespoons golden sultanas
40 whole almonds
1 teaspoon green cardamom seeds

MARINADE
5fl oz (150ml) natural yoghurt
3 tablespoons sunflower oil
4 garlic cloves, crushed
1 tablespoon finely chopped fresh
    mint or 1 teaspoon bottled mint
    sauce

3 tablespoons finely chopped fresh
    coriander
1 teaspoon cummin seeds, roasted
    and ground (page 45)
1 teaspoon garam masala (page 47)
1 tablespoon mild curry paste
    (page 49)
1 teaspoon ground coriander
2 teaspoons ground paprika
1 teaspoon chilli powder
    a few drops of cochineal
1 teaspoon aromatic salt (page 46)

METHOD

1. Pulse the **stuffing** ingredients together in a food processor with enough water to achieve a very thick paste.

2. Mix the **marinade** ingredients together thoroughly.

3. Scrub and peel the potatoes, then rub them with lemon juice. Using an apple corer, create a hole through the whole length of each potato. Fill the hole with the stuffing.

4. Coat each potato with a quarter of the marinade, then carefully wrap each one in foil.

5. Place the potatoes on an oven tray and bake for $1^1/_4$ hours in an oven preheated to 325°F/160°C/Gas 3.

6. Unwrap the potatoes, and keeping them on their foil, put them under the grill at medium heat to finish them off. Cook them until they blacken a little bit, turning once.

7. Serve hot, on a bed of salad, with chutneys and Chupattis (see page 264) or Puris (see page 266).

DHAL NEHRI
—— *Fragrant Lentils* ——

BANGLADESH

This aromatic Bangladeshi lentil dish is enjoyed all over India at any time of day. At breakfast, for example, it would be relished with plain yoghurt and Puris (see page 266).

SERVES 4

INGREDIENTS

6–8oz (175–225g) red masoor
* lentils, split and polished*
4 tablespoons ghee (page 43)
4 garlic cloves, chopped
8oz (225g) onions, chopped
1–3 red cayenne chillies, chopped
6fl oz (175ml) akhni stock
* (page 44)*
1 tablespoon chopped fresh
* coriander*

1 tablespoon garam masala
* (page 47)*
salt
onion tarka (optional, page 44)

SPICES
1 teaspoon panch phoran (page 48)
6 green cardamom pods
6 cloves
2 inch (5cm) piece cassia bark

METHOD

1. Pick through the lentils to remove any grit or impurities. Rinse them several times, then drain and immerse in ample water for 4 hours.

2. Heat the ghee in a 4 pint (2.25 litre) saucepan and stir-fry the **spices** for 20 seconds. Add the garlic, onions and chillies and stir-fry for 5 minutes more.

3. Put the akhni stock in a large saucepan with 6fl oz (175ml) water and bring to a simmer.

4. Drain the lentils and add them and the stir-fry to the saucepan. Simmer for about 30 minutes, stirring as the water is absorbed. The texture should be pourable, not too thick and not too thin.

5. When ready, add the coriander, garam masala, and salt to taste. Garnish with onion tarka if you wish.

FACING PAGE *Clockwise from top: Bangladeshi Fragrant Lentils (above), Pan-fried Flat Bread (page 265), Spicy Vegetable Fritters (page 184) and Green Chilli Curry (page 186)*

GURKHA DHAL
—— *Gurkhas' Lentils* ——

NEPAL

This highly nutritious and delicious dhal is very popular with Gurkha troops. I've had a similar dish at their Church Crookham barracks in Hampshire.

SERVES 4

INGREDIENTS

8oz (225g) moong dhal (whole green lentils)
1 teaspoon ground turmeric
4 tablespoons ghee (page 43) or niter kebbeh (page 43)
4 garlic cloves, crushed
1 inch (2.5cm) cube ginger, grated
1–3 red cayenne chillies, chopped

1 teaspoon green peppercorns (in brine or freeze-dried)
4oz (110g) onion, chopped
1 tablespoon chopped fresh coriander
aromatic salt (page 46)
onion tarka (optional, page 44)

METHOD

1. Pick through the lentils to remove any grit or impurities. Rinse them several times, then drain and immerse in ample water for 4 hours.

2. Drain and rinse, then measure an amount of water twice the volume of the drained lentils into a 4 pint (2.25 litre) saucepan. Bring to the boil.

3. Put in the lentils and turmeric and simmer for about 30 minutes, stirring as the water is absorbed. The texture should be pourable, not too thick and not too thin.

4. During stage 3, heat the ghee or *niter kebbeh* in a karahi. Stir-fry the garlic and ginger for 1 minute. Add the chillies, peppercorns and onion and continue stir-frying for 5–6 more minutes.

5. Just before serving, add the stir-fry to the lentils with the fresh coriander, and aromatic salt to taste. Garnish with onion tarka if you wish, and serve with plain rice, Chupattis (see page 264), a raita (see page 296) and Middle Eastern Vinegared Chillies (see page 294).

Chef's Tip

KETJAP MANIS
Ketjap manis is a sweet thick soy sauce (ketchup) from Indonesia. The Conimex brand is available worldwide. I have specified it in several recipes and it is well worth stocking. If you can't find it, use dark soy sauce with brown sugar added to your taste.

SAJUR TCHAMPUR
—— *Indonesian Vegetable Curry* ——

INDONESIA

Tchampur ('vegetables') come in all shapes and sizes in Indonesia, and many of these exotic varieties are now available in our supermarkets in the West. When you see them, buy them and cook this tasty recipe. Alternatively, choose from the more readily available vegetables I've suggested in the ingredients below.

SERVES 4

INGREDIENTS

2 tablespoons sesame oil
2–4 garlic cloves, crushed
2 inch (5cm) cube galingale or
    ginger, grated
4oz (110g) onion, chopped
8fl oz (250ml) akhni stock (page
    44) or water
1 stalk lemon grass, bruised
2–4 whole red chillies
4 bay leaves
1 inch (2.5cm) cube fresh turmeric
    (chef's tip, page 183)
1lb (450g) total weight chosen
    from:
    Chinese leaves, chopped
    baby sweetcorn, halved
    bean sprouts
    mangetouts, topped and tailed
    fresh whole basil leaves

1 tablespoon brown sugar
1 tablespoon ketjap manis (chef's
    tip, opposite)
salt

SPICES
1 teaspoon Sichuan peppercorns,
    crushed
1 teaspoon aniseed
1–2 star anise
$1/2$ teaspoon ground turmeric

GARNISH
1–2 red chillies, chopped
chopped Macadamia or cashew
    nuts

METHOD

1. Heat the oil in a karahi or wok over a high heat, then stir-fry the **spices** for 20 seconds. Add the garlic and galingale or ginger and continue stir-frying for a further 30 seconds.

2. Add the onion and reduce the heat. Stir-fry for 10 minutes, until the onion becomes translucent and begins to brown.

3. Add the stock or water, the lemon grass, chillies, bay leaves and fresh turmeric and simmer for 10 minutes.

4. Add the vegetables, sugar and *ketjap manis*. Simmer for 1–2 minutes so that the vegetables are still crisp. Add salt to taste. Extract the cube of turmeric.

5. Garnish with chopped red chillies and nuts, and serve with a noodle dish such as *Kaukswe-Kyaw* (see page 61) or a rice dish such as *Nasi Goreng* (see page 240).

BOBOTIE
—— *Vegetable Baked Pie* ——

SOUTH AFRICA

Bobotie is one of South Africa's national dishes. Usually it is a meat (originally wild game) pie, and its baked egg topping is unique. This spicy version only uses vegetables. It also uses two kinds of eggs, as well as nuts and pickle, and includes South Indian spices.

SERVES 4

INGREDIENTS

4 tablespoons ghee (page 43) or
    niter kebbeh (page 43)
2–4 garlic cloves, crushed
2 inch (5cm) cube ginger, chopped
4–6 spring onions, chopped
2–3 leeks, finely chopped
1 tablespoon mild curry paste
    (page 49)
1 pint (600ml) stock
8oz (225g) potatoes, peeled and
    diced
8oz (225g) parsnips, peeled and
    diced
2 sticks celery, finely chopped
1 medium size aubergine, diced
    into small pieces
2 tablespoons Trevor Pack's Chilli
    Chutney (page 295)
4–6 plum tomatoes, quartered
4 slices white crustless bread,
    crumbled
14fl oz (400ml) full cream milk

1 tablespoon tamarind purée
    (page 44)
1 tablespoon chopped fresh
    coriander
aromatic salt (page 46)
6–8 whole quail's eggs, hard-boiled
    and shelled
2 tablespoons whole cashew nuts
1 tablespoon golden sultanas
3 eggs

SPICES
4–6 green cardamom pods
4–6 cloves
1 tablespoon coriander seeds
4 bay leaves
1 teaspoon green peppercorns in
    brine
6–8 dried curry leaves

GARNISH
whole fresh mint or coriander
    leaves

METHOD

1. Heat the ghee or *niter kebbeh* in a karahi or wok. Stir-fry the **spices** for 15 seconds. Add the garlic and stir-fry for 30 seconds. Add the ginger and continue stir-frying for a further 30 seconds. Add the spring onions, leeks and curry paste and, when sizzling, add the stock. Allow this to simmer for 3–4 minutes.

2. Transfer to an oven dish. Add the potatoes, parsnips, celery and aubergine, and place the dish, uncovered, in an oven preheated to 375°F/190°C/Gas 5.

3. After about 20 minutes, remove the dish and add the chutney, tomatoes, bread, milk, tamarind and coriander. Mix well and return to the oven for a further 15 minutes.

4. Remove from the oven once more. By now the mixture should be relatively dry, though by no means dried out. Add aromatic salt to taste. Place the whole quail's eggs, nuts and sultanas on top of the mixture. Hand whisk the eggs and milk in a separate bowl until they are aerated omelette-style. Pour over the vegetables and return to the oven for a final 15–20 minutes.

5. Garnish with mint or coriander, and serve straight from the oven dish with rice and chutney.

BELOW *Left to right: Zanzibar Clove Rice (page 248) and Bobotie (opposite)*

MISHMISHEYA LA KAMA
—— *Spicy Vegetables with Apricot* ——

MAGHREB

Mishmish means 'apricot' in Arabic and the practice of mixing nuts, sweet fruit and savoury spices is common to Algeria and Iran, although they are 3000 miles apart. *La kama* is a popular spice mixture from Tangiers, capital of Morocco. This delightful dish is so tasty and nutritious that all you need with it is rice or couscous and a hot chutney like harissa (see page 293).

SERVES 4

INGREDIENTS

2–3 large carrots
1 large parsnip
1 large potato
1 fennel bulb
2–3 sticks celery
4 tablespoons ghee (page 43) or
   niter kebbeh (page 43)
2–4 garlic cloves, finely chopped
1 inch (2.5cm) cube fresh ginger
8oz (225g) onions, finely sliced
8oz (225g) fresh or dried apricots
   or peaches

aromatic salt (page 46)
2 teaspoons brown sugar (optional)
20 hazelnuts, chopped
20 almonds, chopped
1 teaspoon juniper berries

SPICES (all ground)
2 teaspoons black pepper
1 teaspoon ginger
1 teaspoon turmeric
1 teaspoon cinnamon
$^1/_2$ teaspoon nutmeg

METHOD

1. Prepare the vegetables and cut into 1 inch (2.5cm) cubes.

2. Heat the ghee or *niter kebbeh* and stir-fry the garlic for 1 minute. Add the ginger and stir-fry for a further minute. Add the onions and continue stir-frying for about 5 minutes.

3. During stage 2, mix the **ground spices** with enough water to make a runny paste, then add to the frying pan. Mix well, and stir-fry for 1–2 minutes more.

4. Preheat the oven to 375°F/190°C/Gas 5. Put the vegetables, stir-fried ingredients, and dried apricots or peaches (if using) into a lidded casserole with a little akhni stock or water. Cook for 20 minutes.

5. If using fresh apricots or peaches, peel, halve and stone them during stage 4. If they are very soft, mash with a fork. If firm, use a blender or food processor to purée.

6. Remove the casserole from the oven, stir in the puréed fruit, add aromatic salt to taste, the sugar (optional) and the nuts and berries. Return to the oven for a further 10 minutes and serve.

CHERMOULA POTATOES
—— *Chilli Potatoes* ——

MAGHREB

Chillies are popular in North Africa, and *chermoula* or *tchermila* is a chilli-based paste which is used as a rub-on marinade for meat, poultry and fish (see page 42). Here it is used to coat boiled potatoes in a quick and simple recipe.

SERVES 4

INGREDIENTS

1lb (450g) baby new potatoes
4 tablespoons ghee (page 43)

PASTE
4 garlic cloves
3–4 tablespoons fresh coriander leaves
2 tablespoons fresh mint leaves
1 teaspoon red chilli mash (or more to taste) (pages 286–7)

1 teaspoon green peppercorns (any type)
1 teaspoon aromatic salt (page 46)
20 saffron strands

GARNISH
onion tarka (page 44)

METHOD

1. Wash the potatoes but don't scrub them.

2. Boil them for 10–15 minutes (or until tender).

3. During stage 2 put the **paste** ingredients into a blender or food processor with enough water to create a pourable paste.

4. Heat the ghee in a karahi or wok. Stir-fry the paste for a few minutes, until the water is reduced and the oil is floating. Remove from the heat until stage 5.

5. When the potatoes are cooked add them to the karahi or wok. Stir for a few moments until thoroughly heated, garnish with onion tarka, and serve with roast meat of your choice.

SHEIK-EL-MA'SHI
—— *Stuffed Courgettes* ——

SAUDI ARABIA

Courgettes and gourds are popular all over the Middle East, especially when they are stuffed. You can use courgettes of any size for this, although tiny courgettes make a daintier dish. They are fiddlier to do and you'll need proportionally more courgettes, and slightly less oven time, but the results are worth it. Alternatively, you can use large gourds or marrows, requiring slightly longer baking time.

SERVES 4

INGREDIENTS

4oz (110g) coarse-grained burghul (cracked wheat)
8×6 inch (15cm) long courgettes
3 tablespoons ghee (page 43) or niter kibbeh (page 43)
1 tablespoon baharat *(page 48)*
2–4 garlic cloves, chopped

4oz (110g) onion, finely chopped
3–4 tablespoons chopped fresh mint
1 fresh fennel bulb, finely chopped
1 egg
aromatic salt (page 46)

METHOD

1. Rinse and immediately drain the burghul.

2. Wash the courgettes, then top and tail them. Carefully remove the centre core using an apple corer. Leave about $1/4$ inch (6mm) of skin and flesh all around, and don't pierce the skin or it will probably split during cooking.

3. Finely chop the courgette cores.

4. Heat the ghee or *niter kebbeh* and stir-fry the *baharat* and garlic for 30 seconds. Add the onion and continue to stir-fry for a further 5 minutes. Add the drained burghul, mint, fennel, egg, and aromatic salt to taste. Mix well and cook for a final 5 minutes, then allow to cool.

5. Carefully stuff the courgettes with the cool mixture and line them up side by side on an oven tray.

6. Preheat the oven to 375°F/190°C/Gas 5 and bake them for 15 minutes.

7. Brush the courgettes with a little ghee and sprinkle them with some extra *baharat*. Serve with chutneys and rice or Pitta Bread (see page 257) or Yemeni Spicy Bread (see page 260).

FASOOLI KHADRA
—— *Levantine Runner Beans* ——

LEVANT

Beans are enjoyed all over the Middle East. From the Levant area (Syria, Jordan and the Lebanon) comes this spiced-up version of green beans.

Serve as an accompaniment, with Cayenne Pottage (see page 294) and/or Middle Eastern Vinegared Chillies (see page 294).

SERVES 4

INGREDIENTS

1lb (450g) runner, French, Kenyan
 or other snap beans
1 tablespoon olive oil
2 tablespoons ghee (page 43)
2 garlic cloves, chopped
2 teaspoons harissa (page 293)
4oz (110g) onion, finely chopped

any chopped fresh herbs (e.g.
 parsley, basil and/or oregano)
salt

SPICES
2 teaspoons sesame seeds
2 teaspoons ground cinnamon

METHOD

1. Wash the beans and pull away the scaly 'string' down their length. Chop into bite-size diagonal strips.

2. Immerse them in boiling water and simmer for about 10 minutes. Drain.

3. During stage 2, heat the oil and ghee in a karahi or wok. Stir-fry the **spices** for 1 minute, then add the garlic, harissa and onion and stir-fry for about 5 more minutes.

4. Add the warm beans, and the herbs to taste, and stir-fry until all the ingredients are combined in a dryish mixture. Add salt to taste.

SABZI KORESH
—— *Vegetable Stew* ——

IRAN

This dish originated in ancient Persia. Literally meaning 'sauce poured over rice', it appears at nearly every meal and in many guises. *Korak* is the thicker version, containing meat, poultry or vegetables, and often dried fruit and nuts. Sometimes yoghurt is used and the dish is spiced, but the spicing is subtle and aromatic, never overwhelming and hot. The tastes combine sweet and sour and the textures are soft and crunchy.

SERVES 4

INGREDIENTS

8oz (225g) spinach
3–4 sticks celery
4oz (110g) French, Kenyan or snap beans
4 tablespoons ghee (page 43)
8oz (225g) onions, chopped
1 teaspoon ground turmeric
1 teaspoon ground cinnamon
1/2 teaspoon ground cloves
1/2 teaspoon freshly ground black pepper

4oz (110g) dried apricots and/or prunes and/or fresh cherries
1/2–1 teaspoon sumak (optional)
2–4 loumi (dried limes) or 1 fresh lime, pierced in several places
7oz (200g) canned chickpeas with their liquid
aromatic salt (page 46)

METHOD

1. Prepare the vegetables. After washing, chop the spinach into shreds and the celery into bite-size pieces. Chop the beans into bite-size diagonal strips.

2. Heat the ghee in a karahi to just below smoking point. Stir-fry the onions for 5–6 minutes, then add the turmeric, cinnamon, cloves and pepper, stir-frying for a further 5 minutes.

3. Transfer the stir-fried items to a lidded casserole and mix in the dried fruit if being used (but no fresh fruit yet), the *sumak* (for an ultra-sour taste) and the *loumi*. Place the casserole in an oven preheated to 375°F/190°C/Gas 5, and cook for 10 minutes.

4. Remove, inspect and stir. Add a little water as needed, and stir in the chickpeas and any fresh fruit. Return to the oven for a final 10 minutes minimum, or until cooked to your liking. Add aromatic salt to taste. Serve with rice.

PALAVA NIGER ABUJA
—— *Spinach and Sweet Potato Stir-Fry* ——

NIGERIA

A *palava* means 'a hubbub, a hullabaloo or a commotion' in West Africa, just as it does in England. But the only commotion in this dish is in the stirring. Spinach, nuts, tomatoes and red sweet potato are stir-fried together, giving a gorgeous contrasting green and red appearance. In West Africa they add shrimps or dried smoked fish to their *palava*, but this version is all vegetable. You could substitute chopped fresh red chillies for the chilli mash, if you like.

SERVES 4

INGREDIENTS

12oz (350g) fresh spinach, weighed after stage 1
4 tablespoons groundnut oil
2–4 garlic cloves, chopped
1 inch (2.5cm) cube ginger, chopped
4oz (110g) onion, chopped
12oz (350g) boiled sweet red potatoes, diced into small bite-size pieces

5oz (150g) Pan-Roasted Peanuts (page 60)
1 tablespoon chopped fresh coriander
aromatic salt (page 46)
8oz (225g) plum or cherry tomatoes, puréed
1 red bell pepper, finely chopped
1 tablespoon red chilli mash (pages 286–7)

METHOD

1. Prepare the spinach. Discard unwanted matter, wash, then chop coarsely.

2. Boil, or better, steam the spinach until soft (about 3 minutes). Remove from heat.

3. Heat the oil in a karahi or wok. Stir-fry the garlic for 30 seconds, then the ginger for a further 30 seconds. Add the onion and stir-fry for 5 more minutes.

4. Add the sweet potato, steamed spinach, nuts and coriander, and aromatic salt to taste.

5. Add the tomatoes, bell pepper and chilli mash and continue to stir-fry for about 10 minutes more.

6. Serve with *Jollof* rice (see page 247).

AMADAN KE ABOBIE
—— *Regina's Selfridges Banana Beans* ——

GHANA

Recently I was invited by Selfridges to create a menu for a six-month curry season at their Arena Restaurant. This involved a couple of days working in their kitchen training the resident staff. Head Chef is Regina from Ghana. She hadn't cooked curry before and she thoroughly enjoyed learning the techniques. Suddenly she said, 'Let me show you my favourite Ghanaian dish,' and this is what she cooked. It is essential to use good firm plantains for this dish.

SERVES 4

INGREDIENTS

3–4 *large, ripe, yellow-green peeled plantains*
6 *tablespoons ghee*
2–4 *garlic cloves, chopped*
8oz (225g) *onions, chopped*
12–14 *fresh tomatoes, puréed*
2–4 *fresh habanero red chillies, sliced*
1 *red or green bell pepper, chopped*
20–25 *whole fresh coriander leaves*
14oz (400g) *canned black-eyed beans with their juice*
aromatic salt (page 46)

METHOD

1. Chop the plantains into large bite-size pieces.

2. Heat the ghee in a karahi or wok. Stir-fry the garlic for 30 seconds. Add the onions and stir-fry for about 5 more minutes.

3. Add the puréed tomatoes, chillies and bell pepper and continue stir-frying for a further 5 minutes.

4. Add the plantains, fresh coriander, and beans. Simmer until everything is hot. Add aromatic salt to taste, and serve with *Jollof* rice (see page 247).

CALAS

—— *Bean Ball Fritters* ——

USA

These round fritters originated in West Africa where they are known variously as *Koosay*, *Kusay* or *Akara*. In the seventeenth century they went with slaves to the West Indies and became the *akkra* of the islands. A century later they turned up amongst the Creole American negro population in New Orleans as *Calas*. Sometimes made from rice instead of beans, they are deep-fried, and really simple to make.

MAKES 8

INGREDIENTS

5oz (150g) dry black-eyed lobia beans
2fl oz (50ml) fresh lime juice
6 garlic cloves, crushed
8oz (225g) onions, finely chopped
1 tablespoon red chilli mash (pages 286–7)

1 tablespoon chopped fresh basil
1 teaspoon sugar
1 teaspoon salt
oil for deep-frying

METHOD

1. In a large pan, dry-fry the beans on the stove for 1–2 minutes.

2. Cool, then grind down the beans in an electric coffee grinder or spice mill (see page 45) to create a relatively fine powder or flour.

3. Combine the beanflour and lime juice in a mixing bowl with enough water to make a thickish paste which will drop sluggishly off the spoon. Let it stand for at least 10 minutes, to allow the mixture to absorb all the moisture.

4. Next add the garlic, onion, chilli mash, basil, sugar and salt. Mix in well and leave again for about 10 minutes. Meanwhile, heat the oil in a deep-fryer to 375°F/190°C (chip-frying temperature). This is below smoking point and will cause a drop of batter to splutter a bit, then float more or less at once. Inspect the mixture. There must be no 'powder' left. It must be well mixed, still with a sluggish dropping texture.

5. To cook, simply scoop out an eighth of the mixture and place it carefully in the oil. Place all eight fritters in the deep-fryer, but allow about 10 seconds between each one so that the oil maintains its temperature. Fry for 10 minutes each, turning once. Remove from the oil in the order they went in, drain well and serve with salad, lemon wedges and salsas (see pages 290–92).

FRIJOLES FRITOS
—— *Fried Beans* ——

MEXICO

A Mexican meal is not a meal without beans (*frijoles*). There are many types and colours of Mexican beans. The most popular are black (turtle) beans, pink (pinto) beans, red (kidney) beans and white (lima) beans. One of my favourite recipes is one where cooked beans are fried with chillies, oregano, cummin, salt and pepper. Serve with Tortillas (see page 262) and *Fajitas* (see page 104).

METHOD

1. Dry beans should be soaked for at least 8 hours, then rinsed thoroughly.

2. To cook, simply bring an ample amount of water to the boil (at least three times the amount of water to beans). Simmer for 1–$1^1/_2$ hours (until the beans are tender), stirring occasionally.

3. Heat the oil (or dripping for a better flavour). Add some beans and some liquid and mash them with the back of a spoon as they warm up. Continue this process, stir-frying until all the beans are used up. It is not necessary to use up all the water if too much is left.

FRIJOLES REFRITOS
—— *Refried Beans* ——

MEXICO

The purpose of refrying is mainly to heat up already fried mashed beans.

METHOD

1. Heat some dripping (for the best flavour) or butter in a wok or frying pan.

2. Add the fried beans and stir-fry continuously until they are dry and hot.

PICANTE DE PAPAS
—— *Hot Potatoes* ——

PERU

This delightfully simple Peruvian recipe for spicy potatoes dates from Inca times. It uses new potatoes and Scotch bonnet or habañero chillies (or rocotos if you can get them). So be warned – it really is a *hot* potato recipe.

SERVES 4 as an accompaniment

INGREDIENTS

16–20 cherry-sized baby new
* potatoes*
2 tablespoons light oil
2 teaspoons olive oil
2–4 garlic cloves, crushed
6oz (175g) onion, finely chopped
¹/₂–2 Scotch bonnet or habañero
* chillies, seeds and pith discarded,*
* chopped into rings*

8–12 small cherry tomatoes
1 teaspoon tomato purée
1 tablespoon chopped fresh
* coriander*
1 tablespoon chopped fresh parsley
aromatic salt (page 46)

METHOD

1. Scrub the potatoes. Cook them in boiling water for about 5 minutes.

2. Meanwhile, heat the oils in a karahi or wok. Stir-fry the garlic for 30 seconds. Add the onion and the chilli and stir-fry these for a further 5 minutes.

3. Now add the cherry tomatoes, tomato purée and the drained hot potatoes. Add enough water to prevent sticking and stir-fry for about 5 more minutes.

4. Add the fresh coriander and parsley. Salt to taste and serve as a side dish.

PAPAS ANDEAN
—— *Peruvian Potatoes* ——

PERU

This dish has a distinctive yellow colour. It is a dish from the Peruvian Andes where they use a rare herb, palillo, to achieve the colour. I've used turmeric in the boiling water instead. Try it with Peruvian Roast Pork (see page 107).

SERVES 4

INGREDIENTS

1lb (450g) potatoes
1 teaspoon ground turmeric
3 tablespoons ground nut or
* corn oil*
2–4 green cayenne chillies, chopped
5fl oz (150ml) sour cream
5fl oz (150ml) cottage cheese

aromatic salt (page 46)

GARNISH
chopped Pan-Roasted Peanuts
* (page 60)*
whole fresh coriander leaves
freshly ground black pepper
chilli powder

METHOD

1. Wash, peel and cut the potatoes into bite-size pieces.

2. Bring ample water to the boil in a saucepan. Add the turmeric and potatoes and boil for 10–12 minutes. When they are cooked, drain them.

3. Heat the oil in a frying pan. Add the chillies and stir-fry for about 30 seconds. Add the sour cream and cottage cheese and stir-fry for 1–2 minutes. Add aromatic salt to taste.

4. Add the potatoes to the frying pan and, when completely hot and mixed, put on to individual plates or a serving bowl. Garnish with the chopped peanuts, whole fresh coriander leaves, a twist of black pepper and a sprinkling of chilli powder.

OCAPA
—— *Venezuelan Potatoes* ——

VENEZUELA

This obviously related Venezuelan version of the previous recipe should have an orangey colour. Serve it with Venezuelan Marinated Roast Pork (see page 108).

SERVES 4

INGREDIENTS

1lb (450g) potatoes
1 teaspoon ground turmeric
3 tablespoons ground nut or
* corn oil*
2–4 garlic cloves, finely chopped
1 teaspoon Hungarian paprika
4oz (110g) onion, finely chopped
1–3 orange habanero or Scotch
* bonnet chillies, finely chopped*
1 orange bell pepper, finely
* chopped*

1 tablespoon smooth or crunchy
* peanut butter*
5fl oz (150ml) double cream
8oz (225g) Cheddar cheese, grated
salt

GARNISH
chopped fresh parsley
chopped fresh chives
halved Pan-Roasted Peanuts
* (page 60)*
chilli powder

METHOD

1. Follow stages 1 and 2 of the previous recipe.

2. Heat the oil in a frying pan. Add the garlic and paprika and stir-fry for 30 seconds. Add the onion, chillies and bell pepper. Fry for about 10 more minutes.

3. Add the peanut butter and cream and mix in well. When simmering, add the cheese. Stir continuously until it has melted into the mixture. Add salt to taste.

4. Put the potatoes into a serving dish and pour the mixture over them. Garnish attractively with chopped fresh parsley and chives, halved Pan-Roasted Peanuts and a sprinkling of chilli powder.

OCAPA QUESO
—— *Potatoes in Chilli Cheese Sauce* ——

VENEZUELA

Potatoes, preferably new ones, are the basis of this dish. *Ocapa* is adored all over Latin America, especially in the chilli countries such as Peru and Guatemala. This particular recipe is from Venezuela.

SERVES 4

INGREDIENTS

2 tablespoons corn oil
1 teaspoon ground turmeric
4 garlic cloves, chopped
8oz (225g) onions, chopped
1 teaspoon chopped dried mulato chillies
1 teaspoon chopped dried ancho chillies
1 teaspoon chopped dried pasilla chillies

4 tablespoons cottage cheese
8fl oz (250ml) single cream
salt
1lb (450g) baby new potatoes, cooked

GARNISH
fried pine nuts
whole fresh coriander leaves

METHOD

1. Heat the oil in a karahi or wok. Stir-fry the turmeric for 15 seconds. Add the garlic and continue stir-frying for 30 seconds. Add the onion and the chillies and stir-fry for a further 5 minutes.

2. When this mixture is cool enough put it into a blender or food processor, along with the cottage cheese and cream, and pulse down to a pourable paste.

3. Return the paste to the pan and stir-fry until it thickens (about 3 minutes). Add salt to taste.

4. Pour the sauce over the hot potatoes and garnish with pine nuts and whole fresh coriander leaves. Serve with salsas (see pages 290–2), Tortillas (see pages 262-4) and a meat or prawn main dish.

COLOR LOS VEGOS
—— *Red Coloured Vegetables* ——

CHILE

Color, a chilli sauce from Chile, is a vibrant red mixture of chilli, paprika, tomatoes and garlic, mostly used as a condiment. Here we combine it with a selection of red vegetables.

SERVES 4

INGREDIENTS

3 tablespoons corn oil
3–4 garlic cloves, crushed
4oz (110g) red onion, chopped
2 tablespoons strained red thin chilli sauce (page 287)
1 tablespoon ground Hungarian paprika
2 tablespoons chopped sun-dried tomatoes in oil (chef's tip, page 76)

3–4 plum tomatoes, chopped
½ red cabbage, chopped
12oz (350g) red sweet potatoes (American yam), chopped
2–3 bottled beetroots, chopped
2 tablespoons chopped fresh oregano
salt

METHOD

1. Heat the oil in a karahi or wok over a high heat, then stir-fry the garlic for 30 seconds.

2. Add the onion and reduce the heat. Stir-fry for 10 minutes, until the onion becomes translucent and begins to brown.

3. Add the chilli sauce, paprika and tomatoes and continue to stir-fry until the mixture gets darker, indicating that the water has reduced out (about 5 minutes). Remove from the heat.

4. Now steam or cook the cabbage and sweet potato until tender. When they are ready put them and the beetroot into the karahi, with the fresh oregano, and salt to taste.

5. Stir-fry until thoroughly heated, and serve with Peruvian Roast Pork (see page 107) and Peruvian Potatoes (see page 206).

SEBZELER PLAKI
—— *Baked Vegetables* ——

TURKEY

Plaki means the baking of vegetables in olive oil and herbs and is a standard cooking method in Turkey, Armenia and Greece. It's not unlike a ratatouille and is delicious with a rice dish like *Pilafi* (see page 242).

SERVES 4

INGREDIENTS

8oz (225g) aubergine, chopped
1 tablespoon olive oil
2 tablespoons vegetable oil
4 garlic cloves, chopped
6–7 spring onions, bulbs and leaves
* chopped*
1 fresh red Hungarian paprika
* chilli, chopped*
1 green bell pepper, chopped
1–2 fresh red chillies, chopped
2 tablespoons sun-dried tomatoes
* in oil (chef's tip, page 76)*

8oz (225g) courgettes, sliced
12 black olives, pitted and halved
8oz (225g) Kenyan green beans,
* sliced*
4–5 plum tomatoes, quartered
1 tablespoon chopped fresh
* coriander*
1 tablespoon chopped fresh dill
1 tablespoon chopped fresh parsley
salt

METHOD

1. Soak the chopped aubergine in cold salty water for 1 hour. See chefs' tip on page 113. This leaches out any bitterness. Drain before use.

2. Heat the oils in a wok or large frying pan. Stir-fry the garlic for 1 minute, then the spring onions for about 5 more minutes.

3. Put this stir-fry with all the other ingredients, and salt to taste, in a suitable flat casserole dish.

4. Place the casserole, uncovered, in an oven preheated to 375°F/190°C/Gas 5 and bake for about 20 minutes.

5. Inspect and test the vegetables for tenderness. They may well require a few minutes longer. Add a few splashes of water if necessary to prevent them from getting too dry.

Chef's Tip

CHILLI OR SPRING ONION TASSELS

Tassels are really easy to make and are an attractive garnish that will make any dish look very professional and appetising.

To make a tassel you need a thin-walled vegetable with a thick top at one end and a hollow thin part at the other. Both chillies and spring onions are ideal candidates.

Spring Onion Tassels

1. Peel away any discoloured greenery and then trim off enough of the green part to leave about 2 inches (5cm) attached to the white bulb. Trim off the hairy roots. Wash the spring onions well.

2. Using a small, sharp paring knife, make cuts down the length of the green, away from the bulb, leaving most of the bulb uncut. Turn the onion round a little and repeat the cutting process until all the green part is cut into $1/32$ inch (1mm) threads.

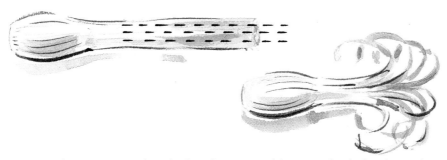

3. Immerse the onions in a bowl of iced water and leave in the fridge for an hour or so. The effect of the chilled water is to tighten the structure which causes the threads to curl backwards.

Chilli Tassels

1. Wash the chillies but leave the stalks on.

2. Make cuts down the length of the chilli, leaving $1/6$–$1/4$ of the chilli uncut at the stalk end.

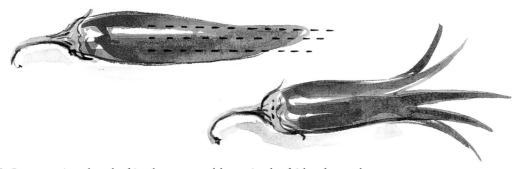

3. Immerse in a bowl of iced water and leave in the fridge for an hour or so.

SAUERKRAUT CHILI
—— *Chilli Pickled Cabbage* ——

POLAND

In the 1970s, I worked in Poland for a while. The Russians were in charge at that time, and many of the Poles I worked with made it abundantly clear that they had little time for Russians or politics. As ever, food proved to be fertile ground for conversation. This dish was first talked about, then sampled, at a hotel in Krakow near the Czech border. Food was very scarce in Poland and I remember that this dish had tripe cooked in it and was served with mashed potatoes.

SERVES 4

INGREDIENTS

2 tablespoons sunflower or light oil
1 teaspoon paprika
2 garlic cloves, crushed
4oz (110g) onion, chopped
1 tablespoon brown sugar
4fl oz (120ml) dark beer
3 tablespoons finely chopped celery
20oz (550g) canned sauerkraut
*   with its juice*

salt
fennel leaves

SPICES
1 teaspoon crushed green
*   peppercorns (fresh or in brine)*
1 teaspoon cummin seeds
1/2 teaspoon celery seeds
4–5 bay leaves

METHOD

1. Heat the oil in a frying pan or wok. Stir-fry the **spices** for 20 seconds. Add the paprika and garlic and stir-fry for 30 seconds more. Add the onion and stir-fry for about 5 more minutes.

2. Add the sugar, beer, celery and sauerkraut, and simmer for about 10 minutes.

3. Add salt to taste, garnish with fennel leaves and serve.

ROT KOHL PIKANT
—— *Spiced Red Cabbage* ——

GERMANY

Germans use few spices in their cooking, but this gorgeous recipe for red cabbage turns a rather ordinary dull vegetable into a gastronomic masterpiece. Note the alcoholic kick!

SERVES 4

INGREDIENTS

1lb (450g) red cabbage, shredded
3–4 bay leaves
6–8 cloves
¹/₂oz (15g) butter
2 teaspoons brown sugar

1 teaspoon coarsely ground black pepper
1 tablespoon Pernod
aromatic salt (page 46)

METHOD

1. Put about 2 pints (1.2 litres) water in a 5 pint (2.75 litre) lidded saucepan, bring to the boil and add the cabbage, bay leaves and cloves.

2. Simmer until the cabbage goes nice and soft (about 20 minutes). Drain and replace the cabbage in the pan, piping hot.

3. Mix in the butter, sugar, pepper and Pernod and leave the cabbage in the saucepan off the heat. Put the lid on and leave to absorb the flavours for about 10 minutes. Add aromatic salt to taste, then serve with potatoes and Chicken Paprika (see page 149).

DAIRY &
EGG DISHES

Here is a selection of cheese and egg dishes, a couple of which also contain meat. There are four types of omelette – one from Japan, another from Java, a third, known as a Magic Pancake Omelette, from Korea, and the fourth a thick oven-baked omelette from Saudi Arabia. I've also included an interesting scrambled egg dish with red chillies, from Oman, a Sri Lankan egg and fenugreek curry, stuffed chillies, and a Mexican favourite – fried eggs on a spicy sauce served on top of tortillas – Huevos Rancheros.

Paneer is a fresh home-made 'cheese' which does not melt when cooked. It resembles compacted cottage cheese and is very common in the subcontinent of India as a vegetarian dish. It is extremely versatile and very easy to make, so do please try it. I've included in this chapter a tasty curry from India that uses paneer as the main ingredient.

OPPOSITE *Clockwise from top: Fried Tortillas with Chilli Sauce (page 58), Mexican Fried Eggs on a Spicy Sauce (page 216) and Chillies Stuffed with Cheese (page 218)*

HUEVOS RANCHEROS
—— *Fried Eggs on a Spicy Sauce* ——

MEXICO

Literally meaning 'the cowboy's (rancher's) egg', this is one of Mexico's finest dishes. They eat it there for breakfast, lunch and tea. It's a great snack or accompaniment to a meal, best eaten with home-made Tortillas (see page 262).

SERVES 4

INGREDIENTS

4 tablespoons light olive oil
2–4 garlic cloves, finely chopped
1/2 teaspoon cummin seeds
4oz (110g) onion, finely chopped
4oz (110g) cherry tomatoes or sun-dried tomatoes (chef's tip, page 76), chopped
1–4 African snub or jalapeno green chillies, chopped

1 teaspoon tomato purée
1 tablespoon chopped fresh oregano
salt
4 eggs
4 home-made tortillas (page 262)
freshly ground black pepper

METHOD

1. Heat 2 tablespoons oil in a frying pan over a high heat, then stir-fry the garlic and cummin seeds for 30 seconds.

2. Add the onion and reduce the heat. Stir-fry for 10 minutes, until the onion becomes translucent and begins to brown.

3. Add the tomatoes, chillies, tomato purée, oregano, and salt to taste, and stir-fry for 3–4 more minutes.

4. In a separate pan, heat the remaining oil and fry the eggs.

5. Place the sauce on the tortillas and the eggs on top. Add a generous twist of black pepper and serve at once.

CREPAS DEL CHILI Y QUESO
—— *Chilli Cheese Crêpes* ——

MEXICO

This delightful Mexican recipe is a triple-decker savoury pancake. The two fillings are a garlic, onion, tomato and chilli *sofrito* or stir-fry on the bottom layer, and spicy cheese and sour cream on the top layer.

SERVES 4

INGREDIENTS

CRÊPES
4oz (110g) plain white flour
2oz (50g) butter, melted, plus extra
    for frying
2 eggs, beaten
1/2 pint (300ml) milk, warmed

FILLINGS
2 tablespoons corn oil
2–4 garlic cloves, finely chopped
4oz (110g) onion, finely chopped
2–3 dried ancho chillies, chopped

4oz (110g) chopped sun-dried
    tomatoes (chef's tip, page 76)
aromatic salt (page 46)
6oz (175g) Cheddar cheese, grated
4fl oz (120ml) sour cream
1 tablespoon green peppercorns in
    brine (strained)
1/2 teaspoon ground cinnamon

GARNISH
fresh dill

METHOD

1. First, make 12 crêpe pancakes (see chef's tip below). Sift the flour into a bowl and mix in the butter, eggs and warm milk. Beat well and leave to stand for about 10 minutes. The batter should be of pouring consistency. In a very hot omelette or griddle pan, heat a little butter. Pour in enough batter to make a thin pancake when 'swirled' around the pan. Cook until set, then turn over and briefly cook the other side. Turn it out. Repeat with the remaining batter.

2. Next make the *sofrito*. Heat the oil. Stir-fry the garlic for 30 seconds then add the onion, chillies and sun-dried tomatoes and stir-fry for about 10 minutes. Add aromatic salt to taste.

3. Put the cheese, sour cream, green peppercorns and cinnamon together in a bowl and mix well.

4. Spread the *sofrito* mixture generously on four crêpes.

5. Now spread the cheese mixture on four further crêpes and place them on top of the first four.

6. Place the remaining four pancakes on top. Garnish with fresh dill and serve.

Chef's Tip

Pancakes of any type can be cooked in advance, stored between layers of foil and refrigerated for a day, or frozen. Thaw, remove foil, and reheat in an oven or microwave.

CHILIS RELLENOS DE QUESO
—— *Chillies Stuffed with Cheese* ——

MEXICO

Stuffed chillies have appeared in several recipes in this book (see Index). The cheese stuffing in this recipe goes really well with chillies – the two were made for each other! The best types of chilli to use are the large New Mexican, the Anaheim or the Hungarian wax. Or, if you can obtain fresh ones, the Mexican poblano. If there is any filling left over after stuffing the chillies, thicken it with flour, divide into four, dip it in the batter and deep-fry it.

SERVES 4

INGREDIENTS

8 large green chillies or bell
   peppers
oil for deep-frying

STUFFING
5oz (150g) Cheddar cheese, grated
3oz (75g) cottage cheese
2–4 garlic cloves, chopped
2 tablespoons yoghurt or sour
   cream
2 tablespoons dried onion flakes
   (chef's tip, page 65)

1–2 tablespoons red chilli mash
   (pages 286–7)
1 tablespoon cummin seeds
$1/2$ teaspoon aromatic salt (page 46)

BATTER
4oz (110g) plain white flour
4oz (110g) cornmeal
2 egg yolks
5fl oz (150ml) milk
$1/2$ teaspoon aromatic salt (page 46)
whites of 2 eggs, beaten stiffly

METHOD

1. Pulse all the **stuffing** ingredients in a food processor or use a mincer to achieve a well-mixed cohesive paste.

2. For the **batter**, put the flour and cornmeal in a bowl, beat in the yolks, then the milk and aromatic salt. Adjust the milk quantity if necessary to achieve a thick batter. Then gently fold in the egg whites.

3. Roast the chillies or bell peppers (see pages 41–2) and, whilst they are warm and soft, peel them and slit them carefully, leaving the stalk on, to create a pocket. Remove the seeds and pith but don't make holes other than the slit if possible.

4. Carefully insert the stuffing. Don't worry if there is some left over (see recipe introduction above).

5. Dip the stuffed chillies/peppers into the batter, ensuring that they are thickly coated. Heat the oil in a deep-fryer to 375°F/190°C (chip-frying temperature) and cook them for about 10 minutes.

6. To serve, place two chillies/peppers per person on each plate. Serve with rice and salsas (see pages 290–92).

BITTARA HODI METHI
—— *Egg and Fenugreek Curry* ——

SRI LANKA

Hard-boiled eggs make great curry subjects, as this recipe from Sri Lanka shows. The eggs are cooked in a tasty combination of fenugreek leaves and coconut milk.

SERVES 4

INGREDIENTS

8 eggs
3 tablespoons sunflower oil
1 red bell pepper, thinly sliced
2–4 green cayenne chillies, thinly sliced
4 tablespoons chopped fresh coriander
6oz (175g) fresh chopped fenugreek leaves, stalks removed, or 2 tablespoons dried fenugreek leaves
14fl oz (400ml) canned coconut milk (page 44)

aromatic salt (page 46)

SPICES
1 tablespoon coriander seeds, roasted and ground (page 45)
2 teaspoons cummin seeds, roasted and ground (page 45)
1 teaspoon ground turmeric
1 teaspoon mango powder (optional)
$1/2$ teaspoon Hungarian paprika

METHOD

1. Put the eggs in a pan of boiling water and simmer for exactly 15 minutes. Remove and shell under the cold tap.

2. During stage 1, heat the oil in a karahi or wok and stir-fry the **spices** for about 1 minute. Add the red bell pepper and the green chillies and stir-fry for about 3 more minutes.

3. Add about 7fl oz (200ml) water and bring to a simmer. Add the fresh coriander and the fresh or dried fenugreek leaves. Simmer for about 10 minutes.

4. By now the eggs should be ready. Quarter them and add them to the karahi, together with the coconut milk. Add aromatic salt to taste. When the curry is simmering, remove from the heat and serve with raita (see page 296) and Parathas (see page 265) and/or plain rice.

FILFIL AHMAR BAIDH
—— *Scrambled Eggs with Red Chilli* ——

OMAN

This recipe from the south of the Gulf combines scrambled eggs with red chilli (*filfil ahmar*) and spices. Oman first became a port of call for Arab sailors en route to India in about 400 AD, when they learned how to use the seasonal monsoon winds. They continued to stop there until the Portuguese opened up a direct trading route in 1500. Oman has remained a spicy nation to this day, as shown by this super scrambled egg recipe. It makes a great teatime snack or sandwich filler.

SERVES 4

INGREDIENTS

1 tablespoon olive oil
2 garlic cloves, chopped
2–3 spring onions
1–3 fresh red cayenne or habanero chillies, chopped
6–8 black olives, pitted and chopped
1 tablespoon chopped sun-dried tomatoes in oil (chef's tip, page 76)
1 tablespoon chopped fresh mint
1 tablespoon chopped fresh chives
6 eggs

aromatic salt (page 46)
freshly ground black pepper

SPICES
1 teaspoon ground coriander
1 teaspoon ground cummin
1/2 teaspoon green cardamom seeds
1/2 teaspoon ground fenugreek seeds

GARNISH
baharat (page 48)
whole fresh coriander leaves

METHOD

1. Heat the oil and stir-fry the **spices** and garlic for 1 minute. Add the spring onions and chillies, and a splash of water to prevent them sticking, and stir-fry for about 5 minutes. Add another splash of water and the olives, sun-dried tomatoes, mint and chives.

2. Beat the eggs lightly with a fork, then pour them over the stir-fry mixture. Reduce the heat. Allow the eggs to start setting, then stir carefully to scramble until ready to serve. Watch that the mixture doesn't burn and stick.

3. Add aromatic salt and pepper to taste, and garnish with *baharat* and fresh coriander. Serve with hot Pitta Bread (see page 257) or cold in sandwiches.

IJJAH BIL TAWABEL
—— *Arabian Omelette* ——

SAUDI ARABIA Don't confuse this with a flimsy French-style omelette. *Ijjah bil Tawabel* is a thick, firmly baked egg concoction packed with vegetables, herbs and spices. It is substantial enough to be a meal in itself, served with a chutney and bread, if you're really hungry. The best way to cook it is to bake it in a round flan tray in the oven.

SERVES 4

INGREDIENTS

melted ghee (page 43)
6 eggs
4oz (110g) frozen peas, thawed
3oz (75g) cooked potato, chopped
1–3 green cayenne chillies, sliced
4oz (110g) red onion, coarsely chopped
4 tablespoons chopped fresh parsley
4 tablespoons chopped fresh mint
¹/₂ tablespoon dried mint

4 tablespoons snipped chives
*2 tablespoons **each** of three or four of the following herbs: chervil, watercress, basil, dill, etc.*
¹/₄ teaspoon ground turmeric
20 saffron strands
aromatic salt (page 46)
black pepper
¹/₄ teaspoon sumak (see page 241)
¹/₄ teaspoon zereshk (see page 241)

METHOD

1. Preheat the oven to 325°F/160°C/Gas 3. Select a flan dish about 8–9 inches (20–23cm) in diameter, preferably non-stick, and brush it with melted ghee.

2. Break the eggs into a bowl and beat with a whisk. Add the remaining ingredients, mix well and immediately transfer to the flan dish. Cover with aluminium foil.

3. Bake for 20 minutes. Remove the foil and bake for a further 20 minutes, then inspect. The top should be light brown, the inside about cooked. If you want it more solid, cook on for a few minutes longer. Serve cut into wedges.

TELUR GORENG
—— *Javanese Omelette* ——

JAVA

The combination of eggs and Indonesian flavourings, such as lemon grass, tamarind, coconut and optional *blachan* shrimp paste creates a very tasty omelette.

SERVES 4

INGREDIENTS

2 tablespoons ghee (page 43)
8 large free range eggs
1 tablespoon coconut milk powder (page 44)
2–4 fresh red cayenne chillies, sliced
1 tablespoon chopped fresh coriander
butter
aromatic salt (page 46)

PURÉE
4 garlic cloves
1 inch (2.5cm) cube galingale or ginger, chopped

2–3 spring onions, bulbs and leaves chopped
1 soft lemon grass bulb, chopped
1/2 teaspoon tamarind purée (page 44)
1/2 teaspoon blachan *shrimp paste* (optional, chef's tip, page 172)
1/2 teaspoon ketjap manis (chef's tip, page 192)
1/2 teaspoon brown sugar

GARNISH
finely chopped fresh basil
fresh grated coconut

METHOD

1. Pulse the **purée** ingredients in a food processor, using enough water to achieve a paste.

2. Heat the ghee in a karahi or wok and stir-fry the purée for 1–2 minutes.

3. Whisk the eggs in a bowl. Add the stir-fried purée, coconut powder, chillies and fresh coriander, and mix in well.

4. Next, heat a dab of butter in a flat frying pan. When it is melted, pour off the excess into the karahi or wok.

5. Give the egg mixture a final brisk whisk, then pour a quarter of it into the frying pan. Deftly roll the egg mixture around the pan with a quick wrist action. Return to the heat. When the egg begins to set, sprinkle on some aromatic salt to taste.

6. Cook for about 1 more minute, then slide the omelette out of the pan, roll it up and keep it warm.

7. Repeat stages 5 and 6 to cook the remaining three omelettes.

8. Garnish with fresh basil and grated coconut, and serve with salad and plain rice.

GULCHUPAN
—— *Magic Pancake Omelette* ——

KOREA

In Korea they fry this dish at the table, having first made a selection of nine ingredients which must always include omelette. Nine, say the Koreans, is a magic number. It is up to the individual to decide how much of each to combine. The items are shredded, stir-fried and wrapped in a rice pancake. I've kept the omelette whole, using it as a 'lining' for the pancake, then wrapping the stir-fried items inside it.

The other eight ingredients could all be vegetables – for example, white radish, water chestnuts, bean sprouts, bamboo shoots, carrots, spring onions, mushrooms and fresh horseradish.

SERVES 4

INGREDIENTS

any 8 items (see above) totalling about 1lb (450g)
2 tablespoons sesame oil
2 garlic cloves, crushed
1 inch (2.5cm) cube ginger, grated
2 teaspoons sesame seeds
1–2 green chillies, finely chopped
8 rice pancakes (see below)

3 eggs
1 teaspoon dark soy sauce

GARNISH
chives or garlic chives
Japanese seven-taste pepper (page 47) or Chinese five-spice powder (page 46) or ten-spice powder (page 47)

Note: Rice pancakes or rice flour discs can be bought frozen from Chinese or Asian stores. To use, thaw the pack enough to peel off the number of pancakes you need. Close the pack, cover with clingfilm, and return to the freezer.

METHOD

1. Shred the eight filling ingredients you have chosen into roughly equal-sized matchsticks.

2. Heat the oil in a karahi or wok. Stir-fry the garlic, ginger, sesame seeds and chillies for 1 minute. Add the shredded items and briskly stir-fry for about 5 minutes or as long as it takes to cook them. Don't overload the wok. Do it in batches if necessary, and mix everything together at the end. Set aside.

3. Steam the rice flour pancakes in a bamboo steamer or a strainer.

4. Beat the eggs and soy sauce together in a bowl and make eight omelettes about 5 inches (12.5cm) in diameter.

5. To serve, make sure everything is hot. Then place each omelette on top of a pancake, arrange some filling down the centre and roll it up. Garnish with chives and a sprinkle of Japanese seven-taste pepper. Serve with soy sauce or *Nuoc Cham* dipping sauce (see page 290).

TAMAGO-YAKI
—— *Japanese Omelette* ——

JAPAN

Most countries have omelettes in their culinary repertoire and Japan is no exception. The Japanese use a rectangular frying pan which creates a neat shape for rolling the omelettes. In the absence of this pan, simply cut the omelette to shape, as described in stage 7.

SERVES 4

INGREDIENTS

2 tablespoons brown sesame oil
1 inch (2.5cm) cube ginger, crushed
leaves of 2–3 spring onions, finely
  chopped
2 teaspoons brown sugar
8 large free range eggs
butter

MARINADE
2 teaspoons bonito (dried fish)
  flakes

2 dried shiitake mushrooms, finely
  chopped
2–3 Japanese santaka chillies,
  chopped
1 teaspoon wasabi
2 tablespoons mirin or sake
  (Japanese wine)
1 teaspoon soy sauce

METHOD

1. Mix together the **marinade** ingredients and refrigerate for about 2 hours (see page 42).

2. To cook, heat the oil in a karahi or wok. Stir-fry the ginger and spring onion for 2 minutes. Add the marinade and, when sizzling, add the sugar. Almost at once, take off the heat and keep until stage 5.

3. Whisk the eggs in a bowl.

4. Next, heat a dab of butter in a flat frying pan. When it is melted pour off the excess into the karahi.

5. Give the egg mixture a final brisk whisk, then pour an eighth of it into the frying pan. Deftly roll the egg mixture around the pan with a quick wrist action, to achieve a thin omelette. Return to the heat. When the egg begins to set, spread on an eighth of the stir-fry.

6. Cook for 1 minute longer, then slide the omelette out of the pan.

7. To achieve a tidy roll, trim two opposite sides of the omelette, saving the offcuts for some other use. Roll up the omelette quite tightly.

8. Repeat with the other seven omelettes. Serve hot or cold with a dipping sauce, such as *Nuoc Cham* (see page 290), and other Japanese dishes.

TORI-MAKI
—— *Chicken Omelette* ——

JAPAN

Chicken (*tori*) is of prime importance to the Japanese, as they hardly eat any red meat. You can add some shredded cooked chicken to the previous omelette to create *Tori-Maki*. Simply follow the previous recipe but replace one of the eggs with a cooked skinned chicken breast which has been cut into small even cubes about $^1/_4$ inch (6mm) in size. Add the chicken at stage 5. Then follow stages 6–8.

CHILLI IN THE HOLE

ENGLAND

This is based on the peculiarly English dish of Toad in the Hole, which consists of sausages baked into a Yorkshire pudding batter. Quite how the name came about, nor which is 'toad' and which is 'hole' is obscure. At the suggestion of Heather, my editor, the sausages are replaced by chillies for a spicy hot version of a traditional English dish. It sure is a great idea. It is mandatory to serve it with Beef Casserole with Horseradish and Mustard (page 122).

SERVES 4 as an accompaniment

INGREDIENTS

oil
4oz (110g) plain flour
1 egg
8fl oz (250ml) milk

$^1/_2$ teaspoon salt
freshly ground black pepper
6–8 chillies, whole

METHOD

1. Preheat the oven to 425°F/220°C/Gas 7.

2. Put enough oil in a roasting tin to cover the bottom and lap a bit up the sides, and place in the hot oven for about 10 minutes.

3. Meanwhile, sift the flour into a large mixing bowl. Make a well in the middle.

4. Beat in the egg and, gradually, the milk, using a balloon whisk. An electric mixer will do this in seconds. Add the salt, and pepper to taste.

5. Take the roasting tin out of the oven, place the chillies in the hot oil, and pour the batter around them. Return to the oven for 25 minutes or until risen and browned. Serve cut into pieces.

KHARA SOTI BOTI KABAB
—— *Spicy Meat Kebabs Enrobed In Omelette* ——

INDIA

This is a Parsee dish (Parsees are Zorastrian ex-Persians living in India) consisting of cooked succulent kebabs, still on their skewers, enrobed with omelette. The picture below tells the story.

Serve two skewers per person with a wet curry or two, plus rice and/or Indian bread. Alternatively, it can make an excellent stand-alone starter served on a bed of salad. A vegetarian version follows on page 228.

SERVES 4

INGREDIENTS

32 cubes of lean lamb or beef,
  about 1¹/₄ inches (3cm) square
4–5 tablespoons ghee (page 43)
2–4 garlic cloves, crushed
1 inch (2.5cm) cube fresh ginger,
  finely chopped
¹/₂ teaspoon ground turmeric
1 teaspoon chilli powder
2 teaspoons mild curry paste
  (page 49)
4oz (110g) onion, very finely
  chopped
8 bamboo skewers, cut to fit your
  frying pan and soaked in water
  for 1 hour

4 eggs

MARINADE
6fl oz (175ml) milk
1 tablespoon brown sugar
1 tablespoon soy sauce
2 garlic cloves, crushed
1 teaspoon garam masala (page 47)
¹/₂–1¹/₂ teaspoons chilli powder
1 teaspoon aromatic salt (page 46)

GARNISH
fresh coriander leaves

1. Mix together the marinade ingredients in a non-metallic bowl. Immerse the meat and marinate for 24–60 hours (see page 42).

2. Heat 2 tablespoons ghee in a flat frying pan and stir-fry the garlic for 30 seconds. Add the ginger and continue to stir-fry for 30 seconds more. Add the turmeric and chilli powder and when mixed in, the curry paste. Add the onion and the meat together with its marinade and simmer and stir-fry on a low heat for 15–20 minutes, or until the meat is tender and cooked.

3. Allow it to become cool enough to handle, then thread four pieces of meat on to each skewer, with gaps between each piece. Transfer any spare sauce to a saucepan and keep warm. Clean the frying pan.

4. Break the eggs into a bowl and beat with a whisk.

5. Heat a teaspoon of ghee in a non-stick frying pan. When hot, pour in one eighth of the egg mixture and swirl round to coat the pan, as if making a thin omelette. Place a hot kebab in the centre of the omelette and fold over the top and bottom edges of the omelette to enclose the kebab. The egg will adhere to the kebab as it cooks and sets.

6. Repeat with the remaining skewers and egg. When all are cooked, pour over any remaining sauce. Garnish with coriander leaves and serve as a starter on top of a salad, or as part of a main course on a bed of rice with an accompanying vegetable curry

FACING PAGE *Spicy Meat Kebabs Enrobed in Omelette (above). Behind is a bunch of flowering garlic chives*

ALOO BOTI KHARA KABAB

INDIA

For a vegetarian version of the previous recipe, substitute cooked potatoes (no need to marinate them) for the meat. In stage 2, reduce the cooking time to a few minutes only, then follow the rest of the instructions, as for meat.

PANEER
—— *Indian Cheese* ——

INDIA

Paneer is remarkably versatile. The recipe below produces a bright white neutral flavoured product, which can be used crumbled or cut to any shape. 'Solid' rather than crumbled paneer can be marinated for 2–6 hours to absorb flavour and colour. Then it can be deep- or shallow-fried, grilled or barbecued.

MAKES about 8oz (225g)

INGREDIENTS

4 pints (2.25 litres) full-cream milk (not UHT) *4–6 tablespoons any vinegar or lemon juice*

METHOD

1. Choose a large pan. If you have one of 12 pint (6.75 litre) capacity, the milk will only occupy a third of the pan and won't boil over (unless the lid is on).

2. Bring the milk slowly to the boil. Add the vinegar or lemon juice, stirring until it curdles – when the curds separate from the whey.

3. Strain into a clean tea towel placed on a strainer over a saucepan or bowl. Fold the tea towel over and press through the excess liquid – the **whey**. Keep for later use as stock.

4. Now place the curds – from now on called paneer – on to the draining board, still in the tea towel. Press it out to a circle about $^1/_2$ inch (1cm) thick. Place a flat weight (the original saucepan full of water, for instance) on the tea towel and allow it to compress the paneer.

5. If you want **crumbly paneer**, remove the weight after 30–45 minutes and crumble the paneer. If you want the paneer to be solid, keep the weight on for $1^1/_2$–2 hours. Then cut the paneer into cubes.

SAAG DAL PANEER CURRY
—— *Spinach & Lentil Curry with Indian Cheese* ——

INDIA

Here is a combination of ingredients which goes together like a magical trinity. The creamy yellow smoothness of the lentils, the golden crispy nuggets that are the deep-fried paneer pieces, and the deep green shreds of spinach not only look good, but linked together with spices, they taste good too.

SERVES 4

INGREDIENTS

6oz (175g) red masoor lentils, split and polished
4 tablespoons light oil
2 garlic cloves, crushed
6oz (175g) onion, finely chopped
2 tablespoons garam masala (page 47)
1 tablespoon tomato purée
6oz (175g) fresh spinach, chopped and cooked

aromatic salt (page 46)
oil for deep-frying
about 8oz (225g) solid paneer (page 228), cut into cubes

SPICES
2 teaspoons cummin seeds
1 teaspoon black mustard seeds
1–2 teaspoons chilli powder
1/2 teaspoon ground turmeric

METHOD

1. Pick through the lentils for unwanted matter, then soak them for about an hour. Rinse well and drain.

2. Bring 2 pints (1.2 litres) of water to the boil, then add the lentils. After a couple of minutes stir them and reduce the heat to simmer. As soon as they are no longer sticking to the bottom of the pan, leave them to simmer for 45 minutes.

3. Towards the end of stage 2, heat the oil to high heat in a wok or karahi. Stir-fry the **spices** for 10 seconds. Add the garlic and continue to stir-fry for a further 30 seconds. Then add the onion, lower the heat and continue to stir-fry for 10–15 minutes until the onion browns.

4. Add the garam masala and tomato purée and enough water to create a paste-like consistency.

5. As soon as the lentils are cooked strain off any excess lentil water (keep it for future stock) and add the lentils to the stir-fry together with the cooked spinach. Add aromatic salt to taste.

6. Heat the oil in a deep-fryer to 375°F/190°C and carefully immerse the paneer, piece by piece to prevent sticking. Fry for about 5 minutes.

7. Drain the paneer and add it to the lentil and spinach curry. Stir well and serve fairly promptly with rice or bread.

RICE DISHES

Rice is now universally popular and apart from being nutritionally superb, it is both filling and satisfying. Even more importantly, it is the most perfect medium for flavouring and spicing. Mastering the art of cooking rice is a skill well worth achieving. Many people feel that rice cooking is beyond them, complaining that they always seem to end up with a stodgy result. I have found that instructions on packets do not always work, so my advice to these people is to ignore them and to follow my methods.

I am convinced that anyone can cook rice who is capable of boiling water, telling the time and hearing the timer ping. You may need to practise a few times, but once you've got it mastered there will be no going back. The most important rule of all is to allow enough time. Always cook the rice first not last and, especially if the particular recipe requires fluffy grains, allow it to stand after cooking to dry off.

Here are 20 simply sensational rice dishes from around the world, including many national dishes like Spain's paella, Italy's risotto, Africa's jollof, Greece's pilafi, India's pullao, Malaysia's nasi goreng, and American Cajun's jambalaya. These are just some of the colourful tasty rice dishes waiting for you to try.

OPPOSITE *Clockwise from top: Chilean Red Coloured Vegetables (page 209), Chillies Stuffed with Rice (page 251) and Cuban Beans and Rice (page 252)*

PLAIN RICE BY BOILING

This is the quickest way to cook rice, and it can be ready to serve in just 15 minutes from the water boiling. Two factors are crucial for this method to work perfectly. Firstly, the rice must be Basmati rice. Patna or long-grained, quick-cook or other rices will require different timings and will have neither the texture nor the fragrance of Basmati. Secondly, this is one of the few recipes in this book which require precision timing. It is essential that for its few minutes on the boil you concentrate on it or else it may overcook and become stodgy.

A 3oz (75g) portion of dry rice provides an ample helping per person; 2oz (50g) will be a smaller but adequate portion.

INGREDIENTS *8–12oz (225–350g) Basmati rice*   *2–3 pints (1.2–1.75 litres) water*

METHOD

1. Pick through the rice to remove grit and impurities.

2. Boil the water. It is not necessary to salt it.

3. Whilst it is heating up, rinse the rice briskly with fresh cold water until most of the starch is washed out. Run boiling kettle water through the rice at the final rinse. This minimises the temperature reduction of the boiling water when you put the rice into it.

4. When the water is boiling properly, put the rice into the pan. Start timing. Put the lid on the pan until the water comes back to the boil, then remove the lid. It takes 8–10 minutes from the start. Stir frequently.

5. After about 6 minutes, taste a few grains. As soon as the centre is no longer brittle but still has a good *al dente* bite to it, drain off the water. The rice should seem slightly undercooked.

6. Shake off all the excess water, then place the strainer on a dry tea towel which will help remove the last of the water.

7. After a minute place the rice in a warmed serving dish. You can serve it now or, preferably, put it into a very low oven or warming drawer for at least 30 minutes. As it dries, the grains will separate and become fluffy. It can be held in the warmer for up to 90 minutes. Or it can be cooled and reheated in a wok (quickly stir-fry without any oil).

PLAIN RICE BY ABSORPTION

Cooking rice in a pre-measured ratio of water which is all absorbed into the rice is undoubtedly the best way to do it. Provided that you use Basmati rice, the finished grains are longer, thinner and much more fragrant and flavourful than they are after boiling.

The method is easy, but many cookbooks make it sound far too complicated. Instructions invariably state that you must use a tightly lidded pot and precise water quantity and heat levels, and never lift the lid during the boiling process, etc. However, I lift the lid, I might stir the rice, and I've even cooked rice by absorption without a lid. Also, if I've erred on the side of too little water, I've added a bit during 'the boil'. (Too much water is an unresolvable problem, however.) It's all naughty, rule-breaking stuff but it still seems to work.

It's useful to know that 10oz (300g) is 2 teacups dry rice, and 20fl oz (1 pint/570ml) is about $1^1/_3$ volume of water to 1 of rice. This 10:20 ratio (or 2 teacups : 1 pint) combination is easy to remember, but do step the quantities up or down, as required, in proportion. For small appetites, for instance, use 8oz (225g) rice : 16fl oz (450ml) water to serve four people. For large appetites use 12oz (350g) rice : 24fl oz (685ml) water.

Cooking rice by absorption does need some practice, but after a few goes you'll do it without thinking. Here is my foolproof method.

INGREDIENTS

10oz (300g) Basmati rice
20fl oz/1 pint (570ml) water

2 tablespoons ghee (page 43)

METHOD

1. Cover the rice in ample water and soak for about 10 minutes.

2. Rinse it until the water runs more or less clean, then drain.

3. Measure and pre-boil the water or, for tastier results, use 10fl oz (300ml) each of milk and water.

4. Heat the ghee in a heavy lidded pan. Add the drained uncooked rice and very gently (so as not to break the grains), stir-fry for 30 seconds.

5. Add the boiling water, or milk and water, to the rice and stir well.

6. As soon as it starts bubbling put the lid on the pan and reduce the heat to under half. After about 3 minutes, inspect. You should see that all the water has disappeared and that there are little holes or craters on the surface of the rice. Carefully spoon the rice to one side to check that all the water has gone from the bottom of the pan. If not, replace the lid and leave for a bit longer. When it has, stir the rice well, ensuring that it is not sticking to the bottom. Now taste. It should not

be brittle in the middle. If it is, add a little more hot water and return to the heat.

7. Once it reaches this stage, remove the pan from the heat and place it in a warm place, such as a warming drawer or oven preheated to its lowest setting. This should be no lower than 175°F/80°C and no higher than 210°F/100°C (about Gas $^1/_8$). You can serve the rice at once, but the longer you leave it, the more separate the grains will be. Thirty minutes is fine, but it will be quite safe and happy left for up to 90 minutes. Or it can be cooled and reheated in a wok (quickly stir-fry without any oil).

CHILLI RISOTTO
—— *Italian Rice* ——

ITALY

Although it was used in Roman cookery, with the decline of the empire, rice was forgotten in Italy. The Arabs reintroduced it when they took southern Italy in the ninth century. Their long-grained Pullao/Pilaf recipes would have been enjoyed at that time. Centuries later Spain captured southern Italy and Paella became standard fare. However, it was the northern Italian traders of Genoa and Venice who in medieval times began to exchange their goods for Indian and Persian rice. It is not surprising that they eventually started to grow their own. Today Italy's thriving rice-growing district lies in the foothills of the Alps, in the Lombardy plains.

In the northern cities of Genoa, Milan and Venice you are more likely to find rice dishes than you would in the south of Italy where pasta reigns supreme. You will certainly find Risotto.

I love the word Risotto – I always think it means besotted with rice. I certainly am besotted with Italy's stupendous rice dish. Unlike the fluffy birianies and pullaos, a genuine Risotto should be slightly sticky – though not starchy or glutinous.

You must use short, round-grained rice for Risotto – the very best of which is Carnaroli (largest-grain, and most expensive and difficult to find). Vialone Nano is next best. Third and most readily available (and highly acceptable) is Arborio.

Unlike the previous Paella dish, Risotto is constantly stirred (caressed, some might say) during its cooking. We actually want to release some of the starch in order to create this clinging texture. The traditional way is to add the liquid in several batches, allowing each to reduce before adding the next. This requires constant attention and frequent gentle stirring to prevent sticking and burning.

As in other recipes, I have included a few spicy additions.

SERVES 4

INGREDIENTS

1 tablespoon olive oil
1oz (30g) butter
2–4 garlic cloves, sliced
4oz (110g) onion, finely chopped
2–3 tablespoons cooked Sicilian
 Spicy Mince (optional, page 115)
4oz (110g) cooked shrimps
 (optional)
1 tablespoon sun-dried tomatoes in
 oil (chef's tip, page 76)
2 teaspoons tomato purée
1 teaspoon red chilli mash
 (pages 286–7)
2 teaspoons pesto sauce
16fl oz (450ml) thin clear stock
 (any type)
10oz (300g) risotto rice

4fl oz (120ml) dry white wine
1 teaspoon saffron, strands
 separated
1 tablespoon chopped fresh
 oregano
1 tablespoon chopped fresh parsley
aromatic salt (page 46)

SPICES
4–5 green cardamom pods
6–7 cloves
2 inch (5cm) piece cassia bark

GARNISH
whole fresh oregano leaves
a few sprigs of parsley
grated Mozzarella or Parmesan
 cheese

METHOD

1. Heat the oil and butter in a large saucepan. Add the **spices** and stir-fry for 10 seconds. Add the garlic and stir-fry for 30 seconds more, then add the onion and stir-fry for about 5 minutes. Add the mince and shrimps if using, and the sun-dried tomatoes, tomato purée, chilli mash and pesto sauce.

2. During stage 1, bring the stock to a simmer in its own pan.

3. Stir the rice into the stir-fry and, when sizzling, add a cupful of stock, and all the wine and saffron. Stir, bring to a simmer, then lower the heat and stir now and again until the stock is absorbed (about 3 minutes).

4. Repeat stage 3 (minus the wine and saffron) until all the stock is used up. Note that as the rice softens the absorption time speeds up.

5. Add the oregano and parsley and fork everything together. Add aromatic salt to taste, then let the risotto stand in a warm place for at least 10 minutes.

6. If you wish, you can mould each portion of risotto by pressing it gently into an oiled bowl, then easing it out on to the dining plate. Garnish with whole fresh oregano leaves, a few sprigs of parsley and some grated Mozzarella or Parmesan cheese.

Note: As rice varies batch to batch it may require a little less stock than specified to achieve perfectly cooked, creamy, yet al dente risotto. In the unlikely event that it requires more and you've run out, use boiling water

ARROZ CON AZAFRAN
—— *Spanish Saffron Rice* ——

SPAIN

The Arabic Moors brought saffron (they called it *zafran*) to Spain in the ninth century. The Arabs use ghee and long-grained rice. Spain's version uses olive oil and Spanish short-grained rice. Note the use of both turmeric and saffron to create colour and fragrance.

SERVES 4

INGREDIENTS

10oz (300g) Spanish short-grained
  rice
2 tablespoons olive oil
2 garlic cloves, chopped
2oz (50g) onion, finely chopped
1/2 teaspoon ground turmeric

1 teaspoon saffron, strands
  separated
20fl oz (570ml) boiling water

GARNISH
grated fresh coconut (page 43)
pan-roasted peanuts (page 60)

METHOD

1. Follow the recipe on pages 233–4, adding the garlic and onion as soon as the oil is hot in stage 4. Stir-fry for about 5 minutes, then add the rice.

2. Add the turmeric and saffron with the boiling water and follow the recipe on pages 233–4 to its end.

3. Garnish with grated fresh coconut and roasted peanuts, and serve.

PAELLA
—— *Spanish Rice* ——

SPAIN

Since the Arabic Moors brought rice, and one of their favourite rice dishes, *Pullao*, to Spain over 1000 years ago, the Spanish have made rice their own with Paella, the direct descendant of Pullao. Spain is now a major rice-growing nation. The rice is stubby, fat, almost round, short-grained and marketed abroad as 'Spanish rice'.

Paella can only be cooked by absorption, preferably in a lidless paella pan (*paelleria*) or frying pan see pages 233–4. Its colour must be achieved by using saffron, never turmeric. Apart from the mandatory rice, the dish included anything that had been trapped that day – rabbit, fowl, wild birds, etc. Fishermen would use the fruits of the sea. Today, anything goes.

The meat, poultry and seafood should be par-cooked first, then added to the pan as the rice cooks.

SERVES 4

INGREDIENTS

4 tablespoons olive oil
4 small chicken drumsticks, skin on
4 uncooked king prawns, shell on
20–24 uncooked tiny brown
 shrimps, shell off
4–6 fresh mussels, shell on
4–8 fresh cockles, shell on
1oz (30g) butter
2–4 garlic cloves, chopped
4oz (110g) onion, finely chopped
2 tablespoons chopped bell pepper
1–3 red cayenne chillies, chopped
1 tablespoon sun-dried tomatoes in
 oil (chef's tip, page 76)
20–24fl oz (600-685ml) boiling
 water

1 teaspoon saffron strands
$1/2$ teaspoon aromatic salt (page 46)
salt
10–12oz (300–350g) Spanish rice
4oz (110g) chorizo (page 105),
 chopped
4oz (110g) mixed vegetables (peas,
 sweetcorn, carrot, beans)

SPICES
4–6 green cardamom pods
4–6 cloves
2 inch (5cm) piece of cassia bark

GARNISH
lemon wedges
sprigs of parsley

METHOD

1. Heat the oil in a large frying pan or paella pan (see chef's tip on page 238). Sear the chicken legs for 5 minutes, turning frequently to achieve an even browning. Remove them and set aside.

2. Using the same liquid, do the same to the king prawns. After 5 minutes add the shrimps, mussels and cockles, and stir-fry for 3–4 more minutes. Drain and set aside, returning the liquid to the pan.

3. Heat the liquid with the butter. Stir-fry the garlic for 30 seconds. Add the onion and stir-fry for 5 minutes. Add the bell pepper, chillies and sun-dried tomato and, when sizzling, the measured boiling water. Add the **spices**, saffron, and aromatic salt to taste, and stir well. Allow this mixture to simmer for a few minutes to bring out the saffron colour.

4. Run a kettle of boiling water through the rinsed rice, strain well, then add the rice to the pan. Let it come back to the boil.

5. Place the chicken, shellfish, chorizo and vegetables in the bubbling liquid on top of the rice.

6. Either lower the heat and let the paella cook on top of the stove or place it, uncovered, in an oven preheated to 375°F/190°C/Gas 5. If cooking on the stove, turn off the heat altogether as soon as the water disappears (after 5–6 minutes).

7. Either way, do not stir. (Doing so disturbs the surface of the rice and releases starch, making the dish sticky.) Leave it alone for about 20 minutes, then test a grain or two. It should be cooked *al dente*, but not brittle. Leave it for a few more minutes, off the heat, then serve in its cooking dish garnished with lemon wedges and parsley.

ABOVE *Paella*
(*pages 236–7*)

Chef's Tip

A *paella* pan is made from carbon steel and is flat and shallow. This shape is perfect for cooking rice by absorption, providing that the heat is evenly applied all over the bottom of the pan. This is ideal when one has a large hotplate but gas and electric rings tend to localise the heat in hot spots, causing the rice to stick and even burn in places. This can be eased considerably by placing the pan a little above the heat, on a wok stand, for example. Also, make sure the paella pan base is not larger than the heat source ring. Having said all this, I find that my largest cast-iron Le Creuset frying pan works perfectly in direct contact with the heat even though it is much larger than the heat source. The cast-iron distributes the heat evenly all over the pan.

RICE AND PEAS

WEST INDIES

This dish is synonymous with the West Indies. It is the unofficial national dish. You'll find it on every island, in every homestead, hotel and hostelry. It is, of course, very nourishing, the peas being pulses (yellow split peas), giving ample protein when combined with rice for fibre, and spices for flavouring. It is also economical (minimal meat being optional) and makes a meal on its own. Above all it is delicious. Try it and see.

SERVES 4

INGREDIENTS

7oz (200g) yellow split peas
24fl oz (685ml) akhni (page 44) or
  other stock
2 tablespoons ghee (page 43)
1 teaspoon green peppercorns,
  crushed
3–4 garlic cloves, crushed
2–3 slices bacon plus fat, chopped
4oz (110g) onion, chopped
1–2 red habanero chillies, chopped

1 tablespoon chopped sun-dried
  tomatoes (chef's tip, page 76)
7oz (200g) Basmati or long-grained
  rice
aromatic salt (page 46)

GARNISH
chopped fresh chives
chopped fresh parsley

METHOD

1. Search through the split peas to remove grit and any impurities, and soak them in ample water for 8–12 hours.

2. Put the stock in a pan and bring to the boil. Add the split peas and simmer for 30 minutes.

3. Heat the ghee in a heavy lidded pan on high heat, then stir-fry the green peppercorns for 20 seconds. Add the garlic and bacon and continue stir-frying for a further 30 seconds. Add the onion, chillies and sun-dried tomatoes and reduce the heat. Stir-fry for 10 minutes, until the onion becomes translucent and begins to brown.

4. Cover the rice in ample water and soak for about 10 minutes. Rinse well and drain thoroughly.

5. Add the rice to the stir-fry and gently (so as not to break the grains) stir into the mixture.

6. Add the simmering stock, split peas, and aromatic salt to taste, and follow the absorption recipe on pages 233–4.

7. Garnish with chopped chives and parsley, and serve.

NASI GORENG

—— *Malaysian Fried Rice* ——

MALAYSIA

Nasi simply means 'rice', *go* 'fried' and *reng* 'Malay' and 'Indonesian'. You'll find this dish all over the East Indies. You'll also find it in Indonesian restaurants all over Holland.

SERVES 4

INGREDIENTS

8–12oz (225–350g) Basmati rice
$1/2$ teaspoon ground turmeric
2 tablespoons ghee (page 43)
2 garlic cloves, crushed
2 inch (5cm) cube galingale or ginger, chopped
several pieces cooked chicken, skinned and boned
4oz (110g) cooked prawns, shell off
1 tablespoon chopped fresh coriander
1 tablespoon chopped fresh basil
3–4 tablespoons cooked peas

PASTE
3 garlic cloves

3–4 spring onions, bulbs and leaves chopped
1 large soft lemon grass bulb, chopped
$1/2$ teaspoon tamarind purée (page 44)
$1/2$ teaspoon blachan *shrimp paste* (chef's tip, page 172)
$1/2$ teaspoon ketjap manis (chef's tip, page 192)
$1/2$ teaspoon brown sugar
1–4 teaspoons sambal manis (page 288)

GARNISH
finely chopped fresh basil
fresh grated coconut (page 43)
chopped Macadamia or cashew nuts

METHOD

1. Pulse the **paste** ingredients in a food processor or blender, using enough water to make a purée.

2. Cook the Basmati rice by either the boiling or the absorption method (see pages 232 and 233–4), adding the turmeric before the rice goes into the water. It can be hot or cold but it must be as fluffy as possible.

3. Heat the ghee in a karahi or wok. Stir-fry the garlic for 30 seconds, add the galingale or ginger and fry for a further 30 seconds. Add the paste and briskly stir-fry for 1–2 more minutes.

4. Add the chicken, prawns, coriander, basil, peas and the rice. Stir carefully to mix thoroughly. Garnish with basil, coconut and chopped nuts, and serve.

POLLOU
—— *Persian Rice* ——

Iran was historically a trading crossroads between Asia and the Mediterranean. Rice cooking has therefore been a part of Iranian culture for at least 2500 years, having been brought there from northern India and China. Iran elevated rice to the highest culinary heights with the perfection of the Pollou. This was later to become India's Pullao, Turkey's Pilav, the Greek Pilafi and Spain's Paella. The Pollou is best cooked by absorption using Basmati rice. If you can obtain it, use Iranian *dom-siyah* (black-tailed) rice, a fragrant Basmati variety.

The great thing about Pollou is that you can add any ingredients – nuts and dried fruit are typically Persian, and that's what I've used here, but legumes, vegetables, meat and seafood can all be used.

This list of ingredients is deliberately Persian. *Zereshk* (barberry) is a particularly sour berry and *sumak* is another sour berry in powder form. Alternatively use lime juice and sour bottled redcurrants.

SERVES 4

INGREDIENTS

8–12oz (225–350g) Basmati or Iranian rice
3 tablespoons ghee (page 43)
3–4 zardaloo (dried apricots in clear honey), chopped
1 tablespoon fresh pomegranate seeds (optional)
1¹/₂ teaspoons dried zereshk *(barberries), soaked in water for 1 hour*
1 tablespoon green pistachio nuts, chopped
1 tablespoon almonds, chopped
¹/₂ teaspoon sumak *powder (optional)*
30 saffron strands, separated

SPICES
4 green cardamom pods
4 cloves
¹/₂ teaspoon caraway seeds
¹/₂ teaspoon aniseed
2 inch (5cm) piece cassia bark
20–24fl oz (600–685ml) boiling water

GARNISH
a little melted ghee
whole green pistachio nuts
whole toasted almonds
fresh chopped chives
orange wedges

1. Pollou is best cooked by the absorption method, so please follow the recipe on pages 233–4 to the end of stage 3.

2. Heat the ghee in a large saucepan and stir-fry the **spices** for 30 seconds. Then add the rice as described in stage 4 on page 233.

3. Add the remaining ingredients, with the measured boiling water, and follow the recipe to its end. Garnish and serve.

PILAFI

—— *Greek Fried Rice* ——

GREECE

This tasty rice is slightly sticky because it uses short-grained rice. It is a derivative of the Indian Pullao, the Iranian Pollou and the Turkish Pilav. These, however, use long-grained rice. Like Italian Risotto, you can serve each portion of this from a mould if you wish. It's good with Shashlik Kebabs (see page 110) or Moussaka (see page 112).

SERVES 4

INGREDIENTS

8–12oz (225–350g) Italian Arborio
  risotto rice
1 tablespoon olive oil
1oz (30g) butter
2–4 garlic cloves, chopped
4–6 black olives, pitted and
  chopped
3–4 chopped sun-dried tomatoes in
  oil (chef's tip, page 76)

several sprigs of parsley, chopped
1 teaspoon green peppercorns
  (fresh or in brine)
4fl oz (120ml) white wine
16fl oz (450ml) akhni stock (page
  44)
aromatic salt (page 46)

METHOD

1. Soak the rice for 5 minutes, then wash it several times. Drain.

2. Heat the oil and butter in a large saucepan and stir-fry the garlic for 30 seconds. Add the olives, sun-dried tomatoes, parsley and peppercorns and, when sizzling, the white wine.

3. Cook the rice as in stages 2–6 of the risotto recipe (see page 235).

4. Add aromatic salt to taste, and serve.

FACING PAGE *Greek Fried Rice (above) with Pitta Bread (page 257) and black olives*

FILFIL PILAV
—— *Chilli Fried Rice* ——

<u>CYPRUS</u>

From Turkish Cyprus comes this rather more robust creamy variation of Pilafi. Its flavours derive from a mixture of vinegared chillies and hummus. Serve with Shashlik Kebabs (see page 110) and Pitta Bread (see page 257).

SERVES 4

METHOD

Use exactly the same ingredients as the previous recipe, minus the olives and peppercorns.

   In their place substitute:

INGREDIENTS

3–4 Middle Eastern Vinegared Chillies (page 294)

2 tablespoons fresh or canned hummus

BOOMBA TAMARTA BHAAT
—— *Bombay Tomato Rice* ——

INDIA

Try this tasty colourful recipe to flavour already-cooked plain rice, which can be cold 'leftovers' or rice especially cooked for this dish. Serve with a lentil dish and/or Puris (see page 266) for a truly satisfying and very inexpensive meal.

SERVES 4

INGREDIENTS

3 tablespoons ghee (page 43)
2 garlic cloves, chopped
1 tablespoon garam masala paste (page 49)
4oz (110g) onion, chopped
2 tablespoons chopped sun-dried tomatoes in oil (chef's tip, page 76)
4oz (110g) canned chopped tomatoes

4oz (110g) frozen and thawed spinach leaves, chopped
1 teaspoon dried fenugreek leaves
1 tablespoon chopped fresh coriander
1 1/2lb (675g) cooked plain rice
aromatic salt (page 46)

METHOD

1. Heat the ghee in a karahi or wok. Stir-fry the garlic for 30 seconds. Add the garam masala paste and stir-fry for a further 30 seconds. Add the onion and continue stir-frying for 5 minutes.

2. Add the sun-dried tomatoes, canned tomatoes, spinach, fenugreek and fresh coriander. When sizzling, add just enough water to keep it from sticking, and continue to cook for 5–6 minutes.

3. Add the rice, little by little being the easiest way to mix it, and heat it through. Add aromatic salt to taste, and serve.

ALU CHOLE PULLAO
—— *Curried Potato and Chickpea Rice* ——

PAKISTAN

This healthy nutritious vegetarian dish makes a meal in itself. It's a favourite of cricketer Imran Khan's. Serve with Trevor Pack's Chilli Chutney (see page 295) and a raita (see page 296).

SERVES 4

INGREDIENTS

2 tablespoons ghee (page 43)
1 garlic clove, finely chopped
1 inch (2.5cm) cube ginger,
   chopped
4oz (110g) onion, finely chopped
2 tablespoons mild curry paste
   (page 49)
10oz (300g) Basmati rice
14oz (400g) canned baby potatoes
14oz (400g) canned chickpeas
1 tablespoon chopped fresh
   coriander
salt

SPICES

1½ teaspoons cummin seeds
½ teaspoon coriander seeds
½ teaspoon fennel seeds
4–6 green cardamom pods
2–4 bay leaves
2 inch (5cm) piece cassia bark

GARNISH

2–3 tablespoons almonds, chopped
0–4 fresh green chillies, sliced
   lengthways and briefly grilled

METHOD

1. Heat the ghee in a heavy lidded casserole dish. Stir-fry the **spices** for 1 minute. Add the garlic and ginger and briskly stir-fry for a further minute. Mix in the onion and curry paste. Reduce the heat and leave to go golden, stirring occasionally. (This will take a further 10 minutes.)

2. Pick through the rice to remove unwanted matter. Rinse several times in cold water until it runs clear. Leave to soak in ample cold water.

3. Pour the liquid from the canned potatoes and chickpeas into a measuring jug. Add water so that the liquid totals 1 pint (600ml). Bring to the boil in a separate pan.

4. Drain the rice and add to the casserole, carefully stirring and mixing. Add the potatoes, chickpeas and fresh coriander. When sizzling and hot, add the boiling liquid.

5. Keep the heat high until the liquid starts simmering, stirring all the time. Then reduce the heat, put the lid on and leave to cook for 10 minutes.

6. Place the pot in an oven preheated to its lowest heat for at least 30 minutes. After this, remove and stir the rice with a fork to aerate it and let the steam escape. Add salt to taste. It can now be served or returned to the oven for a further 30–60 minutes. Garnish with chopped almonds and green chillies, and serve.

ARROZ DE COCO
—— *Coconut Chilli Rice* ——

ANGOLA

The Hispanic name indicates that this is another Portuguese-influenced dish. You'll find minor variations on this theme all round coastal Africa.

SERVES 4

INGREDIENTS

3 tablespoons ghee (page 43)
4oz (110g) onion, finely chopped
2 tablespoons sun-dried tomatoes in oil (chef's tip, page 76)

1–3 habanero chillies, sliced
8–12oz (225–350g) Basmati rice

METHOD

1. Heat the ghee in a karahi or wok. Stir-fry the onion for about 10 minutes until golden. Add the sun-dried tomatoes and chillies and continue stir-frying for a further 5 minutes.

2. The rice is best cooked by the absorption method so please follow the recipe on pages 233–4.

3. Add the washed and drained rice to the stir-fry, carefully mixing together. Now add the boiling water and follow the recipe to its end.

JOLLOF
—— *West African Rice* ——

You'll find this tasty rice dish all over West Africa. It probably originated after the Arabs brought rice here over 1000 years ago. At that time the whole area, then called Jollof, was ruled by a king. The dish can include meat, chicken, fish, eggs or just vegetables. Here I've used ham and vegetables. The Portuguese brought chillies and tomatoes to West Africa, and they are now an integral part of Jollof rice.

SERVES 4

INGREDIENTS

3 tablespoons ghee (page 43)
2–3 slices rindless streaky bacon, chopped
4oz (110g) onion, finely chopped
1–3 red habanero chillies, sliced
1 teaspoon green peppercorns in brine
1 tablespoon chopped sun-dried tomatoes in oil (chef's tip, page 76)

5oz (150g) chopped plum or cherry tomatoes
1–2 slices ham, chopped
8–12oz (225–350g) Basmati rice
1/2 teaspoon ground turmeric
1/2 teaspoon paprika
5oz (150g) cooked mixed peas, sweetcorn and diced carrots
aromatic salt (page 46)

METHOD

1. Heat the ghee in a karahi or wok and stir-fry the bacon for 3 minutes. Add the onion and continue stir-frying for 5 minutes. Add the chillies, peppercorns, sun-dried tomatoes, fresh tomatoes and ham, with 7fl oz (200ml) water, and leave to simmer until the water is reduced and the mixture quite thick.

2. Boil the rice (see recipe on page 232), adding the turmeric and paprika before the water boils.

3. Once the rice is strained (note the gorgeous orange colour), combine it with the simmering items and mix well.

4. Mix in the peas, sweetcorn and diced carrots (at this stage to retain their colours). Add aromatic salt to taste.

5. Leave the rice to dry (see stage 7 on page 232) and serve.

ZANZIBARI CHELLAU
—— *Clove Rice* ——

ZANZIBAR

Native to the Molucca Islands in Indonesia, cloves are now mainly harvested in Zanzibar, Madagascar and Grenada. Zanzibar is a tiny, otherwise insignificant island off the East African coast, opposite Tanzania. The chillies, though popular locally, can be reduced or even omitted from this simple recipe.

SERVES 4

INGREDIENTS

8–12oz (225–350g) Basmati rice
2 tablespoons ghee (page 43)
8–10 plump cloves, gently crushed
1–4 habanero chillies (any colour),
  sliced

GARNISH
fresh grated coconut (page 43)
pan-roasted peanuts (page 60)

METHOD

1. This rice is best cooked by the absorption method so please follow the recipe on pages 233–4.

2. As soon as the ghee is hot at stage 4, add the cloves and chillies, stir-fry for about 15 seconds, then add the rice and follow the recipe to its end.

3. Garnish with grated coconut and pan-roasted peanuts, and serve.

JAMBALAYA

USA

Louisiana has been the rice bowl of America since the crop was brought there by the Spaniards in the seventeenth century. This is a rice-based dish to which everything and anything to hand is added Cajun-style. As to the word Jambalaya, the best explanation is that the dish was influenced by those early Spanish settlers who brought their Paella with them to the New World. Ham (*jamon* in Spanish) was usually an ingredient, hence Jambalaya. Unlike Paella which is golden in colour, Jambalaya is reddish from the tomatoes. The *chorizo* sausage from Spain has evolved into the chaurice of Louisiana.

SERVES 4

INGREDIENTS

1lb (450g) main ingredients (see stage 1)
10oz (300g) long-grained rice
2oz (50g) butter or lard
2 garlic cloves, chopped
3oz (75g) finely chopped spring onions (bulbs and leaves)
1–3 red habanero chillies, finely chopped
2 tablespoons chopped sun-dried tomatoes in oil (chef's tip, page 76)
1 tablespoon tomato purée

6–8 cherry tomatoes, quartered
3–4 tablespoons white wine
1 pint (600ml) fish or vegetable stock or water
2 medium sticks celery, finely chopped
1 tablespoon chopped fresh oregano
1 tablespoon chopped fresh thyme
aromatic salt (page 46)

GARNISH
a few fronds of fresh dill or fennel

METHOD

1. Make a selection of ingredients from cooked chicken, meat, shrimps, oysters, ham, bacon and *chorizo* (see page 105) which, when prepared and chopped into bite-size pieces, weigh a total of 1lb (450g).

2. Cover the rice in ample water and soak for about 10 minutes.

3. Heat the butter or lard in a karahi over a high heat, then stir-fry the garlic for 30 seconds.

4. Add the spring onions, chillies, sun-dried tomatoes, tomato purée, cherry tomatoes and white wine and reduce the heat. Stir-fry for 10 minutes, until the onion becomes translucent and begins to brown.

5. Add your meat and seafood selection and stir-fry until about half-cooked.

6. Rinse the rice until the water runs more or less clear. Drain thoroughly.

7. Add the rice to the stir-fry and, when thoroughly mixed, transfer everything to a heavy lidded pan.

8. Bring the stock or water to the boil and stir it into the pan.

9. Follow the absorption recipe on pages 233–4 from stage 6 to the end, adding the celery, oregano, thyme, and aromatic salt to taste, when the water is absorbed.

10. Garnish with the fresh dill or fennel, and serve. Jambalaya is a satisfying meal in itself and needs no accompaniment, except perhaps an appropriate chilli chutney or sauce.

DIRTY RICE

USA

The Cajuns have a wicked sense of humour. If you ask a Cajun, as I have done, why they call this particular dish 'dirty', like as not they'll make up some gobbledegook about using swamp water to cook it with. The truth is simply that the dish contains chicken giblets which, when simmered and ground, are quite dark in colour.

SERVES 4

INGREDIENTS

3–4 bay leaves
8oz (225g) chicken liver, heart and kidney (chef's tip), finely chopped
1oz (30g) butter or lard
2–3 garlic cloves, chopped
3–4 spring onions, chopped
2 sticks celery, finely chopped

1 red bell pepper, finely chopped
2–3 green cayenne chillies, finely chopped
1¹/₂lb (675g) plain boiled rice
1 tablespoon chopped fresh parsley
1 tablespoon chopped fresh basil
salt

METHOD

1. Bring 5fl oz (150ml) water to the boil, add the bay leaves and the chicken offal. Simmer for about 20 minutes. Cool and pulse in a food processor or blender to make a pourable paste.

2. Heat the butter or lard in a karahi or wok over a high heat, then stir-fry the garlic for 30 seconds.

3. Add the onion, celery, bell pepper and green chillies and reduce the heat. Stir-fry for 10 minutes, until the onion is translucent and brown.

4. Add the rice and the paste and stir-fry until heated right through, then add the parsley and basil, and salt to taste.

Chef's Tip

CHICKEN HEART, LIVER AND KIDNEY
These tiny delicacies are delightful in certain recipes (see *Yakitori*, page 75, for example). The problem is that one often needs several of each. The solution is to collect them in an airtight box in the freezer, adding to the collection each time you buy a chicken. When you have enough – thaw and use.

CHILIS RELLENOS CON ARROZ
—— *Chillies Stuffed with Rice* ——

MEXICO

Large chillies stuffed with spicily enhanced rice are dipped in batter and deep-fried. Great at parties and you can vary the fillings (see pages 101 and 156). Spare filling can be thickened with flour, battered and fried.

SERVES 4

INGREDIENTS

8 large chillies or bell peppers
oil for deep-frying

STUFFING
6oz (175g) cooked rice
2oz (50g) cooked sweetcorn
1oz (30g) cooked black beans
2–4 garlic cloves, chopped
2 tablespoons yoghurt or sour cream
2 tablespoons dried onion flakes (chef's tip, page 65)
1–2 tablespoons red chilli mash (pages 286–7)

1 tablespoon chopped fresh coriander
1 teaspoon cummin seeds
1/2 teaspoon aromatic salt (page 46)

BATTER
4oz (110g) plain white flour
4oz (110g) cornmeal
2 egg yolks
5fl oz (150ml) milk
1/2 teaspoon aromatic salt (page 46)
whites of 2 eggs, beaten stiffly

METHOD

1. Pulse all the **stuffing** ingredients in a food processor or use a mincer to achieve a well-mixed cohesive paste.

2. For the **batter**, put the flour and cornmeal in a bowl, beat in the yolks, then the milk and aromatic salt. Adjust the milk quantity if necessary to achieve a thick batter. Then gently fold in the egg whites.

3. Roast the chillies or bell peppers (see pages 41–2) and, whilst they are warm and soft, peel them and slit them carefully, leaving the stalk on, to create a pocket. Remove the seeds and pith but don't make holes other than the slit if possible.

4. Carefully insert the stuffing. Don't worry if there is some left over (it depends on the size of your chillies/peppers). We'll use it later.

5. Dip the stuffed chillies/peppers into the batter, ensuring that they are thickly coated. Heat the oil in a deep-fryer to 375°F/190°C (chip-frying temperature) and cook them for about 10 minutes.

6. To serve, place two chillies/peppers per person on each plate. Serve with rice and salsas (see pages 290–2).

MOROS Y CRISTIANOS
—— *Beans and Rice* ——

CUBA

This dish should really be called 'Black Beans and White Rice', although the Spanish name is more colourful. Literally meaning 'Moors and Christians', the recipe was invented 1000 years ago when the Moors invaded Spain and then settled there successfully for centuries. Far from being racist, this dish expresses the integration of black and white, in culinary as well as cultural terms. Cuba was one of the islands 'discovered' by Columbus, and this dish has been particularly Cuban since those days. Curiously, it has vanished without trace from mainland Spain.

SERVES 4

INGREDIENTS

2 tablespoons corn oil
2–3 bay leaves
2 garlic cloves, finely chopped
2–3 rashers smoked streaky
   rindless bacon, finely chopped
4oz (110g) onion, finely chopped
8oz (225g) Spanish round-grained
   rice

7oz (200g) canned black beans

GARNISH (OPTIONAL)
sun-dried tomatoes in oil cut
   into thin strips (chef's tip,
   page 76)
whole fresh coriander leaves

METHOD

1. Heat the oil and the bay leaves in a karahi or wok and stir-fry the garlic for 30 seconds. Add the bacon and continue to stir-fry for another minute. Add the onion and stir-fry for a further 5 minutes.

2. The rice is best cooked by the absorption method so please follow the recipe on pages 233–4.

3. Add the washed rice to the stir-fry and carefully mix them together. Now add the boiling water and follow the rice recipe to the end of stage 5.

4. Strain the beans (keep the liquid for future use as stock) and add them to the rice.

5. Finish off the rice, following stage 6 of the recipe on pages 233–4.

6. You may wish to garnish this dish with contrasting red and green items, such as sun-dried tomatoes and whole fresh coriander leaves.

Note: Canned beans are immensely convenient. However, purists may prefer to cook dry black beans for this recipe, using black (turtle) beans or black soya beans. Allow 6 hours' soaking and about 2 hours' simmering.

ANJU
—— *Rice Cake* ——

BRAZIL

A kind of Brazilian rice bread, it seems 'heavy' at first sight, but it's filling and tasty. Serve with any Brazilian dish or *Vatapa* (see page 162).

INGREDIENTS

*10oz (300g) hot or cold plain
  cooked rice
5oz (150g) butter
2–3 spring onions, bulbs and leaves
  finely chopped*

*1 tablespoon chopped fresh
  coriander
$^1/_2$ teaspoon aromatic salt
  (page 46)*

METHOD

SERVES 4

1. Put the rice in a food processor or blender with enough water to make a thick pourable paste.

2. Heat the butter in a karahi or wok. Add the spring onions and fresh coriander and stir-fry for about 3 minutes.

3. Add the rice paste, and aromatic salt to taste, and stir-fry until it can thicken no further.

4. Put the mixture into a flat dish or mould. When cold, slice and serve.

BREADS

Some of the world's nations traditionally eat only rice as their main staple – for example the peoples of South India, Sri Lanka and the Indian Ocean. Others eat rice with noodles – China, Thailand, Burma and Indo-China. None of these people have bread. Conversely, some traditionally eat wheat breads and never have rice – for example northern Indian, Pakistani and Nepalese peoples. It used to depend on what crops grew in which region.

The easy availability of imported rice or wheat has blurred these distinctions somewhat in recent years, and most people now have a choice of either rice or wheat staples, or both. But old traditions die hard and I am struck by how similar breadmaking traditions are in, say, Mexico and India. Here methods have remained unchanged through dozens of centuries. In Mexico small, round, flat cornmeal tortillas are dry-fried on convex steel pans called *comals*, and in India small, round, flat wheat chupattis are dry-fried on convex steel pans called *tavas*. It is remarkable how these and other breads have developed independently.

Here's my selection of hot and spicy breads, including traditional items plus, I believe, some innovatory surprises such as Chilli Bread and Naan Bread Rolls.

OPPOSITE *From top to bottom: Ethiopian Millet Bread (page 261), Turkish Crispy Bread (page 258), Tortillas made with yellow maize flour and blue maize flour (pages 262–3), Yemeni Spicy Bread (page 260) and Naan Bread (page 266). Corn varieties are nearly as diverse as chillies in size, colour and number. The corns here are complete with husks and range from 2 inches (5cm) to 10 inches (25 cm).*

BASIC DOUGH MAKING

Before we get down to the individual breads, it is important to study basic dough-making techniques. Once you have mastered the method you will confidently produce perfect bread. The principal secret lies in the first kneading, or mixing, of the basic ingredients – flour and water. This requires patient and steady mixing either by hand or by machine, transforming the tacky mass of flour and water into a dough. It should be elastic without being sticky and should feel satisfying to handle. It should also be pliable, springy and soft.

Below are the basic methods for making unleavened and leavened dough.

UNLEAVENED DOUGH

INGREDIENTS

flour types and quantities as given in specific recipes

METHOD

1. Choose a large ceramic or glass bowl and put in the flour.

2. Add warm water, little by little, and work it into the flour with your fingers. Soon it will become a lump.

3. Remove it from the bowl and knead it with your hands on a floured board or work surface until the lump is cohesive and well combined.

4. Return it to the bowl and leave it for 10–15 minutes, then briefly knead it once more. It will now be ready to use in the recipes.

LEAVENED DOUGH

INGREDIENTS

flour types and quantities as given in specific recipes
fresh yeast or natural yoghurt

METHOD

1. Dissolve the fresh yeast in a little lukewarm water.

2. Put the flour in a *warmed* bowl, make a well in the centre and pour in the yeast. (Non-vegans can use yoghurt in the absence of yeast, except for deep-fried breads which require yeast in order to rise.)

3. Gently mix the yeast into the flour, and add enough warm water to make a firm dough.

4. Remove from the bowl and knead on a floured board until well combined. Return to the bowl and leave it in a warm place for a couple of hours to rise.

5. Your dough, when risen, should have doubled in size. It should be bubbly, stringy and elastic.

6. Knock back the dough by kneading it down to its original size.

PITTA BREAD
—— *Greek/Turkish Oval Bread* ——

GREECE

Probably the most celebrated bread from the Middle East is the Pitta Bread, that delicious, oval-shaped, flat bread with the pocket, so convenient for holding food. Pitta is a variant of *Khoubiz*, the flat bread found all over the Middle East, the main difference being its shape. Indeed in Syria, the Pitta is called *Khubz Shami* or *Aiysh Shami*, whilst in the Gulf it is called *Khubz Arabi*. The traditional Pitta shape is an oval about 8×6 inches (20×15cm) and $1/_8$ inch (2–3mm) thick. It must always have a pocket, called *mutbag*.

Pittas are easy enough to make, and the way to achieve the pocket is to knead the dough well, leaving it to rise and expand in a warm place, and then bake in a hottish oven. If the pocket is not required, prick the rolled-out bread with a fork. An Armenian variation of Pitta is *Pideh*; it uses wholemeal flour, and white sesame seeds are pressed on to the dough before baking.

MAKES 6

INGREDIENTS

2oz (50g) fresh yeast   *$1^1/_2$lb (675g) plain white flour*

METHOD

1. Follow the leavened dough-making recipe, opposite, to stage 6.

2. Divide the dough into six pieces and then roll into oval shapes as described above. Leave to rise whilst the oven heats up to 400°F/200°C/Gas 6.

3. Put the discs on floured oven trays. Bake for 8–10 minutes. Serve hot.

Note: Pittas can be frozen when cold. To reheat, simply pop them in the toaster.

KAVGIR
—— *Turkish Crispy Bread* ——

TURKEY

The earliest bread was made from unleavened brown flour, when man first learned to cultivate wheat about 9000 years ago. Flour and water were made into dough which was rolled into thin discs and cooked in a charcoal oven. Variations are to be found all over the Middle East. *Kavgir*, the Turkish variant, is a relative newcomer, having been developed by the first civilised settlers to come to the area, the Hittites, in 2500 BC. The cooked discs are eaten at once or they are further dried in the sun to make them crisper. After this treatment they can be stored in a lidded earthenware pot for months. An Iranian variant is called *Lavash*. Serve with dishes from Turkey (see Menus).

MAKES 8

INGREDIENTS

1lb (450g) wholemeal flour

about 4–8fl oz (100–225ml) warm water

METHOD

1. Divide the dough into eight pieces and roll out into discs around 9 inches (23cm) diameter by $1/8$ inch (3mm) thick.

2. Place the discs on floured oven trays and bake in an oven preheated to 400°F/200°C/Gas 6 for 10–20 minutes.

3. When cool, they can be broken into pieces and stored like biscuits in an airtight tin. If they lose their crispness re-bake for a few minutes.

RED INDIAN FRY BREAD

USA

I had all manner of preconceptions as to what Indian sour bread might be. I finally encountered it at the Chili Festival at Tucson. A very old Navaho Red Indian woman was sitting behind a tent in the shade of a tree shaping pliable white dough into balls about tennis ball size, and lining them up in a big oven tray like soldiers. She then covered the balls with a damp tea towel to prevent them drying up in the fierce midday sun. Another very old woman, but not quite so old, maybe the first woman's daughter, would every now and then take one of the balls and deftly slap it into a disc between her hands. It took her but moments to achieve a perfect circle about 12 inches (30.5cm) in diameter.

This she slipped into a vast and well-used karahi sitting above a gas flame, in which was simmering oil. At once the bread puffed up, like those sherbet flying saucers we used to buy as children. Within seconds, using tongs, she withdrew it from the oil. It was pale golden and highly tempting. The third member of the team, maybe a grandson, offered a choice of chili or beans with the bread.

So what we had here was a combination of two Asian Indian techniques – leavened white dough (Naan Bread-style) deep-fried like a giant Puri. This Red Indian bread had clearly evolved somewhere in the mists of time without any reference to Asian Indian techniques. Come to think of it though, this giant white leavened Puri goes fabulously well with curry (why didn't they think of it?), while Naan and Parathas go equally well with chili and the other savoury dishes in this book.

Because most of us don't have deep-fryers large enough, I've had to make the discs smaller than those I enjoyed in Tucson. These are about 8 inches (20cm) in diameter.

MAKES 4

INGREDIENTS

2oz (50g) fresh yeast (yoghurt will not puff up)
1¹/₂lb (675g) plain white flour

lukewarm water
oil for deep-frying

METHOD

1. Using the yeast, flour and water, follow the recipe for leavened dough (page 256).

2. Divide the dough into four equal parts.

3. Roll each part into a circle, at least ¹/₄ inch (6mm) thick.

4. Preheat the oil in a deep-fryer to 375°F/190°C (chip-frying temperature) and immerse one disc at a time. It should puff up quickly. Turn when it does, and remove after 30 seconds. Serve at once.

SALUF BI HILBEH
—— *Yemeni Spicy Bread* ——

THE YEMEN

Arabia's standard flat, slightly leavened bread is to be found all over the Middle East, and elsewhere. Yemen, at the junction of the Red Sea and the Indian Ocean, has been a maritime trading station linking Arab and Indian sailors for thousands of years.

Consequently, the Yemenis adore the spices of India. For example in this recipe they spread *hilbeh*, a paste made from fenugreek, chillies and other spices, on to their bread before baking it.

MAKES 4

INGREDIENTS

1lb (450g) strong white flour
1oz (25g) fresh yeast
4–8fl oz (100–225ml) warm water

PASTE
2 tablespoons fenugreek seeds
4 tablespoons vegetable or olive oil
4 garlic cloves, crushed

4oz (110g) onion, finely chopped
1 teaspoon char masala (page 48)
2oz (50g) chopped fresh coriander
3–4 chopped sun-dried tomatoes in oil (see chef's tip, page 76)
3 tablespoons lemon juice
2–6 fresh green chillies, destalked and chopped

METHOD

1. First make the **paste**. Pick through the fenugreek seeds, removing grit, etc. Put them in a bowl with 5fl oz (150ml) water, and leave for at least 12 hours or overnight. They will swell and become quite soft.

2. Heat the oil, and fry the garlic for 1 minute. Add the onion and fry that for 3 more minutes, stirring frequently. Strain the fenugreek seeds, then add them to the frying pan, stirring for 3 more minutes. Add the char masala and the fresh coriander. Stir for another 3 minutes, then allow to cool.

3. Put the flour and yeast in a food processor or blender and add sufficient water to make a purée when pulsed together.

4. Add the cooled fried mixture and pulse again to obtain a thicker purée.

5. Divide the dough into four pieces and make into balls. Roll each into a disc about 9 inches (23cm) in diameter. Leave to rise while the oven heats up to 400°F/200°C/Gas 6.

6. Put the discs on to floured oven trays. Prick them with a fork to prevent them rising.

7. Spread each with a quarter of the paste.

8. Bake for 8–10 minutes. Serve hot, with Arabic dishes (see Menus).

INERJA
—— *Millet Bread* ——

ETHIOPIA

Ethiopia's best-known bread, *Inerja*, is made pancake-fashion from a fermented millet batter. This gives it a gorgeous sour taste, and an aerated bubbly texture. They use huge *tava* (griddle) pans to produce *Inerja* the size of tablecloths.

Traditionally the food is placed communally on this 'cloth' and diners use the *inerja* in place of cutlery to scoop up the food.

Here the bread is 'cut down to size', so to speak, producing breads the size of the average pancake. Serve with African dishes.

MAKES 4–6

INGREDIENTS

4oz (110g) millet flour　　　　*salt*
2oz (50g) plain white flour　　　*oil for frying*
1 teaspoon fresh yeast

METHOD

1. Mix the ingredients together with enough lukewarm water to make a smooth, easily pourable, pancake batter. Leave overnight in a warm place, so that it ferments very slightly.

2. To cook, stir the batter and add salt to taste.

3. Heat a few drops of oil in a tava or flat non-stick frying pan. Pour in sufficient batter which, when 'swilled' around the pan, makes a thin pancake. Pour off any excess – the thinner the better. Cook until it sets. Turn if necessary (a really thin one won't need it) and repeat. The whole process takes about 1 minute. Remove from the pan and serve. (See also chef's tip on page 217).

Blue tortillas being cooked on a comal in Mexico

TORTILLAS

MEXICO

Crisp triangular Tortilla chips in packets are now as familiar and widely available as potato crisps. It is the maize flour which gives them their distinctive flavour, but of course there is much more to Tortillas than packet chips.

The Tortilla (pronounced tor-teeyar) is Mexico's national bread. It appears in many forms (see chef's tip opposite). The basis is always a 5 inch (12.5cm) diameter thin disc which is dry-fried on a steel griddle pan called a *comal*, just like Indian Chupattis, which they closely resemble, cooked on a *tava*.

Tortillas are really easy to make. They are soft, not crisp, and eaten at once, they taste fresh and delicious.

MAKES 8

INGREDIENTS

7oz (200g) cornmeal
1 egg

¹/₂ teaspoon salt
lukewarm water

METHOD

1. Mix the cornmeal, egg and salt in a mixing bowl. Add sufficient lukewarm water (little by little) to make a dough which collects all the flour and detaches from the bowl.

2. Knead it well and let it stand for 20 minutes or so.

3. Divide into eight parts, and roll each one into a 5 inch (12.5cm) disc.

4. Heat a *tava* or frying pan until very hot. Using no oil, cook each Tortilla for a few minutes on both sides.

Chef's Tip

TORTILLA VARIATIONS

Maize or sweetcorn comes in many shapes, sizes and colours. Yellow, pink and black are equally common. The corn is dried on the cob, which makes the kernels easier to get off. The corn is ground down to make *massa* or cornmeal. One type of black cob makes 'blue' flour. This is a pastel turquoise colour and makes remarkable tortillas (see photo opposite). Other black cobs make greyer flour and the tortillas are black.

Tacos are tortillas which are deep-fried to become crisp, then folded over and used to hold fillings.

Tortilla chips (Tostaditos) are tortillas cut into segments, then deep-fried. Enchiladas are tortillas which are fried, rolled around a filling, then baked. Empanadas are tortillas filled with a stuffing, folded and sealed like a turnover, then baked. Burritos are soft tortillas folded into a cup shape and filled with stuffing. Raspadas are very thin tortillas, and Tostadas are cooked raspadas.

Although wheatflour tortillas are found in northern Mexico, cornmeal is more authentic and has a unique flavour. It is available from better delis.

WHITE FLOUR CHUPATTIS OR TORTILLAS

INDIA

The White Flour Chupatti is a relatively recent development in India where, until modern milling, they always used brown flour. As far as I can tell, it is identical in every respect to the White Flour Tortilla (which was traditionally made from cornmeal and stretches equally far back in time). Both these breads were developed without any apparent reference to each other as thin 5–6 inch (12.5–15cm) discs, dry-fried on flat griddle pans.

MAKES 8

INGREDIENTS

1lb (450g) plain white flour   *hot water*

METHOD

1. Using the flour, follow the recipe for unleavened bread on page 256 to make a dough.

2. Divide the dough into eight equal parts, and shape each one into a ball. On a floured work surface, roll each ball into a thin disc about 6 inches (15cm) in diameter.

3. Heat a *tava* or frying pan until very hot. Test it by dropping a tiny bit of flour on the bottom of the pan. If it turns brown at once the pan is ready.

4. Using no oil, cook the Chupatti on one side. Turn it over and cook on the other side. Serve as hot as possible.

PARATHAS
—— *Pan-Fried Flat Bread* ——

INDIA

The Paratha is unleavened bread, a flat disc about 7 inches (18cm) in diameter. Flaky and delicious, it is many people's favourite Indian bread. The trick is to make it very light, and the trick to that is to trap air in the dough by creating layers in it – like puff pastry. This 'sausage technique' predates Western puff pastry by 2000 years or more. When shallow-fried in ghee the Parathas should end up crispy on the outside, yet still soft and 'melt-in-the-mouth' on the inside.

MAKES 4

INGREDIENTS

1lb (450g) plain white flour   *about 7 tablespoons melted ghee (page 43)*

METHOD

1. Follow the recipe for unleavened bread on page 256.

2. Add 4 tablespoons melted ghee, and mix well into the dough.

3. Divide the dough into four equal lumps. Shape the first lump into a long sausage, then flatten it into a strip about 12×3 inches (30×7.5cm).

4. Apply further melted ghee to the strip, then roll it from the long side to make a 'snake'. Gently flatten the snake with a rolling pin back into a strip of the same dimensions as above. You now have layered dough.

5. Cut the strip into two long strips about 12×1¹/₂ inches (30×4cm).

6. Now coil one strip around itself into a shape like a three-dimensional ice-cream cone. Lightly press it down with your hand, brush it with ghee and coil the second strip on top in the same shape.

7. Sprinkle extra flour on to the cone and again lightly press it down, then very lightly roll it out to a disc about 7 inches (18cm) in diameter. It should be obviously flaky and layered.

8. Heat a further 2 tablespoons ghee on a *tava* (griddle pan) or large frying pan and fry the Paratha until it is hot. Lift it out with tongs. Add more ghee and repeat on the other side. Keep in a warming drawer or very low oven. Repeat to make the remaining three Parathas. Serve as hot and fresh as possible.

PURIS
—— *Deep-fried Puff Bread* ——

INDIA

India has taken the art of making unleavened bread to great heights with puris, small discs which puff up when deep-fried. They are light and delicious.

MAKES 16

INGREDIENTS

1lb (450g) ata or wholemeal flour   *oil for deep-frying*
1 tablespoon melted ghee (page 43)

METHOD

1. Make a soft dough for unleavened bread, following the recipe on page 256. Add the ghee and mix well into the dough.

2. Divide into four, then divide each part into four again – it's the easiest way of getting 16 similar sized pieces.

3. Shape each into a ball, then roll out to a 4 inch (10cm) disc.

4. Preheat the oil in a deep-fryer to 375°F/190°C (chip-frying temperature) and immerse one disc at a time. It should puff up quickly. Turn when it does, and remove after 30 seconds. Serve at once.

NAAN BREAD

INDIA

Naan is the very well known and popular leavened flat bread (about 8 inches/20cm long by 6 inches/15cm wide) which originated in Persia (as the *Nane Lavash*) and travelled into India to become a constant companion to tandoori cooking.

The naan is itself cooked in the tandoori oven, which gives it a distinctive smoky flavour. It sticks to the oven wall, and the force of gravity produces its 'teardrop' shape. Here we use a grill and fake the tear shape.

MAKES 4

INGREDIENTS

2oz (50g) fresh yeast, or 3   *1¹/₂lb (675g) plain white flour*
  tablespoons yoghurt   *1 teaspoon wild onion seeds*
lukewarm water   *melted ghee (page 43)*

METHOD

1. Using the yeast or yoghurt, water and flour, follow the recipe for leavened dough on page 256. Add the seeds.

2. Divide the dough into four equal parts.

3. Roll each part into a teardrop shape at least $^1/_4$ inch (6mm) thick.

4. Preheat the grill to three-quarters heat, cover the rack pan with foil, and set it in the midway position.

5. Put the Naan on to the foil and grill it. Watch it cook (it can easily burn). As soon as the first side develops brown patches, remove it from the grill.

6. Turn it over and brush the uncooked side with a little melted ghee.

7. Return it to the grill and cook until it is sizzling. Remove.

8. Repeat stages 5–8 with the other three naan. Serve at once.

DOMINIQUE'S NAAN BREAD ROLLS

INDIA

These rolls can be served on any occasion. Try them with soup or cheese, for example.

MAKES 12

INGREDIENTS

2oz (50g) fresh yeast or 3 tablespoons natural thick yoghurt
lukewarm water

1$^1/_2$lb (675g) plain white flour
1 teaspoon wild onion seeds
melted ghee (page 43)

METHOD

1. Using the yeast or yoghurt, water and flour, follow the recipe for leavened dough on page 256. Add the seeds.

2. Divide the dough into twelve equal parts, and roll into balls. Leave the balls to rise while the oven heats up to 400°F/200°C/Gas 6.

3. Put the balls on floured oven trays. Prick them with a fork to prevent them rising, brush with melted butter ghee, then bake for 8–10 minutes. These are best eaten hot (leave them for about 10 minutes before serving). Or they can be eaten cold but make sure you serve them within 8 hours of baking.

THE ULTIMATE GARLIC BREAD

<u>UK</u>

This is garlic bread with a difference. Instead of spreading a mixture of garlic and butter on already cooked bread, which you then rebake, this totally antisocial recipe incorporates chopped fresh garlic chunks into the dough, which are baked in, imparting flavour throughout the bread. Purists may wish to split open the cooked bread and spread with garlic butter before wrapping in foil and returning to the oven for a couple of minutes. They'll have a delicious, potent double-garlic bread, but possibly no friends!

MAKES 6 rolls

INGREDIENTS

2oz (50g) fresh yeast
some lukewarm water
1¹/₂lb (675g) strong white flour

4 or more garlic cloves, peeled and
    quartered
1 teaspoon aromatic salt (page 46)

METHOD

1. Using the yeast, water and flour, follow the recipe for leavened dough on page 256, kneading in the garlic and aromatic salt at stage 4.

2. Divide the dough into six equal pieces, and roll each into a sausage. Place on a floured baking tray and leave to prove in a warm place while the oven heats up to 400°F/200°C/Gas 6.

3. Bake for 8–10 minutes. These are best eaten hot (leave them for about 10 minutes before serving). Or they can be eaten cold but make sure you serve them within 8 hours of baking.

HEATHER'S CHILLI BREAD

<u>UK</u>

This is heavenly inspiration from Heather my editor, who has become first a curryholic and now a chilehead as the result of editing all my books! Amongst the many clever things she has thought of is this recipe.

Simply chop up any fresh chillies (the type and quantity is your choice) and incorporate them into the bread dough. Remember to wear disposable gloves whilst kneading the dough if chilli hurts you (see page 41). When we tasted the examples we had made for the photo on page 41, Heather had tears running down her cheeks, which I sincerely hope was from the joy of sampling her first Chilli Bread!

Simply follow the previous recipe for garlic bread, substituting chopped fresh chilli for garlic.

CHILLI PINWHEELS

This is an invention of mine and I hope you like it! It's a kind of Swiss roll, using white bread and red chilli paste.

INGREDIENTS

1 fresh small white loaf
1 tablespoon red chilli mash
  (pages 286–7)

3 tablespoons tomato ketchup
1 tablespoon tomato purée
oil for deep-frying

METHOD

1. Cut the crusts off the bread and splash a little water on the bread which is left.

2. Press it as flat as you can, then roll it to create a thin rectangle about $^1/_2$ inch (1.25cm) thick.

3. Mix the chilli mash, tomato ketchup and purée together, then spread the mixture all over the rectangle. Roll up from the long side, Swiss roll style.

4. Cut into slices, and secure each pinwheel with a wooden (not plastic – it will melt) cocktail stick. Heat the oil in a deep-fryer to 375°F/190°C (chip-frying temperature) and cook for about 4 minutes, until golden brown.

5. Place on kitchen paper to drain off excess oil. Serve hot or cold as a snack or in place of bread with your meal.

CURRY PINWHEELS

Substitute 2 tablespoons mild curry paste (see page 49) for the chilli mash and follow the above recipe. For hotter curry pinwheels, use both the mild curry paste and the chilli mash.

SWEET THINGS & DRINKS

Perhaps it is not surprising that the traditional cooking of both the Old and New Worlds has relatively few cooked desserts. I am sure that many of us will agree that, having worked our way through a meal of delicious spicy appetisers, soups, main courses, rice and chutney, we have little room for a further course. The ancients enjoyed a wide variety of fresh fruit and they knew how to preserve it. Fruit is perfect at any time, especially for dessert.

This selection of desserts and drinks may well be small, but it contains some remarkable and unusual goodies which chile-heads will delight in. Green Chilli Ice Cream is one, and Deep-Fried Ice Cream another. Chocolate makes its appearance in the Indian ice cream, *kulfi*, and in the astounding confectionery, Chocolate-Enrobed Garlic, as well as the even more remarkable Chocolate-Enrobed Chilli.

I have also included drinks in this chapter, ranging from chilled yoghurt drinks – *Lhassi* – to accompany a curry, to hot Spicy Mulled Wine.

OPPOSITE *Clockwise from top: Syrupy Banana (page 274), Breakfast Puff Bread (page 273), Chutney Mary's Bitter Chocolate Kulfi (page 274) and Hot Fruit Compote (page 272)*

HOT FRUIT COMPOTE

ENGLAND

Fruit is quartered, spiced and baked on a low heat. When cooked it is laced with brandy and can be served with ice cream or Sweet and Sour Yoghurt (see page 281). This choice of fruit is only an example, which you can change to suit yourself.

SERVES 4

INGREDIENTS

3¹/₂fl oz (100ml) water
4 fresh peaches
4 fresh apricots
4 fresh Victoria plums
4oz (110g) fresh raspberries
2oz (50g) fresh blackcurrants
4 canned peaches, quartered
3¹/₂fl oz (100ml) syrup from the canned peaches

about 3 tablespoons apricot or cherry brandy
freshly grated nutmeg

SPICES
4–6 cloves
4–6 green cardamom pods
6 inch (15cm) cinnamon quill

METHOD

1. Bring the water to a simmer in a small pan. Add the **spices** and simmer for about 5 minutes. This both softens the spices and releases the volatile oils.

2. Stone and quarter the fresh peaches, apricots and plums. Put them into a baking dish, add the raspberries and blackcurrants, the spices with the water, and the canned peaches with their syrup. Place the dish, uncovered, in an oven preheated to 375°F/190°C/Gas 5.

3. Inspect after 20 minutes to see whether the fruit is soft (test with a skewer). Cook further if needed and, when ready, mix in the alcohol. Serve more or less at once with some freshly grated nutmeg sprinkled over the top.

Note: This recipe deliberately omits sugar, producing a gorgeously tart compote which contrasts with a sweet accompaniment. Those with a sweet tooth can mix in sugar to taste before cooking (and after if needed).

CHOTA HAZRI MEETHI PURI
—— *Breakfast Puff Bread* ——

INDIA

Crispy deep-fried puffy Puris, hot and tempting, can be drizzled with honey and served with yoghurt to make an irresistible breakfast dish – or dessert.

MAKES 16

INGREDIENTS

16 freshly made Puris (page 266)
icing sugar for dusting

clear honey
thick plain yoghurt

METHOD

1. Follow the recipe on page 266 to make the Puris.

2. As soon as each one comes out of the deep-fryer, dust it with icing sugar.

3. Drizzle honey over them all and serve with plain yoghurt or the sweetened version in the next recipe.

MOIRA BANANA
—— *Syrupy Banana* ——

INDIA

A few years ago I gave a recipe for Moira Banana in my book *Curry Club Favourite Restaurant Curries*. It produces a sweet dark treacly sauce. Since then Dominique has cooked it dozens of times for guests at our curry cookery courses at The White House Hotel, Williton, Somerset. Her version is much more delicate in colour and flavour. It's very popular with our guests, and with the owners of the hotel, Dick and Kay Smith. So, for them and for you too, here's the new recipe. Try to get the gorgeous little apple bananas if you can or else use ordinary ones.

SERVES 4

INGREDIENTS

4 tablespoons golden sultanas, chopped
2 tablespoons hazelnuts, chopped
$^{1}/_{2}$ teaspoon green cardamom seeds, crushed
4 tablespoons light brown Demerara sugar

2 tablespoons melted ghee (page 43)
8 ripe apple bananas or 4 ordinary ripe bananas
4 tablespoons sweet sherry
plenty of really thick cream

METHOD

1. Using a smallish non-stick saucepan, combine everything except the bananas, sherry and cream. Stir this over a low heat until you get a runny syrupy texture. This can be set aside for reheating later, or used at once.

2. Before serving, peel and cut the bananas lengthwise and diagonally into bite-size pieces, and place them on side plates.

3. Add the sherry to the sauce and pour over the bananas.

4. Dollop the cream (Cornish is best) on top, and serve.

CHUTNEY MARY'S BITTER CHOCOLATE KULFI

INDIA

This recipe comes from the renowned Chutney Mary restaurant in London. Namita Panjabi, Director of Cuisine at the restaurant, broke her rule about not giving out recipes when a young curry fan wrote to me. He had enjoyed Bitter Chocolate Kulfi on a visit to Chutney Mary to celebrate passing his school entrance exam, but was disappointed when his mother's attempts to recreate the recipe failed.

Kulfi is Indian ice cream. It has been made since Mogul times and creates a harder ice cream than Western methods. It is traditionally frozen in a kulfi mould, which produces a cone-shaped ice cream. To make your own mould, see the chef's tip.

SERVES 4

INGREDIENTS

4 pints (2.25 litres) full cream milk
5oz (150g) bitter chocolate (chef's tip, page 135)
5oz (150g) brown sugar

3–4 drops vanilla essence
a pinch of ground cardamom
a pinch of salt
2fl oz (50ml) single cream

METHOD

1. Boil the milk in a thick-bottomed pan, preferably non-stick, over a low heat, stirring constantly, until it has reduced to one-third of its volume. I'm afraid this will take about 1½ hours, and you must not stop stirring or the milk will boil over and burn. So get yourself a stool and a good novel!

2. Add the chocolate, sugar, vanilla, cardamom and salt and stir until the chocolate has completely melted.

3. Let it cool and add the cream. Transfer to a freezer-proof bowl and place in the freezer for at least 1 hour. Remove the bowl and mash the semi-frozen mixture with a fork, to break up any large ice crystals. It should be slushy, cold and viscous.

4. Spoon into kulfi moulds, if you have them, and freeze. You will have to prop up the moulds with bags of frozen peas, or whatever you have in the freezer, but do make sure they stay upright so that they freeze into a proper cone shape.

Chef's Tip

To achieve a traditional kulfi cone shape without using a kulfi mould, simply make a cone from cooking paper (ie: baking parchment or greaseproof paper). The top diameter is around 2½ inches (6.5cm); the bottom of the cone must be turned up (to close the cone). Hold the cone together with sticky tape. Do not be tempted to use kitchen foil as this will not peel off after the kulfi has frozen.

DEEP-FRIED ICE CREAM

INDIA

I met this great innovation when I last went to India. It was at a wedding reception in Delhi. The bride and groom's parents did 'something important' in the Indian government, and the place was crawling with Maharajas, movie stars, ministers and machine-gun armed police. The guest list exceeded 2000 and catering was dispensed with some alacrity and no queuing from a number of marquees. The choice of dishes was vast, the quality superb. The sweets' tent was no exception. From a huge choice of traditional Indian and modern international sweets, this one, Deep-Fried Ice Cream, had to be the Oscar winner. The secret to the success of this amazing technique performed in front of us, was speed. Once you have enrobed the ice cream in a thick coat of creamy coconut, give it 10 seconds **and no more** in the deep-fryer. Make sure you use clean oil in the deep-fryer, unless you want your ice cream with a hint of chips or pakora!! Serve at once and you'll be the talk of the town!

SERVES 4

INGREDIENTS

4oz (110g) sweet desiccated coconut
5fl oz (150ml) single cream

1 tablespoon plain white flour
8 scoops ice cream, any flavour
oil for deep-frying

METHOD

1. Mix the sweet desiccated coconut with the cream and the flour. You should achieve a paste which will drop off the spoon, but not too fast.

2. Heat the oil in a deep-fryer to 375°F/190°C (chip-frying temperature).

3. Wash your hands under cold water – to clean and cool them. Scoop out some ice cream. Place it in your hand and quickly compress it to achieve an airless sphere, the size of a ping-pong ball.

4. Briskly roll it in the paste to get a thorough coating.

5. Lower it into the hot oil.

6. Remove it after about 10 seconds and serve at once, following with the others as soon as they are ready. The coating should be golden and hot, the ice cream still freezing.

BEIGNETS

USA

Every gourmet should visit New Orleans, the seat of Creole and Cajun cookery, now becoming popular worldwide. Less known, outside Louisiana, are Beignets and the place to eat them is the Café du Monde in the French Quarter. That's all they serve – Beignets, with coffee, iced coffee, tea, chocolate or soft drinks.

Not only can you eat them there at any time of day and much of the night, you can also watch them being made through a window. The place seats about 200 and probably has 20 waiters at work at any one time. The turnover of customers is so fast that the waiters seldom stop walking from kitchen to customer and back again, balancing huge trays on one hand.

I would hazard a guess that the place serves 5000 customers a day. That's a lot of Beignets. The place is buzzing with atmosphere, considerably enhanced by busking jazz musicians. So what is a Beignet? Pronounced by the locals bay-nyay, they are a kind of doughnut, but so light as to be almost non-existent. Rectangular in shape and deep-fried to a golden colour, they are served piping hot, crispy on the outside, soft as feathers inside and swathed in icing sugar. I must warn you that once you're hooked on Beignets there's no going back!

MAKES 16

INGREDIENTS

$^1/_2$oz (15g) fresh yeast
7oz (200g) plain white flour
5fl oz (150ml) milk
1 large egg, beaten

1 tablespoon caster sugar
$^1/_2$ teaspoon salt
oil for deep-frying
icing sugar

METHOD

1. Follow the leavened dough recipe on pages 256–7, adding the milk, egg, sugar and salt to the flour at the beginning of stage 3.

2. Continue to stage 6.

3. On a floured work surface, roll out the dough to a thickness of about $^1/_4$ inch (6mm). Cut into rectangles about 2×3 inches (5×7.5cm). (Roll out any spare offcuts and cut more rectangles.) Cover and leave to rise for another hour.

4. To cook, heat the oil in a deep-fryer to 375°F/190°C (chip-frying temperature). Fry in batches until they go golden (about 2 minutes), turn and fry the other side.

5. Remove them from the oil and drain on kitchen paper. Dredge with a landslide of icing sugar and serve hot.

GREEN CHILLI ICE CREAM

USA

'Yuk! Sounds crazy – sounds disgusting!' you may be saying. Well it isn't, believe me. I met this green jalapeno chilli ice cream at Tucson Arizona's annual chili festival. Astonishingly, it was delicious, the sweetness of the ice cream contrasting admirably with the heat of the chilli. I've specified African snub chillies – they're not too hot. Jalapeños are equally good.

SERVES 4

INGREDIENTS

4 large eggs
3½oz (100g) caster sugar
½ teaspoon aromatic salt (page 46)
1 teaspoon vanilla essence
1 teaspoon custard powder

15fl oz (500ml) full cream milk
4 tablespoons double cream
4 tablespoons evaporated milk
2–3 green African snub chillies,
   finely chopped

METHOD

1. Using a hand or electric whisk, mix the eggs, sugar, aromatic salt, vanilla and custard powder together.

2. Put the milk, cream and evaporated milk together in a pan. Bring it to just under boiling point, then transfer to a large heatproof glass bowl which fits comfortably over a saucepan of boiling water.

3. Once the milk is simmering, whisk in the egg mixture. Keep whisking until the mixture is thick enough to coat a spoon. Allow it to cool. Now add the chopped chillies, mixing thoroughly.

4. Place in the freezer for about 3 hours. Remove and mix thoroughly. Repeat this process 1 hour later to break down the ice crystals. Do this two or three times, then leave to freeze properly until you wish to use it. Allow it about 15–20 minutes to soften a little before serving. Dip your ice cream scoop into warm water between each scoop.

Note: If you have an ice cream maker, churn it according to the instructions until you get the required texture, and serve.

CHOCOLATE-ENROBED GARLIC

USA

I expect you've already said, 'This is not for me . . .' but wait. Here's the ultimate substitute for the after-dinner mint! These were on sale at California's celebrated Gilroy Garlic Festival. Do warn your guests what they are biting into – they may not be everyone's cup of tea!

MAKES 12

INGREDIENTS

12 *plump top-quality garlic cloves, peeled*
2fl oz (50ml) grenadine syrup
2fl oz (50ml) port

a pinch of aromatic salt (page 46)
2oz (50g) bitter chocolate (chef's tip, page 135)

METHOD

1. Put the garlic cloves in a non-metallic bowl with the grenadine, port and aromatic salt. Cover and microwave for 2$\frac{1}{2}$ minutes. If you don't have a microwave, marinate the garlic cloves in the mixture overnight, then transfer to a pan and simmer for 8–10 minutes.

2. Remove the cloves from the syrup and allow them to cool.

3. Wash 12 paperclips, then partially open them out to form a walking-stick shape. Poke the straight end of each clip into a garlic clove.

4. Melt the chocolate (see chef's tip, page 135).

5. Dip each garlic clove into the chocolate, coat well, then hang it up somewhere to set. A wire cooling rack, raised and supported by a couple of tin cans is ideal.

6. After a couple of hours, they're ready to eat. Serve chilled with coffee and/or liqueurs after the meal.

BELOW *Chocolate-Enrobed Chillies and Garlic (above and page 280). Underneath the plate are cardamom seeds, fennel seeds, cloves and betel nuts coated in edible silver leaf (vark), from India*

CHOCOLATE-ENROBED CHILLIES

USA

This is closely related to the previous recipe, but here we use 'roasted' chillies. A delicious contrast in tastes, but for real heat-lovers only. You could also use fresh chillies, and vary the chocolate coating from bitter plain, to milk, to white chocolate. These ones aren't for the children!

MAKES 12

INGREDIENTS

12 small dried red bird chillies   2oz (50g) bitter chocolate

METHOD

1. Put the chillies into a preheated frying pan on the stove.

2. Dry-fry, stirring continuously, for about 1 minute. Allow to cool.

3. Follow stages 3–6 of the previous recipe.

PINA COCADA
—— *Mexican Pineapple Dessert* ——

MEXICO

Not to be confused with Pina Colada, this Mexican pudding, served chilled, combines fresh pineapple chunks with a sauce made from pineapple juice and coconut.

SERVES 4

INGREDIENTS

7fl oz (200ml) pineapple juice,   1 tablespoon cornflour
  canned or bottled   2 teaspoons sugar
8oz (225g) coconut milk powder   1 teaspoon vanilla essence
  (page 00)   1 fresh pineapple, flesh cut into
1 tablespoon desiccated coconut   bite-size cubes

METHOD

1. Mix the pineapple juice with the coconut milk powder, coconut, cornflour, sugar and vanilla in a small saucepan.

2. Heat and stir until the sauce thickens.

3. Cool, add the pineapple chunks, and serve chilled.

MEETHI MALAI-DAHI
—— *Sweet and Sour Yoghurt* ——

INDIA

Serve this on its own as a light syllabub dessert, or use it as a cream substitute, serving it in dollops to accompany other sweet dishes.

MAKES about 14fl oz (400ml)

INGREDIENTS

15 saffron strands
3 tablespoons warm milk
6fl oz (175ml) thick plain yoghurt
6fl oz (175ml) sour cream
2 tablespoons clear honey

$^1/_2$ teaspoon ground green cardamom seeds

GARNISH
freshly grated nutmeg

METHOD

1. Mix the saffron with the warm milk in a bowl. Leave it to infuse for 10 minutes.

2. Combine all the ingredients, including the saffron, in a mixing bowl. Whisk (electrically or by hand) until it is quite light.

3. Serve garnished with freshly grated nutmeg.

LHASSI NAMKEEN MIRCHI
—— *Savoury Yoghurt Drink* ——

INDIA

Served cold, this is a traditional Indian beverage to accompany a curry, and it is popular in Indian restaurants over here.

MAKES 1$\frac{1}{2}$ pints (900ml)

INGREDIENTS

8fl oz (250ml) plain yoghurt
1 pint (600ml) water
4 ice cubes
$\frac{1}{2}$ teaspoon ground white pepper

1–2 green chillies, chopped
(optional)
salt

METHOD

Simply put everything into a blender, and blend together. Serve with more ice cubes if you wish.

LHASSI MEETHI
—— *Sweet Yoghurt Drink* ——

INDIA

The sweet version of *lhassi*, which is equally delicious with curry. Serve icy cold.

MAKES 2$\frac{1}{2}$ pints (1.4 litres)

INGREDIENTS

$\frac{1}{2}$ pint (300ml) plain yoghurt
$\frac{1}{2}$ pint (300ml) milk
1 pint (600ml) water

4 drops rosewater
3 teaspoons sugar
$\frac{1}{2}$ pint (300ml) crushed ice

METHOD

Put all the ingredients except the ice into a blender, and blend for about 1 minute at high speed. Add crushed ice, and serve in glasses.

FRUIT LHASSI
Follow the instructions for *Lhassi Meethi*. Add 2–3oz (50–75g) of any fruit of your choice – before blending if you want it smooth, or after blending if you want a drink with some texture. Try fresh strawberries or mango.

TEQUILA AND MEZCAL

MEXICO

Mexico's national alcoholic beverage was around for centuries before the Spanish came on the scene. Its name derives from the town of Tequila in central Mexico. Made from the sap of a plant called the century plant, which resembles a yucca, it is at least 80 per cent proof.

Tequila is taken in a ritualistic way. It is served in a small glass, the rim of which is wiped with a wedge of lime. Salt is sprinkled on the back of your left hand and you take a little salt on the tip of your tongue and sip away. Alternatively, you knock the salt straight into your mouth, suck the lime and down the tequila in one shot.

Tequila is usually drunk as a chaser with a non-alcoholic accompaniment. Sangritta is one. You could be forgiven for thinking it was tomato juice. In fact it is orange juice with chilli and, chased with tequila, it's fantastic (see page 284). Then there is the celebrated Tequila Sunrise in which Tequila is chased with a glass of orange and grenadine, and the Margarita, which is a lime juice and Cointreau chaser. (Often the chaser and the Tequila are mixed and served in the same glass.)

Mezcal is another Mexican drink now becoming known to the outside world. It is made from the agave or maguey cactus. This crystal-clear schnaps-like spirit's greatest claim to fame is that each bottle also contains an agave worm (the cactus maggot). This maggot is top of the pops with Mexicans! They eat it roasted and ground and mixed with salt, and they deep-fry it to create *Gusanos de Maguey*.

SANGRITTA

MEXICO

Not to be confused with Sangrilla, the sweet fruity drink, Sangritta is spicy and savoury. It looks like tomato juice, but its surprising secret is that it is made from orange juice and chillies. Mexicans would use serrano and pequin chillies mixed. Here I am using chilli sauce. Serve it chilled with Tequila or on its own. Either way it is a refreshing alternative to tomato juice.

MAKES 1 pint (600ml)

INGREDIENTS

¹/₂ pint (300ml) fresh orange juice
2 tablespoons vinegar (any type)
1 teaspoon Tabasco sauce or
  strained thin chilli sauce
  (page 287)

salt
sugar (optional)

METHOD

1. Mix the orange juice and vinegar with ¹/₂ pint (300ml) cold water.

2. Add chilli sauce, salt and sugar to taste.

3. Add ice cubes and serve.

SPICY MULLED WINE

ENGLAND

I wonder if, like me, you've ever bought those little white muslin bags containing the spices needed to make mulled wine. I did so recently and discovered that for £7.50 I was in possession of a transparent box containing a red, green and white purse, which each contained three little white muslin bags inside which were mulling spices.

I opened one of each to discover slightly varying quantities of cloves, allspice, dried ginger and cassia bark fragments. I realised then that the value of all nine bags probably did not exceed a few pence. So my advice to you is to make up your own spice kits, and save a fortune! You'll have all the spices you need in stock.

This is a very fruity spicy mulled wine. Without the 'sawdust' it comes out very bright and clear. It uses minimal water but feel free to add more if you want a more diluted taste. By the way, don't wait until Christmas for this treat. It's grand on any cold day or night.

SERVES 4

INGREDIENTS

750ml (1 bottle) cheap, full-bodied
   red wine
1/2 tangerine, peeled and chopped
1/2 lemon, peeled and chopped
6fl oz (175ml) grenadine syrup
2 tablespoons cherry brandy
1 tablespoon Scotch whisky

SPICES
3 teaspoons cloves
1 teaspoon ground allspice
   (optional)
1×6 inch (15 cm) cinnamon quill
1 teaspoon grated fresh ginger
   (optional)

METHOD

1. Put the wine, tangerine, lemon, grenadine and **spices** in a saucepan and bring to a simmer. Do not let it boil.

2. Simmer for 15 minutes.

3. Add the spirits. Strain, discarding the solids, and serve.

Note: If you have a thermos flask to hand it will keep the wine warm for longer.

SPICY MULLED CIDER
Simply use cider in place of the red wine in the previous recipe. The other ingredients and the recipe method remain the same.

CHUTNEYS, SAUCES &
CONDIMENTS

This chapter contains a collection of no less than 37 recipes, 33 of which are based on chilli! There are dipping sauces, chilli purées and pastes, chilli oil, chilli vinegar, salsas, and chutneys, each with its own unique and individual characteristic. Most require minimal preparation and no cooking. Some must be used at once, others will keep indefinitely if bottled in sterilised jars that have plastic-coated lids, not metal ones which would corrode. To sterilise jars, wash thoroughly in a dishwasher, or the hottest water you can get, then let them drain and dry without wiping them. When dry, place in the oven at the lowest heat for 10 minutes.

To counter all this chilli heat, I've also included some yoghurt-based cold chutneys (raitas) which are cooling to the mouth and will act as an antidote to the heat.

RED CHILLI OIL

You can buy this attractive red oil at ethnic stores and delis. Or you can save a fortune and make it yourself. It can be used in any recipe, in place of the cooking oil mentioned, to add a little extra heat and piquancy.

MAKES 12 floz (350ml)

1/2 pint (300ml) soya oil
3 floz (75ml) walnut oil
10 red cayenne chillies, chopped

1. Heat the oil in your wok or karahi over a low heat. Add the chillies and simmer for about 5 minutes. Take off the heat and allow to cool.

2. Strain the oil, pressing the solids against the strainer to extract more colour. Discard the solids and pour the oil into sterilised bottles for use as required.

RED CHILLI VINEGAR

This is also expensive to buy but cheap and easy to make. Using distilled malt vinegar, which is transparent, the chillies create a pretty rosy tint. Red chilli vinegar can be used in any recipe that requires vinegar.

MAKES 1 pint (600ml)

1×1 pint (600ml) bottle distilled malt vinegar
about 12 fresh red cayenne chillies, chopped

1. Transfer the contents of the bottle of vinegar into a non-metallic jug. Retain the bottle.

2. Put the chillies into the jug. Cover and leave for a few days.

3. Mash the chillies, strain off the vinegar (discarding the solids) and pour it into sterilised bottles.

RED CHILLI MASH 1

With every respect to Tabasco and all the other bottled sauces, I greatly prefer my own. It is much hotter and it contains no salt and minimal vinegar. It is simple to make, can be used at once and keeps for ever. You can use it both as a condiment and as an ingredient. If you like, use red habañeros instead of cayenne chillies to get that delightful apple taste.

MAKES 2lb (900g)

2lb (900g) fresh red cayenne chillies
distilled malt vinegar

1. Cut off the stalks, then pulse the chillies in a blender or food processor, using enough vinegar to make it mulch.

2. Store in sterilised airtight jars.

GREEN CHILLI MASH

This can be made in precisely the same way, using fresh green chillies in place of red. It will start off bright green but will gradually get darker and less bright.

RED CHILLI MASH 2

This variation uses the tiny dried bird chillies (pequins or tepins will do) that you can buy in packets. They are ultra-hot and delicious.

MAKES 1¼lb (600g)

10oz (300g) dry red bird chillies
about ½ pint (300ml) distilled malt vinegar

1. Cram sterilised jars with the chillies. Top up with the vinegar. Put airtight lids on and leave for about 2 weeks.

2. By now the chillies will be very soft and can be pulsed in a food processor. You may need to add a little more vinegar to achieve a good even texture.

COOKED RED CHILLI MASH

This is a variation on the previous recipes. The finished mash is cooked in oil, which changes the taste and colour, to make another pleasant chilli accompaniment. It can be eaten straight away and keeps indefinitely.

MAKES 8oz (225g)

8fl oz (250ml) oil (any type)
8oz (225g) red chilli mash (see page 286 and above)

1. Heat the oil in a wok or karahi.

2. Add the chilli mash carefully. It will splutter and give off hot chilli fumes! Stir-fry briskly for 3–4 minutes. It will get darker in colour.

3. When the oil floats off it means all the water has been cooked out and the chilli mash is ready. Bottle it in sterilised airtight jars, topping each one up with hot oil.

STRAINED THIN CHILLI SAUCE

This ultra-hot chilli sauce is simplicity itself to make. Being thin, it can be used to sprinkle over food. Unlike Tabasco, it contains no salt.

MAKES 16fl oz (500ml)

8oz (225g) red chilli mash (see page 286 and left)
at least 8fl oz (250ml) distilled malt vinegar

1. Put the mash in a large bowl and add the vinegar, mixing well.

2. Put the mixture into a large strainer over another bowl and carefully press the mash against the strainer.

3. When it appears to be dryish, put the dry mash back into the first bowl and add a little more vinegar.

4. Repeat stage 2 and leave it to drain.

5. Discard the dry mash and pour the sauce into sterilised bottles.

THIN GREEN CHILLI SAUCE

This is made in exactly the same way as red, using fresh green chilli mash in place of red.

DELUXE THIN CHILLI SAUCE

The previous recipe is for pure unadulterated chilli sauce. This one gives a rather more sophisticated (though less hot because it is diluted) chilli sauce.

MAKES 10 fl oz (300ml)

*8fl oz (250ml) strained thin chilli sauce
(page 287)*
1 teaspoon garlic powder
2fl oz (50ml) red wine
1/2 teaspoon salt

Simply mix the ingredients together and pour into sterilised bottles.

SAMBAL OELEK
Indonesian Hot Chilli Sauce

Indonesians and Malaysians adore hot food and their word for condiment (*sambal*) is used in several parts of the world. This one, *Sambal Oelek*, is tart and hot and goes with any dish in this book (well maybe not the desserts!). It will keep indefinitely.

MAKES 4oz (110g)

4 tablespoons red chilli mash 1 or 2 (pages 286–7)
1 tablespoon tamarind purée (page 44)
1 tablespoon brown sugar
1 tablespoon ketjap manis (page 192)
1 teaspoon aromatic salt (page 46)

Mix together and serve.

SAMBAL MANIS
Sweet Chilli Purée

This delicious chilli preserve from Indonesia requires careful cooking. Its texture is like thick jam, its colour chestnut reddy brown, its flavour enhanced by almost caramelised sugar and shrimp paste. Correctly made, it will keep indefinitely.

MAKES around 12fl oz (350ml)

2fl oz (50ml) corn or groundnut oil
8oz (225g) onions, very finely chopped
2 tablespoons brown sugar
*2 tablespoons strained thin chilli sauce
(page 287)*
1 teaspoon blachan shrimp paste (chef's tip, page 172)
1 teaspoon tamarind purée (page 44)
1 teaspoon aromatic salt (page 46)

1. Heat half the oil in a wok or karahi over a low heat. Stir-fry the onions and sugar for at least 15 minutes. Don't let them burn but do get them good and golden.

2. Blend them in a food processor with the chilli mash, shrimp paste, tamarind, salt and enough water to create a thick pourable paste.

3. Heat the remaining oil over a low heat and stir-fry the purée for a further 10–15 minutes (ensuring it never sticks by adding water bit by bit), until the oil floats above the purée. Pour into sterilised bottles.

CABAI HIJAN MANIS
Sweet Chilli Sauce

One of my absolute favourite sauces is Lingham's Chilly (*sic*) Sauce. Made by a company established in 1908, it is described as 'a mild piquant relish and appetiser of delightful flavour'. This sticky crimson nectar is bottled in Malaysia but is available worldwide. This is my own version.

MAKES 12fl oz (350ml)

8oz (225g) caster sugar
2 tablespoons strained thin chilli sauce (page 287)
1 teaspoon aromatic salt (page 46)

1. Boil 1/2 pint (300ml) water, add the sugar and simmer until you get a thickish syrup.

2. Add the strained thin chilli sauce and the salt, mixing well.

3. When cool it should be pourable – if it is too thick add a little water. Pour into sterilised bottles and use as required.

NAM PRIK
Thai Hot Chilli Sauce

From heat-loving Thailand comes a series of chilli varieties, the hottest of which is a miniature cayenne about 1 inch (2.5cm)long. These are now becoming available at ethnic stores, so I've used them here. Ordinary red cayennes can be substituted. Incidentally *prik* means 'hot' and *nam* means 'liquid'. This version will keep indefinitely and is good with Thai Spring Rolls (see page 70).

MAKES about 12fl oz (350ml)

8oz (225g) tiny Thai red cayenne chillies
6 garlic cloves, crushed
3fl oz (75ml) bottled lemon juice
3fl oz (75ml) distilled malt vinegar
1 tablespoon brown sugar
1 teaspoon nam pla fish sauce (chef's tip, page 172)
1 teaspoon aromatic salt (page 46)

1. Destalk the chillies.

2. Place all the ingredients in a blender or food processor and blend to a purée. Pour into sterilised bottles.

CHINESE CHILLI SAUCE

Ask for chilli sauce at a Chinese restaurant and you'll most likely be given this. It resembles tomato ketchup in texture, though it is rather more orangey in colour. It is an invention of Hong Kong restaurateurs. This recipe makes sufficient to bottle and it will keep indefinitely. Chinese vinegar enhances the taste. In its absence use distilled malt vinegar.

MAKES 12oz (350g)

8oz (225g) fresh red cayenne chillies
4fl oz (125ml) Chinese white rice vinegar
1 teaspoon salt
1 teaspoon white sugar
1 teaspoon cornflour

1. Destalk the chillies, then slit them lengthways. Remove the seeds and any white pith.

2. Soak the chillies overnight in the vinegar and salt.

3. Next day put them into a blender or food processor and pulse into a fine purée.

4. Add the sugar and cornflour and enough water to give a pourable consistency. Pulse briefly to mix. Put into sterilised jars.

CHINESE CHILLI AND GARLIC SAUCE

Add 2 teaspoons garlic powder to the mix at stage 4.

CHINESE CHILLI AND GINGER SAUCE

Add 1 teaspoon ginger powder to the mix at stage 4.

SICHUAN CHILLI SAUCE

In the western Chinese province of Sichuan (or Szechuan) the people grow enormous quantities of chillies. You can sometimes buy these fresh in Chinese shops. They are a gorgeous deep crimson red colour. If you can't get fresh, use dry Sichuan chillies always available in Chinese shops (see *Note* below).

MAKES 18fl oz (550ml)

2 tablespoons vegetable oil
4 garlic cloves, finely chopped
1 inch (2.5cm) cube fresh ginger, finely chopped
1oz (30g) onion, finely chopped
8oz (225g) fresh Sichuan red chillies
2fl oz (50ml) Chinese red rice vinegar or red wine vinegar
1 tablespoon brown sugar
2 tablespoons tomato ketchup
2 tablespoons Chinese yellow rice wine (optional)
2 teaspoons salt

1. Heat the oil in a wok or frying pan.

2. Add the garlic and ginger and stir-fry for 30 seconds, then add the onion and stir-fry for a further minute.

3. Add the chillies and the vinegar and simmer for 10 minutes. Add a little water as needed to prevent it drying up.

4. Add the remaining ingredients and simmer for 5 more minutes.

5. Remove from the heat and, when cool, blend in a food processor or blender with sufficient water to make a smooth-textured sauce. Pour into sterilised bottles.

Note: If using dried Sichuan chillies, 6oz (175g) is sufficient. Soak them in a jar for 24 hours in enough water to cover them. Add the chillies and their soaking water to the pan at stage 3.

KOCHUJAANG
Chilli Paste

This hot sweet thick dark red chutney is to Koreans what mustard is to Westerners. In Korea they ferment the paste. Here is a simpler recipe.

MAKES 2oz (50g)

2 tablespoons red soybean paste
1 tablespoon brown Muscovado sugar
1 tablespoon red chilli mash 1 (pages 286–7)
1/2 teaspoon aromatic salt (page 46)

Mix together and serve.

NUOC CHAM
Vietnamese Chilli Dip

This chilli-based dipping sauce goes well with Thai Spring Rolls (see page 70). The use of fish sauce (*nuoc mam* in Vietnam – *nam pla* in Thailand) works well.

MAKES 4 fl oz (120ml)

2 tablespoons nuoc mam *fish sauce (page 172)*
2 tablespoons fresh lime juice
2 tablespoons red chilli mash 1 (pages 286–7)

1 tablespoon sugar
1/2 teaspoon soy sauce

Mix together and serve.

SALSA ROJA
Mexican Red 'Hot' Chutney

Salsas, meaning 'sauces', are chilli-based chutneys served cold. Mexicans eat salsa from breakfast to bedtime. They eat it on its own, or as an accompaniment. This is known as red salsa because of the colour of its ingredients.

MAKES 6oz (175g)

2 or more habanero/Scotch bonnet chillies or 3 red Anaheim chillies
1 red tomato (golfball size)
2 tablespoons finely chopped Spanish onion
1/4 red bell pepper
2 garlic cloves
1 tablespoon fresh coriander
1 tablespoon olive oil
1 tablespoon distilled malt vinegar, dry sherry or tequila
salt
freshly milled black pepper

1. Finely chop all the vegetables and herbs. Add the oil and vinegar and sufficient water to make the texture you require. You can use a food processor, but pulse briefly. Do not purée.

2. Add salt and pepper to taste and serve cold.

OPPOSITE *A wide selection of hot sauces, pastes and pickles collected by the author from all over the world. Here are over 100 different examples, the largest of which are the massive 1 gallon (3.78 litre) jars from Blue Dragon and Louisiana Gold. Tabasco, who also produce a gallon jar, make the smallest commercially available jar at* 1/8*fl oz (3.5ml). The standard 2fl oz (50ml) bottle contains 720 drops. The* 1/8*fl oz bottle contains 45 drops, and the gallon jar a massive 57,600 drops. At one drop a day that would last 158 years!*

PICO DE GALLO
Special Salsa

I came across this salsa at Mexico's best taco bar, Tacqueria El Pastorcito, owned by Signor Espinosa. *Pico de Gallo* literally means 'rooster's beak', and this is the name given to a red, curved, pointed Mexican chilli.

MAKES 6oz (175g)

4 or more green cayenne chillies
2 canned or fresh plum tomatoes
2 tablespoons chopped onion
1 tablespoon chopped fresh coriander
salt to taste

Follow the same method as the previous recipe.

SALSA VERDE
Mexican Green 'Hot' Chutney

This chutney is known as green salsa because of its green ingredients. For a 'drunken' version use dry sherry, dry white wine or tequila in place of the vinegar.

MAKES 6oz (175g)

1 large green Anaheim chilli
1 green tomato, golfball size
2 tablespoons finely chopped Spanish onion
1/4 green bell pepper
2 garlic cloves
1 tablespoon chopped fresh coriander
1 tablespoon olive oil
1 tablespoon distilled malt vinegar, dry sherry or
  tequila
salt
freshly milled black pepper

1. Roast and peel the chilli (pages 41–2).

2. Follow the same method as for Mexican Red 'Hot' Chutney (see page 290).

MANZANO SALSA
Apple Chilli Chutney

The manzano or rocoto chilli is a relative of the habanero. It is apple-shaped, the size of a small plum and golden yellow in colour. It has large black tasty seeds, and the flavour of apples. This chilli, common in Mexico, is unavailable in the UK and scarce in the USA. I've used yellow habanero/Scotch bonnet chillies with a little apple as a substitute.

MAKES 6oz (175g)

4–5 yellow habanero/Scotch bonnet chillies
2–3 slices apple, peeled and diced
2 tablespoons finely chopped onion
1 1/2 tablespoons lime (or lemon) juice
salt

Follow the same method as for Mexican Red 'Hot' Chutney (see page 290).

CHILE RAJAS
Chilli Chutney with Cream

A tasty chilli chutney served cold. The sour cream gives a fine contrast to the hot spices. It will only keep for a few days in the fridge.

MAKES enough for several servings

2 dried pancho or mulato chillies
1 tablespoon corn oil
1 smallish red onion, finely chopped
3fl oz (85ml) sour cream
aromatic salt (page 46) to taste

1. Soak the chillies in water overnight, then strain, discarding the stalks and seeds. Chop the chillies finely.

2. Heat the oil in a frying pan and stir-fry the onion for 5 minutes.

3. Allow to cool. Add the sour cream, and aromatic salt to taste. Chill and serve.

PIRI-PIRI
Chilli Sauce

You'll find *piri-piri* in Portugal, Brazil and parts of Africa. *Piri-piri* is the African word for chilli, although this sauce is also known as *jindungo* in some parts. You can add a splash to soups and sauces, or use it as a condiment, or to cook with. See Piri-Piri Curry (page 125) and Piri-Piri Diabole (pages 168–9). This *piri-piri* will last indefinitely, though I suspect it will be consumed faster than you think.

MAKES 1¼lb (560g)

1¼lb (560g) red chilli mash 1 (pages 286–7)
  using dry or fresh bird chillies if possible
3fl oz (85ml) olive oil

Fill sterilised jars up to seven-eighths full with chilli mash, and top up with the olive oil. Shake well to mix and leave for a month or so to 'mature'.

HARISSA
Hot Red Chilli Purée

This is a hot spicy chilli sauce which accompanies most North African savoury dishes, especially Couscous (see page 129).

MAKES 2–4 servings

2 tablespoons tomato purée
¼ teaspoon ground cummin
1 tablespoon red chilli mash 1 (pages 286–7)

Mix together and serve.

BERBERE/BARIBARAY

This complex mixture of spices and chilli is only a few steps removed from curry powder. To the Ethiopian cook it is indispensable, both in cooking (see page 165) and as a dip or chutney. Spoon measures are heaped.

MAKES about 3½oz (100g) dry mix

6 teaspoons (30g) extra hot chilli powder
6 teaspoons (30g) onion powder
2 teaspoons (10g) garlic powder
1 teaspoon (5g) ginger powder
1 teaspoon (5g) salt
½ teaspoon (2½g) ground green cardamom seeds
½ teaspoon (2½g) ground coriander seeds
½ teaspoon (2½g) ground fennel seeds
½ teaspoon (2½g) ground fenugreek seeds
½ teaspoon (1⅓g) ground cinnamon
½ teaspoon (1¼g) ground cloves
½ teaspoon (1¼g) ground mace
4–5 tablespoons red wine
2 tablespoons niter kebbeh (page 43) or ghee
  (page 43)
1 tablespoon finely chopped fresh mint
1 tablespoon finely chopped fresh basil
1 tablespoon finely chopped fresh coriander
3 tablespoons honey

1. Blend the dry ingredients together and store in an airtight jar until required.

2. To make the paste, use about one-third of the dry mix (33g). Add the wine and make a runny paste.

3. Heat the *niter kebbeh* in a karahi or wok. Carefully, to avoid being splattered, add the paste and stir-fry for 3–4 minutes. Add the fresh herbs and the honey, and when they are all blended remove from the heat.

STOMACHIC MANDRUM

I found this West Indian recipe in an Edwardian spice book. Apparently it is an aid to digestion!

MAKES enough for 1 generous serving

6–8 fresh bird chillies
2 inch (5cm) piece cucumber, peeled and sliced
  into matchsticks
2–3 whole spring onions, chopped
3–4 tablespoons Madeira

Mix everything together and enjoy!

DILLOCK
Cayenne Pottage

In Abyssinia they make this pottage in large quantities and place it in a gourd shell suspended from the roof of the kitchen, where it keeps. They take small amounts as required.

MAKES 1 serving

3 teaspoons cayenne pepper
1/2 teaspoon aromatic salt (page 46)
2 tablespoons gram flour (besan)
2 tablespoons mustard oil
1 teaspoon black mustard seeds

1. Combine the cayenne, salt and flour with enough water to make a runny paste.

2. Heat the oil in a karahi or wok. Add the mustard seeds and stir-fry for 20 seconds. Carefully, to avoid being splattered, add the paste. Briskly stir-fry until the water is cooked out, the oil floats and the colour has gone darker. Serve hot or cold.

CHITOR DIN
Hot Shrimp Chilli Pickle

This cooked chilli chutney comes from African Guinea. Elsewhere in West Africa there are variations on the theme, some of which are called *Mako Tuntum*. Cook all the water out in plenty of oil and this will keep indefinitely, like any pickle. Dried shrimps are available in Chinese and Asian stores.

MAKES about 12 oz (350g)

12 garlic cloves, crushed
1oz (30g) dried onions (chef's tip, page 65)
2oz (50g) dried shrimps
3 tablespoons red chilli mash 1 (pages 286–7)
2 teaspoons aromatic salt (page 46)
8fl oz (250 ml) corn oil

1. Blend all the items (except the oil) in a food processor, using enough water to make a runny paste.

2. Heat the oil in a karahi or wok over a high heat. Then, carefully, to avoid being splattered, add the paste. Stir-fry for about 10 minutes, lowering the heat as the water reduces. It's ready when the colour has gone darker and all the oil floats on top of the paste. Bottle in sterilised airtight jars.

BIBER TURSU or QALI FILFIL
Middle Eastern Vinegared Chillies

Bottled vinegared chillies are easy to make and they keep indefinitely, so you can help yourself whenever you wish. Yum Yum!

MAKES 1 1/2 lb (675g)

1lb (450g) green cayenne chillies
1/2 pint (300ml) distilled malt vinegar

1. Rinse and dry but do not destalk the chillies.

2. Choose suitable sterilised screw-top jars and cram them full of the chillies.

3. Pour the vinegar into the jars to the brim. Shake them to burst air-pockets and top up if necessary. Leave in a dark place for 3–4 days. Inspect and top up with vinegar if needed. Leave for at least 4 weeks before using.

TORSHI FILFIL
Pickled Vegetables with Chilli

Pickles have been around for thousands of years in the Middle East. Originally fruit or vegetables were pickled to last only a few months for use over the non-growing period, and so were often pickled unblanched. But if the pickle is to be kept for six months or more, the fruit or vegetables should be blanched. The vinegar to water ratio should also be stepped up to 1:1 or the water even omitted. This reduces the chance of the item going off, though it will not be as crisp.

Typical pickling vegetables are aubergine, carrots, celery, green beans, cucumber, cauliflower, mixed vegetables and green tomato.

1lb (450g) vegetables of your choice (see above)
10 garlic cloves, halved
6 red chillies, chopped

PICKLING LIQUID
8fl oz (250ml) distilled malt vinegar
16fl oz (500ml) water
2 tablespoons salt

1. Clean and prepare the vegetables and slice them into strips, quarters or squares.

2. Put as many of the vegetables as you can into suitable sterilised screw-top jars. Divide the garlic and red chillies between the jars.

3. Mix the vinegar, water and salt to make the **pickling liquid** and pour it into the jars. Jiggle the jars around to burst any air-pockets, then top up until each jar is full to the brim. Store, preferably in the dark. Keep any spare pickling liquid in its own jar, for future use.

4 Examine the pickle after 48 hours. Often, more liquid is needed to top it up. Keep for at least 2 weeks before eating.

TREVOR PACK'S CHILLI CHUTNEY

Trevor Pack is a Curry Club member. He attended one of my cookery courses and was kind enough to bring some bottles of chilli chutney made from home-grown chillies.

MAKES about 2lb (900g)

1/2 pint (300ml) vegetable oil
6 garlic cloves, crushed
2 inch (5cm) piece ginger, grated
1lb (450g) fresh red or green chillies, chopped
3 large onions, chopped
1/2 pint (300ml) distilled malt vinegar
1 tablespoon salt
1 tablespoon Muscovado sugar

SPICES
4 tablespoons ground cummin
2 tablespoons ground turmeric
1 tablespoon curry powder

1. Add enough water to the **spices** to make a pourable paste.

2. Heat the oil in a wok or karahi over a high heat. Add the garlic and ginger and stir-fry for 3 seconds. Add the paste and stir-fry for 3–4 minutes until it darkens and the oil floats.

3. Ladle off the oil into another pan and heat. Add the chillies and onion and stir-fry for 10–15 minutes, adding water from time to time to prevent sticking.

4. Combine the paste, vinegar, salt and sugar with the chillies and onion. Simmer for 10–15 minutes, stirring occasionally. Cool a little.

5. Transfer to sterilised hot jars and cover with airtight lids. It can be eaten at once but will improve with age, keeping indefinitely.

NARIAL CHATNI
Coconut Chutney

Here is a quick version of a chutney which is widely adored in South India and Sri Lanka.

SERVES 4 as a chutney

6 tablespoons unsweetened desiccated coconut
6 tablespoons milk
1 teaspoon mustard oil
2 teaspoons light (eg. sunflower) oil
2 teaspoons mustard seeds
1 teaspoon sesame seeds
6–8 fresh or dried curry leaves
1/2 teaspoon salt
coconut milk powder

1. Mix the desiccated coconut with the milk and leave it covered in the fridge for 6 hours.

2. Heat the oils and stir-fry the seeds, leaves and salt for 30 seconds.

3. Add the coconut and stir-fry for 2–3 minutes. Add enough water to make it quite loose.

4. Now mix in sufficient coconut milk powder to achieve a thickish creamy texture to your

liking. Put it into a bowl, cover and chill for up to but no longer than 2 hours.

BANGARA BHAT
A Cooling Chutney

Served chilled, this is a tasty soothing chutney.

SERVES 4
3oz (75g) Greek or thick yoghurt
2oz (50g) cooked plain rice
1 teaspoon mustard oil
2 teaspoons sesame oil
1 teaspoon mustard seeds
aromatic salt (page 46)

1. Heat the yoghurt and rice and mash together to break the rice grains, but not pulp them.

2. Heat the oils in a karahi or wok and flash-fry the mustard seeds for 20 seconds. Remove from the heat.

3. Stir in the yoghurt and rice. Allow to cool, then add salt to taste. Chill and serve.

TANDOORI RAITA

A very long time ago India discovered that yoghurt was the antidote to chilli heat. Mixtures of yoghurt with savoury ingredients are called raitas. This one is a tart, spicy raita which goes well with any spicy dish.

MAKES 7 fl oz (200ml)

5fl oz (150ml) Greek or thick yoghurt
2 teaspoons clear vinegar
1 teaspoon bottled curry paste
1 teaspoon tomato purée

Mix everything together. Chill and serve.

CHILLI RAITA

Because not everyone wants an antidote to chilli heat.

MAKES 5fl oz (150ml)

5fl oz (150ml) Greek or thick yoghurt
1/2–1 habañero chilli, finely chopped

Mix everything together. Cover and leave in the fridge for up to 48 hours to allow the chilli to impregnate the yoghurt. Serve.

HERBAL RAITA

Add 1 tablespoon each of chopped fresh coriander, mint and basil, and 1/3 teaspoon aromatic salt (page 46) to the yoghurt instead of the chilli. Chill and serve.

PAT'S SPICY VINAIGRETTE

Not only is this much tastier than any commercial vinaigrette product I've met, it is also much cheaper. Make in quantity and store in a decorative bottle with stopper.

MAKES 2 1/4 pints (1 litre)

2 tablespoons white granulated sugar
4 teaspoons salt
2 teaspoons yellow mustard powder
2 teaspoons ground white pepper
2 tablespoons tomato ketchup
5fl oz (150ml) light (eg. sunflower) oil
2 tablespoons best quality olive oil
7fl oz (200ml) distilled (clear) malt vinegar
3 1/2fl oz (100ml) bottled lemon juice
8fl oz (250ml) white wine
red chilli mash (optional, pages 286–7)
approx 7fl oz (200ml) water (enough to top up the bottle)

1. Using a suitable funnel in the neck of your chosen storage bottle, first insert the dry items – the sugar, salt, mustard powder, and pepper. Next add the tomato ketchup and now wash these items down the funnel with the oils, vinegar, lemon juice and wine. Add red chilli mash to taste for a hotter vinaigrette.

2. Put the stopper on the bottle and shake thoroughly. Top up with the water and it is ready to use. Shake well before every use.

GLOSSARY

A

Ajwain or Ajowain – Lovage seeds (India)

Allspice – Native to the West Indies. Related to the clove family, the seed resembles small dried peas. Called allspice because its aroma seems to combine those of clove, cinnamon, ginger, nutmeg and pepper. Also called *pimento* (Spain), *seenl* (India)

Aniseed – Small deliciously flavoured seeds resembling fennel seeds

Asafoetida – A rather smelly spice

Ata or Atta – *Chupatti* flour. Fine wholemeal flour used in most Indian breads. English wholemeal is a suitable alternative

B

Bahar Hah Hilu – Allspice (Middle East)

Bargar – The process of frying whole spices in hot oil

Basmati – The best type of long-grain rice

Bay leaf – Aromatic spice. Used in leaf form fresh or dried, and also dried and ground

Besan – See *Gram flour*

Bhajee or Bhaji – Dryish mild vegetable curry

Bhoona or Bhuna – The process of cooking the spice paste in hot oil. A *bhoona* curry is usually dry and cooked in coconut

Bindi – Okra or ladies' fingers (India)

Blachan – see Shrimp Paste

Bonito – Dried fish sold in blocks or shavings. Used to flavour stocks and soups or as a garnish

C

Cardamom, Green – Green pods containing aromatic black seeds. One of the most aromatic spices. Used whole or ground in savoury and sweet dishes

Caraway Seeds – Small thin black seeds resembling black cummin seeds in appearance, but not in taste, which is sweet and aromatic. It is a European spice – appearing in Germanic savoury dishes

Cassia bark – The corky brown outer bark of a tree with a sweet fragrance, related to cinnamon. Comes in pieces or quills. Less fragrant and cheaper than cinnamon, but stands up to more robust cooking

Celery Seeds – Small round greeny grey seeds, a bit like aniseed or lovage in appearance, but quite savoury in taste

Chana – Type of lentil. See *Dhal*

Chilli Bean Sauce – Fermented black soya beans ground to a thick paste with chilli powder

Chilli Oil – Szechwan pepper and chilli fried into oil

Chupatti – A dry 6 inch (15cm) disc of unleavened bread. Normally griddle-cooked, it should be served piping hot. Spelling varies eg *Chuppati*, *Chapati* etc

Clove – Dark brown, 'nail-shaped' spice (from the Latin *clavus* meaning nail). The rounded head of the clove is an unopened flower bud.

Comal – Mexican steel griddle pan used to dry-fry tortillas

Coriander – used widely in Chinese and Indian cookery. The leaves of the plant can be used fresh and the seeds whole or ground

Cornmeal – Mexican ground maize (sweetcorn) to create a flour called *masa harina* or cornmeal. It is available in yellow or blue (made from black maize) and is essential for tortilla making. Note: European cornflour is made from corn grains and cannot be substituted for cornmeal.

Couscous – Processed semolina grains which require steaming

Cummin or Cumin – *Jeera*. There are two types of seeds: *white* and *black*. The white seeds are a very important spice in Indian cookery. The black seeds (*kala jeera*) are nice in pullao rice and certain vegetable dishes. Both can be used whole or ground

Curry leaves – *Neem* leaves or *kari phulia*. Small leaves a bit like bay leaves, used for flavouring

Cus cus – See Poppy seed

D

Dalchini or Darchim – Cinnamon

Dhal – Lentils. There are over 60 types of lentil, some of which are very obscure. Like peas, they grown into a hard sphere measuring between $1/2$ inch (1cm) (chickpeas) and $1/8$ inch (3mm) (urid). They are cooked whole or split with skin, or split with the skin polished off. Lentils are a rich source of protein and when cooked with spices are extremely tasty. The common types are *Chana* (resembling yellow split peas, used to make gram flour/ besan); *kabli chana* (chickpeas); *masoor* (the most familiar orangey-red lentil which has a green skin); *moong* (green-skinned lentil, used also make bean sprouts); *toor*, or *toovar* (dark yellow and very oily); and *urid* (black skin, white lentil)

F

Fennel – *Sunf* or *soonf* (India). A small green seed which is very aromatic, with aniseed taste

Fenugreek – *Methi* (India). This important spice is used as seeds and in fresh or dried leaf form. It is very savoury and is used in many Northern Indian dishes

Fish sauce – *Nam-pla* (Thai), *Nga-pya* (Burmese), *Patis* (Philippine). It is the runny liquid strained from fermented anchovies, and is a very important flavouring agent

Five-Spice Powder – *Ng heung fun* or *Wu hsiang fen*. A mixture of five aromatic spices: used in Chinese and Malay cooking. Usually ground. A typical combination would be equal parts of cinnamon, cloves, fennel seeds, star anise and Szechuan pepper

G

Galingale or Galangel – A tuber

related to ginger which comes in varieties called greater or lesser. It has a more peppery taste than ginger (which can be substituted for it). It is used in Thai cooking where it is called *kha*, and in Indonesian (*laos*) and Malay (*kenkur*). It is available in the UK in fresh form (rare), dried or powdered

Garam masala – Literally hot mixture. This refers to a blend of spices much loved in northern Indian cookery. The Curry Club garam masala contains nine spices

Garlic Chives – (herb). Flat-bladed leaf. Its leaves are larger than ordinary chives but it has, as its name states, a garlicky taste. Also called Chinese chives.

Ginger – A rhizome which can be used fresh, dried or powdered

Gram flour – *Besan*. Finely ground flour, pale blonde in colour, made from chana (see *Dhal*). Used to make *pakoras* and to thicken curries

Grenadine syrup – A syrup made from pomegranates. Used as a mixer for drinks and cocktails

K

Kabli chana – Chickpeas. See *Dhal*
Kalongi – *See* Wild onion seeds
Kapi – Shrimp paste (Thai)
Karahi – *Karai, korai* etc. The Indian equivalent of the wok. The *karahi* is a circular two-handled round all-purpose cooking pan used for stir-frying, simmering, frying and deep-frying – in fact it is highly efficient for all types of cooking. Some restaurants cook in small *karahis* and serve them to the table with the food sizzling inside
Karela – Small, dark green, knobbly vegetable of the gourd family
Ketjap manis – Indonesian version of soy sauce. It is sweeter and slightly sticky. The Conimex brand is available worldwide. If you can't find it, used dark soy sauce with brown sugar added to your taste
Kulfi – Indian ice cream
Kus Kus (India) – See poppy seed

L

Lassi or Lhassi – A refreshing drink

made from yoghurt and crushed ice. The savoury version is *lhassi namkeen* and the sweet version is *lhassi meethi*
Lemongrass – *Takrai* (Thai), *serai* (Malay). A fragrant-leafed plant which imparts a subtle lemony flavour to cooking. Use ground powder (made from the bulb) as a substitute
Lime Leaves – *Markrut* or citrus leaves. Used in Thai cooking, fresh or dried, to give a distinctive aromatic flavour
Limu Omani or Loumi or Noomi – Dried whole limes, or ground limes used to give sour taste to savoury dishes (Iranian)
Loumi – See *Limu Omani*
Lovage – *Ajwain* or *ajowain* (India). Slightly bitter round seeds

M

Mace – *Javitri* (India). The outer part of the nutmeg
Mango Powder – *Am chur* (India). A very sour flavouring agent
Masala – A mixture of spices which are cooked with a particular dish. Any curry powder is therefore a masala. It can be spelt a remarkable number of ways – massala, massalla, musala, mosola, massalam etc
Masoor – Red lentils. See *Dhal*
Mattar – Green peas (India)
Meethi – Sweet (India)
Methi – Fenugreek (India)
Mezzeh – Mixed hors-d'oeuvre (Middle East)
Mirch – Pepper or chilli (India)
Mirin – Sweet Japanese wine
Miso – Japanese red soya bean paste. See Soya
Mollee – Fish dishes cooked in coconut and chilli (India)
Mooli – Large white radish
Moong – Type of lentil. See *Dhal*
Mustard Oil – This lightly flavoured oil is popular in southern India. European regulations require manufacturers to state 'for external use only' on the packaging, as excess erucic acid can cause allergies. However you would need to consume several pints a day for it to have an adverse effect. As recipes call for

only a teaspoon or two, there is no danger of that. The safest thing is to buy mustard blend oil, or to dilute it yourself with another oil
Mustard seeds – Small black seeds which become sweetish when fried

N

Nam Pla – *See* Fish sauce
Naan or Nan – Leavened bread baked in the tandoor. It is teardrop shaped and about 8–10 inches (20–25cm) long. It must be served fresh and hot (India)
Nga-Pi – Shrimp paste (Burma)
Nga-Pya – *See* Fish sauce
Nigella – Wild onion seeds
Noomi – See *Limu Omani*
Nori – See Seaweed
Nutmeg – Hard, round, pale brown spice ball. Native to South East Asia, it was introduced to the West by the earliest Arab and Chinese traders

P

Papadom – Thin lentil flour wafers. When cooked (deep fried or baked) they expand to about 8 inches (20cm). They must be crackling crisp and warm when served. They come plain or spiced with lentils, pepper, garlic or chilli
Paratha – A deep-fried bread
Patis – See Fish sauce
Patna – A long-grained rice
Phal or Phall – A very hot curry (the hottest), invented by restaurateurs
Pistachio nut – *Pista inagaz* (India). A fleshy, tasty nut which can be used fresh (the greener the better) or salted
Plaki – Cooking style. Fish or vegetable cooked in olive oil with herbs, tomato and garlic. It originated in Byzantine times and is still eaten in Greece, Turkey and Armenia
Poppy seed – *Cus cus* or *Kus Kus* (India). White seeds used in chicken curries, blue seeds used to decorate bread. (Not to be confused with the Moroccan national dish cous-cous, made from steamed semolina)
Pulses – Dried peas and beans, including lentils
Puri – A deep-fried unleavened bread

about 4 inches (10cm) in diameter. It puffs up when cooked and should be served at once

R

Rajma – Red kidney beans (India)

Ras el Hanout – Celebrated Moroccan spice mix

Rice Wine, Chinese – Red, white or yellow. Distinctive in flavour and good in cooking to get an authentic flavour. In its absence, substitute any wine or sherry

Rice Vinegar, Chinese – Red, white or yellow. Similar remarks to the above wine. This vinegar which is made from the wine is sweetish and sticky. Wine vinegar and a little brown sugar can substitute

Roti – Bread (India)

S

Saffron – *Kesar* or *zafron* (India). The world's most expensive spice, used to give a recipe a delicate yellow colouring and aroma

Sake – Dry Japanese wine, used in cooking or as table wine. Often served warm in special small cups

Samneh or Smen – Clarified butter (Middle East)

Samak – Fish (Middle East)

Sambals – A Malayan term describing the side dishes accompanying the meal

Samosa – The celebrated triangular deep-fried meat or vegetable patties served as starters or snacks

Seaweed – Popular in Japanese cooking, assisting with both savoury taste and texture. Nori is one type, Wakame, Lavar and Agar Agar are others

Sesame Oil – Extracted from roasted white sesame seeds. Dark. Wasted on heavy cooking

Sesame Seeds – Small, flat, round, pale cream seeds. These come in other colours, including red, brown, and black, the latter being used in Japanese cooking. The cream seed (called white) is used in China. It is also pressed into an oil and mixed into a paste, called *tahini*

Shrimps – Dry or Dehydrated. Very popular in Malaysia and Indo China. Available in packets, these little browny-pink shrimps can be used whole after rehydration or ground to a powder.

Shrimp paste – *Blachan* (Malay), *Nga-Pi* (Burmese), *Kapi* (Thai). Very concentrated block of compressed shrimps. A vital flavouring for the cooking of those countries

Smen – Clarified butter (Middle East)

Soy Sauce – This is available in two main varieties. Thick or dark soy sauce is the thicker, darker and less salty of the two, and thin or light soy sauce is, obviously, thinner, lighter and more salty. Dark soy sauce gives a reddish brown colour to dishes, while light soy sauce would be used when it is important for the food to be light in colour. The Japanese version is called Shoya sauce, and the Indonesian *ketjap* or *kecap manis* (sic)

Star anise – A pretty star-shaped aromatic spice

Sumak, Summak – Dried berries (Middle East)

Sechwan Pepper – or *Flower pepper*. Reddy brown. Dried berry of a shrub. Aromatic rather than hot. One of the ingredients of Chinese five-spice powder

T

Tagine – Type of slow-cooked stew (Morocco)

Tamarind – *Imli* (India). A date-like fruit used as a chutney, and in cooking as a souring agent

Tandoori – A style of charcoal cooking originating in north-west India (what is now Pakistan and the Punjab)

Tarka – Garnish of spices/onion

Tava or Tawa – A heavy, almost flat, circular wooden handle griddle pan used to cook Indian breads and to 'roast' spices. Also ideal for many cooking functions from frying eggs and omelettes to making pancakes, etc

Tikka – Skewered meat, chicken or seafood, marinated then barbecued or tandoori baked

Tindaloo – See Vindaloo

Toor or Toovar – A type of lentil. See *Dhal*

Turmeric – Fine yellow powdered spice. Native to South Asia, turmeric is a rhizome which, like ginger, can be cooked fresh but is usually encountered ground. A very important Indian spice, used to give the familiar yellow colour to curries. Use sparingly or it can cause bitterness

U

Urid – A type of lentil. See *Dhal*

V

Vanilla – Native to Latin America. Long, very thin, dark, shrivelled, firm pods. These impart a unique flavour to cooking. Vanilla essence is a substitute, but there is nothing like the real thing

Vark or Varak – Edible silver or gold foil (India)

Vindaloo – A fiery hot dish from Goa. Traditionally it was pork marinated in vinegar with potato (*aloo*). In the restaurant is has now come to mean just a very hot dish. Also sometimes called *bindaloo* or *tindaloo* (even hotter)

W

Wasabi – A powder (or paste) supposed to be made from Japanese green horseradish, though often made from ordinary horseradish and food colouring. Available from specialist stores

Wild Onion Seeds – *Kalongi* (India). Small irregular jet-black nuggets. Also known as Nigella

Y

Yahni – Arab method of cooking. Meat or vegetables braised in oil with onion, then simmered with water to make a stock. Used from Egypt to Iran (and a derivative *yakni*, in India) see *Akhni*

Z

Za'faran – Saffron (Middle East)

Zafron – Saffron (India)

Zardaloo – Dried apricots in honey (Iran)

Zeera – Cummin (India)

Zereshk – Also known as barberry. A particularly sour berry, available in dried form. Soak in water for 1 hour before use (Iran)

USEFUL ADDRESSES

All the following suppliers will deal with international orders, but please make contact with the supplier before you order to establish what, if any, additional costs are involved for air freighting or sea mail. Some countries ban the import of food stuffs by mail order, although it rarely applies to dry, canned and bottled goods. Import duty may be payable, although it should not be very high. Contact your local customs and excise office to establish what rules exist.

The Curry Club
PO Box 7
Haslemere
Surrey GU27 1EP UK
Tel: 0428 658 327

Over 300 items (Indian, Thai, Chinese, etc) available, including spices, food, books, cookware. Free leaflets and order forms, but SAE requested.

The Cool Chile Company
34 Bassett Road
London W10 6JL UK
Tel: 081 968 8898

Run by Dodie Miller, specialises in Mexican chillies and other items. Free listings, SAE requested.

El Dorado
6 Upper Deck
Princess Square
Newcastle-Upon-Tyne
Tyne and Wear NE1 8ER UK
Tel: 091-232 9894

Also specialises in Mexican items. SAE requested.

Old Southwest Trading Company
Post Office Box 7545
Albuquerque
New Mexico 87194 USA
Fax: 010-1-505-836-1682

Mexican and American dried chilies, seeds, powders, sauces, food accessories, books etc. Huge chatty catalogue costs $2.

The Chile Shop
109 East Water Street
Santa Fe
New Mexico 87501 USA
Fax: 010-1-505-984-0737

Similar to Old Southwest Trading Company, smaller but different range. Attractive catalogues.

Tabasco Country Store
McLhenny Company

Avery Island
Louisiana 70513-5002 USA

Dozens of Tabasco-labelled goodies (see page 7). Good free colour catalogue.

N'awlins Lous-e-Ana Connection
1031 St Ferdinand Street
Suite B
New Orleans
Louisiana 707117 USA
Tel: 010-1-504-943-3400

Wide range of cajun and creole food products. Free detailed order form. SAE requested.

New Orleans School of Cooking
620 Decatur Street
Suite 107
The Jackson Brewery
New Orleans
Lousiana 70130-1011 USA
Tel: 010-1-504-566-5011

Cajun and Creole food plus big range of cookbooks, gifts, mardi gras items and more. Huge colour catalogue costs $1. Runs cooking courses too.

Redwood City Seed Company
PO Box 361
Redwood City
California 94064 USA

Dried chillies, powder and seeds. Catalogue at small cost.

The Pepper Gal
PO Box 23006
Fort Lauderdale
Florida 3311 USA

Chilli seeds etc. Catalogue at small cost. They also operate the National Hot Pepper Association.

Chile Pepper Magazine
PO Box 4278
Albuquerque
New Mexico 87196 USA

A bi-monthly publication dedicated

to everything and anything about chile! Editor is Dave DeWitt.

The Curry Club Magazine
PO Box 7
Haslemere
Surrey GU27 1EP UK

Quarterly colourful magazine available by subscription. Facts, fun and features all about curry and spicy food. Contains recipes and restaurant information worldwide.

International Connoisseurs of Green and Red Chile
311 N Downtown Mall
Las Cruces
New Mexico 88001 USA

Contact Helen Revels, Executive Director, for details of membership.

The Chile Institute
Box 30003
Las Cruces
New Mexico 88003 USA

Contact Dr Paul Bosland. A serious research unit, at the Mexico State University, whose work includes cultivating and hybridising.

US Department of Agriculture
ARS Plant Introduction Station
1109 Experiment Street
Georgia 30223-1797 USA

This is another serious institution. They maintain a collection of 3,000 different varieties of capsicum seeds, some of which are in growth. Papers published from time to time. Contact Gil Lovel.

INDEX

Page numbers in *italic* refer to the
   illustrations

abay wot (fish stew), 165
Afghanistan, 17
African cookery, 26
African rice, *178–9*, 247
aguates rellenos con cangrejo (crab-stuffed
   avocado), 59
aji de gallina (chilli chicken hotpot), 132–3
aji gazpacho (chilli cold soup), 84
akhni stock, 44–5
alligator sausage, 100, *102*
aloo boti khara kabab, 228
alu chole pullao (curried potato and chickpea
   rice), 244–5
amadan ke abobie (Regina's Selfridges
   banana beans), *178–9*, 202
ambulthial (tuna in tamarind sauce), 157
anju (rice cake), *94–5*, 253
antojitos (spicy heart appetizers), 57
apricot, spicy vegetables with, 196
Arabian omelette, 221
arabiata (Italian chilli sauce), 114, *114*
Arabic fried fish balls, 170
aromatic salt, 46
arroz con azafran (Spanish saffron rice), 236
arroz de coco (coconut chilli rice), 246
asparagus: asparagus and red soy soup,
   50–1, 85
   cream of cashew and asparagus soup,
     86–7, 87
aubergines: moussaka, 112–13
   salting, 113
avocados: chilli, egg and tomato dip, 55, 60
   crab-stuffed avocado, 59
   guacamolé (avocado dip), 58–9

baharat, 48
Balinese fish, *154–5*, 176
banana, syrupy, *270–1*, 274
bangara bhat (a cooling chutney), 296
Bangladesh, 17–18
bean sprout combo, 55, 68
beans: bean ball fritters, 203
   beans and rice, *230–1*, 252
   chili con carne, 97
   fried beans, 204
   refried beans, 204
   Regina's Selfridges banana beans, *178–9*,
     202
beef: beef casserole with horseradish and
     mustard, 122, *123*
   chili con carne, 97–9
   couscous meat stew, 129
   hot red chilli curry, 125
   Mexican stir-fry beef, 104
   Sicilian spicy mince, *114*, 115
   skewered spicy grilled meat, 110
   Thai red beef curry, 126, *127*
beignets, 277
berbere/baribaray, 293
bhindi karhi (Punjabi okra curry), 188
biber tursu (Middle Eastern vinegared
   chillies), 294
bittara hodi methi (egg and fenugreek curry),
   219

blehat samak (Arabic fried fish balls), 170
bobotie (vegetable baked pie), 194–5, *195*
boemboe Bali ikan (Balinese fish), *154–5*,
   176
Bombay tomato rice, *118*, 244
boomba tamarta bhaat (Bombay tomato
   rice), *118*, 244
Brazil, 23–4
Brazilian roast pork, 108–9
breads, 254–69
   basic dough making, 256–7
   breakfast puff bread, *270–1*, 273
   chilli pinwheels, 269
   curry pinwheels, 269
   deep-fried puff bread, 266
   Heather's chilli bread, *102*, 268
   millet bread, *254–5*, 261
   naan bread, 87, *254–5*, 266–7
   pan-fried flat bread, *191*, 265
   pitta bread, *243*, 257
   Red Indian fry bread, 258–9
   tortillas, *78–9*, *254–5*, 262–4
   Turkish crispy bread, *254–5*, 258
   the ultimate garlic bread, 268
   white flour chupattis, *118*, 264
   Yemeni spicy bread, *254–5*, 260
breakfast puff bread, *270–1*, 273
bredie (layered fish and pumpkin stew),
   160–1
Burma, 18
butter: ghee, 43

cabai hijan manis (sweet chilli sauce), 288
cabbage, chilli pickled, 212
Cajun food, 24–5
calas (bean ball fritters), 203
caldo tlapeno (chicken soup with Mexican
   vegetables), *78–9*, 81
capsaicin, 29
caroco (avocado, chilli, egg and tomato dip),
   55, 60
carrot, cheese and chilli croquettes, 52
caruru (shrimps with okra), 168
cashew nuts: cream of cashew and asparagus
   soup, *86–7*, 87
   devilled chilli cashew nuts, 65
cayenne pepper, 39–40
   cayenne pottage, 294
Central America, 23
ceviche (marinated fish), 56, *78–9*
cha gio (crispy crab rolls), 72
char masala, 48
cheese: cheese, carrot and chilli croquettes,
   52
   chilli cheese crêpes, 216–17
   chillies stuffed with cheese, *214–15*, 218
   Indian cheese, 228
   spinach and lentil curry with Indian
     cheese, 229
chermoula potatoes (chilli potatoes), 197
chermoula samak (spicy marinated grilled
   trout), 172
chicken: casseroled coconut chicken, 146
   chicken and prawns in coconut shells,
     130–1, 153
   chicken and shrimp noodles, 61
   chicken in a green hot molé sauce, 136

chicken omelette, 225
chicken paprika, 149
chicken rissoles, *130–1*, 133
chicken soup with lime, *78–9*, 80
chicken soup with Mexican vegetables,
   78–9, 81
chicken with chilli and chocolate, 134–5
chilli chicken hotpot, 132–3
chilli roast chicken, *142–3*, *142*
crispy Malaysian chicken, 152
Guatemalan herbal chicken, 141
Malaysian chicken soup, 82–3
Malaysian fried rice, 240
minced chicken in red molé sauce, 137
offal, 250
paella, 236–7, *238*
skewered grilled chicken, 75
spicy chicken stuffed with curry mince,
   145
chickpea curry, 180
chilaquiles (fried tortillas with chilli sauce),
   58, *214–15*
chile en nogada (pork and walnut-stuffed
   chillies), *102–3*
chile rajas (chilli chutney with cream), 292
chili powder, 40
chilis rellenos con arroz (chillies stuffed with
   rice), *230–1*, 251
chilis rellenos con carne (chillies stuffed with
   meat), 101
chilis rellenos de queso (chillies stuffed with
   cheese), *214–15*, 218
chilis rellenos pescados (chillies stuffed with
   fish), 156–7
chilli jal jeera (hot cummin consommé), 89
chilli powders, 39–40
chillies, 10–11, 27–40
   and sex, 30
   constituents, 28–9
   cultivation, 29–30
   handling, 41
   roasting, 41–2
   Scoville scale, 29
   types, 30–9, *34–5*
   apple chilli chutney, 292
   chili con carne, 96–9
   chilli cheese crêpes, 216–17
   chilli chutney with cream, 292
   chilli fried rice, 243
   chilli in the hole, *123*, 225
   chilli paste, 290
   chilli pinwheels, 269
   chilli potatoes, 197
   chilli raita, 296
   chilli sauce, 293
   chillies stuffed with cheese, *214–15*, 218
   chillies stuffed with fish, 156–7
   chillies stuffed with meat, 101
   chillies stuffed with rice, *230–1*, 251
   Chinese chilli sauce, 289
   chocolate-enrobed chillies, *279*, 280
   coconut chilli rice, 246
   green chilli curry, 186, *191*
   green chilli ice cream, 278
   Heather's chilli bread, *102*, 268
   hot red chilli curry, 125
   hot red chilli purée, 293

Indonesian hot chilli sauce, 288
Italian chilli sauce, 114, *114*
Italian rice, 234–5
Mexican green 'hot' chutney, 292
Mexican red 'hot' chutney, *94–5*, 290
Middle Eastern vinegared chillies, 294
pork and walnut-stuffed chillies, 102–3
potatoes in chilli cheese sauce, 208
red chilli mash, 287
red chilli oil, 286
red chilli vinegar, 286
sangritta, 78–9, 284
scrambled eggs with red chilli, 220
Sichuan chilli sauce, 289–90
special salsa, 292
stomachic mandrum, 293
sweet chilli purée, *63, 154–5*, 288
sweet chilli sauce, 288
tassels, *139*, 211
Thai hot chilli sauce, *127*, 289
thin chilli sauces, 287–8
Trevor Pack's chilli chutney, 295
Vietnamese chilli dip, 290
chin-hin (Burmese sour fish soup), 91
Chinese chilli sauce, 289
Chinese cookery, 20–1
Chinese five-spice powder, 46
Chinese ten-spice powder, 47
chitor din (hot shrimp chilli pickle), 294
chocolate, 11, 135
   chicken with chilli and chocolate, 134–5
   chocolate-enrobed chillies, 279, 280
   chocolate-enrobed garlic, 278–9, *279*
   Chutney Mary's bitter chocolate kulfi,
      270–1, 274–5
chorizo/chourico (spicy sausage), 105
chota hazri meethi puri (breakfast puff
   bread), *270–1*, 273
chupattis, white flour, *118*, 264
Chutney Mary's bitter chocolate kulfi,
   270–1, 274–5
chutney, 290–6, *94–5*
cider, spicy mulled, 285
cochita pibil (marinated roast pork),
   108
coconut, 43–4
   chicken and prawns in coconut shells,
      130–1, 153
   coconut chilli rice, 246
   coconut chutney, 295
   coconut fritters, 69
   creamy coconut lentils, *130–1*, 181
   deep-fried ice cream, 276
   Mexican pineapple dessert, 280
cod: chillies stuffed with fish, 156–7
   fish and shrimp salad, 76
   spicy Japanese fish balls, *50–1, 74*
color los vegos (red coloured vegetables),
   209, *230–1*
cornmeal: tortillas, *78–9, 254–5*, 262–3
courgettes, stuffed, 198
couscous meat stew, 129
crab: crab curry, 177
   crab-stuffed avocado, 59
   crispy crab rolls, 72
crawfish: blackened crawfish, 163
   chilli crawfish, 158–9
   stewed crawfish, 164
Creole food, 24–5
crêpes, chilli cheese, 216–17
croquetas de chili y queso (cheese, carrot and
   chilli croquettes), 52
cummin consommé, hot, 89

curries: baked curried salmon or sea trout,
      171
   chickpea curry, 180
   crab curry, 177
   curried potato and chickpea rice, 244–5
   curry pinwheels, 269
   egg and fenugreek curry, 219
   green chilli curry, 186, *191*
   hot red chilli curry, 125
   Indonesian vegetable curry, *154–5*, 193
   lamb and cashew curry, 120–1
   mild curry blend, 48–9
   mild curry paste, 49
   orange duck curry, 147
   pumpkin curry, 182
   Punjabi okra curry, 188
   scallop curry, 173
   spicy chicken stuffed with curry mince,
      145
   spicy Curaçaoan meat, 124
   spinach and lentil curry with Indian
      cheese, 229
   Thai jungle fowl curry, 148–9
   Thai red beef curry, 126, *127*

dhai kaju gosht (lamb and cashew curry),
   120–1
dhal nehri (fragrant lentils), 190, *191*
dillock (cayenne pottage), 294
dips, 55, 58–60, 293
dirty rice, *139*, 250
Dominique's naan bread rolls, 87, 267
Dover sole: layered fish and pumpkin stew,
   160–1
   marinated fish, 53
drinks: mezcal, 283
   sangritta, 78–9, 284
   savoury yoghurt drink, 282
   spicy mulled wine, 285
   sweet yoghurt drink, 282
   tequila, 283
duck: duck in a sweet and sour sauce, 150–1,
   151
   duck-stuffed quails en croute, 144
   orange duck curry, 147
dum ki batar karsha (duck-stuffed quails en
   croute), 144

East Indies, 19–20
écrevisse étouffée (stewed crawfish), 164
eggs: egg and fenugreek curry, 219
   fried eggs on a spicy sauce, *214–15*, 216
   scrambled eggs with red chilli, 220
   see also omelettes
equipment, 41
European cookery, 12–14

faisinjan koresh (duck in a sweet and sour
   sauce), 150–1, *151*
fajitas (Mexican stir-fry beef), 104
falavda (spicy vegetable fritters), *184–5, 191*
fasooli khadra (Levantine runner beans), 199
fenugreek: egg and fenugreek curry, 219
fihunu mas lebai (grilled garlic fish), *174–5,
   174*
filfil ahmar baidh (scrambled eggs with red
   chilli), 220
filfil pilav (chilli fried rice), 243–4
filo pastry, 71
fish and seafood, 154–77
   Arabic fried fish balls, 170
   ceviche (marinated fish), 56, *78–9*
   marinades, 42

see also cod; trout *etc.*
five-spice powder, 46
frango piri-piri (chilli roast chicken), 142–3,
   142
frijoles fritos (fried beans), 204
frijoles refritos (refried beans), 204
fritters: bean ball, 203
   coconut, 69
   spicy vegetable, *184–5, 191*
frog's legs, battered fried, 140
fruit: fruit lhassi, 282
   hot fruit compote, *270–1*, 272

gaeng ped nua (Thai red beef curry), 126,
   127
gaeng som pet (orange duck curry), 147
galchupan (magic pancake omelette), 223
galinha cafreal (casseroled coconut chicken),
   146
garam masala, 47–8
garam masala paste, 49
garlic: chocolate-enrobed garlic, 278–9,
   279
   garlic soup, 83
   the ultimate garlic bread, 268
garnishes, *139*, 211
ghee, 43
Goa, 16–17
goat or kid: spicy Curaçaoan meat, 124
gohan zoshui (Japanese soup rice), 84–5
goulash (Hungarian paprika stew), 128
Greek fried rice, 242, *243*
guacamolé (avocado dip), 58–9
guajolote molé poblano (turkey in chilli and
   chocolate sauce), *22*, 135
Guatemalan herbal chicken, 141
guinea fowl: Thai jungle fowl curry, 148–9
Gujarat, 16
Gujerati samosas, 66–7
gumbo Creole, 138–9, *139*
Gurkha dhal (Gurkhas' lentils), 192

hae-koon (Thai spring rolls), *63*, 70–1
halibut: spicy Brazilian fish, 161
ham and pork hot pot, *94–5*, 106
harissa (hot red chilli purée), 293
haryali aloo (green herbal potatoes), 185
heart appetizers, spicy, 57
Heather's chilli bread, *102*, 268
herbal raitce, 296
history, 8–13
hot and sour soup, Sichuan, 93
huevos rancheros (fried eggs on a spicy
   sauce), *214–15*, 216
hühn Burgenlander (chicken paprika), 149
hummus: Gujerati samosas, 66–7

ice cream: Chutney Mary's bitter chocolate
   kulfi, *270–1*, 274–5
   deep-fried ice cream, 276
   green chilli ice cream, 278
ijjah bil tawabel (Arabian omelette), 221
imojo (fish and shrimp salad), 76
inche kabin (crispy Malaysian chicken), 152
Indian cheese, 228
Indian cookery, 15–17
Indo-China, 18
Indonesia, 20
Indonesian hot chilli sauce, 288
Indonesian vegetable curry, *154–5*, 193
inerja (millet bread), *254–5*, 261
ingelegde vis (pickled fish), 77
Iranian cookery, 15

Italian chilli sauce, 114, *114*
Italian rice, 234–5

jambalaya, 248–9
Japanese cookery, 21
Japanese fish balls, *50–1*, 74
Japanese omelette, 224
Japanese seven-taste pepper, 47
Japanese soup rice, 84–5
Javanese omelette, 222
jocon (Guatemalan herbal chicken), 141
Jollof (African rice), *178–9*, 247

kaeng pa gai (Thai jungle fowl curry), 148–9
kaju badan (devilled chilli cashew nuts), 65
kakuluo (crab curry), 177
Kampuchea, 19
karamba kulkul issu (chicken and prawns in coconut shells), *130–1*, 153
karela: bitter gourd in yoghurt, 186–7
kari nuoc Phnom Penh (scallop curry), 173
kari patis (curry patties), 64–5
kaushwe-kyaw (chicken and shrimp noodles), 61
kavgir (Turkish crispy bread), *254–5*, 258
kebabs: alligator sausage, 100, *102*
    aloo boti khara kabab, 228
    grilled pork strips with peanut sauce, 62–3, *63*
    skewered grilled chicken, 75
    skewered spicy grilled meat, 110
    skewered swordfish, *166–7*, *166*
    spicy meat kebabs enrobed in omelette, 226–7, *226*
khara soti boti kabab (spicy meat kebabs enrobed in omelette), 226–7, *226*
kilawan (marinated fish), 53
kilich shish (skewered swordfish), *166–7*, *166*
kochujaang (chilli paste), 290
kokis (coconut fritters), 69
Korea, 19
kulfi, Chutney Mary's bitter chocolate, *270–1*, *274–5*
kuroke (spicy Japanese fish balls), *50–1*, 74

lal qila khurma ki Shah Jehan (Shah Jehan's last stew), 117–19, *118*
lamb: lamb and cashew curry, 120–1
    moussaka, 112–13
    Shah Jehan's last stew, 117–19, *118*
    spicy meat kebabs enrobed in omelette, 226–7, *226*
Latin America, 23–4
lechon asado (Peruvian roast pork), *94–5*, 107
leitão recheado (Brazilian roast pork), 108–9
lentils: creamy coconut lentils, *130–1*, 181
    fragrant lentils, 190, *191*
    Gurkhas' lentils, 192
    spinach and lentil curry with Indian cheese, 229
Levantine runner beans, 199
lhassi meethi (sweet yoghurt drink), 282
lhassi namkeen mirchi (savoury yoghurt drink), 282
limes: ceviche, 56, *78–9*
    chicken sopup with lime, *78–9*, 80
    marinated fish, 53
lobster, preparation, 159
logosta rosea afrikana (chilli crawfish), *158–9*

mackerel: sweet and sour fish, *154–5*, 175
Malacca ikan manis (sweet and sour fish), *154–5*, 175
Malaysia, 19–20
Malaysian chicken soup, 82–3
Malaysian fried rice, 240
manzano salsa (apple chilli chutney), 292
marinades, 42
meat dishes, 94–128
    marinades, 42
    see also beef; lamb *etc.*
meethi malai-dahi (sweet and sour yoghurt), 281
Mexican cookery, 21–3
Mexican green 'hot' chutney, 292
Mexican pineapple dessert, 280
Mexican stir-fry beef, 104
mezcal, 283
Middle Eastern cookery, 14–15
millet bread, *254–5*, 261
mirchi ka salan (green chilli curry), 186, *191*
mirchi rasam (pepper soup), 88
mishmisheya la kama (spicy vegetables with apricot), 196
miso shiru (asparagus and red soy soup), *50–1*, 85
Moira banana (syrupy banana), *270–1*, 274
moong chana salat (mixed bean sprout combo), 55, 68
mooqueca (spicy Brazilian fish), 161
Moros y Cristianos (beans and rice), *230–1*, 252
moussaka, 112–13
Mozambiquan chilli prawns, 168–9
murgh cutliss (chicken rissoles), *130–1*, 133

naan bread, 87, *254–5*, 266–7
nam prik (Thai hot chilli sauce), *127*, 289
narial chatni (coconut chutney), 295
nasi goreng (Malaysian fried rice), 240
ne heung fun (Chinese five-spice powder), 46
Nepal, 17
niter kebbeh (spiced ghee), 43
noodles, chicken and shrimp, 61
nuoc cham (Vietnamese chilli dip), 290

ocapa (Venezuelan potatoes), 207
ocapa queso (potatoes in chilli cheese sauce), 208
oil, red chilli, 286
okra curry, Punjabi, 188
omelettes: Arabian, 221
    chicken, 225
    Japanese, 224
    Javanese, 222
    magic pancake omelette, 223
    spicy meat kebabs enrobed in, 226–7, *226*
onions: dried, 65
    onion tarka, 44
orange juice: sangritta, *78–9*, 284
ostiones en adobo (spiced oysters), 54, *55*
oysters, spiced, 54, *55*

paella (Spanish rice), 236–7, *238*
paella pans, 238
palava Niger abuja (spinach and sweet potato stir-fry), *178–9*, 201
pancakes, 217
    chilli cheese crêpes, 216–17
    magic pancake omelette, 223
panch phoran, 48
paneer (Indian cheese), 228

papas Andean (Peruvian potatoes), *94–5*, 206
paprika, 40
    chicken paprika, 149
    goulash, 128
parathas (pan-fried flat bread), 191, 265
parippu (creamy coconut lentils), *130–1*, 181
pastry, spring roll, 71
Pat's spicy vinaigrette, 296
patties, curry, 64–5
peanuts: grilled pork strips with peanut sauce, 62–3, *63*
    pan-roasted peanuts, 60–1
peas, rice and, 239
peppercorns, 9, 89, 109
    pepper soup, 88
Persian rice, *151*, 241
Peruvian potatoes, *94–5*, 206
Peruvian roast pork, *94–5*, 107
Philippines, 20
picante de papas (hot potatoes), *123*, 205
pickled vegetables with chilli, 294–5
pico de gallo (special salsa), 292
pilafi (Greek fried rice), 242, *243*
pilchards: Burmese sour fish soup, 91
pina cocada (Mexican pineapple dessert), 280
pineapple: Mexican pineapple dessert, 280
pipian molé verde (chicken in a green hot molé sauce), 136
piri-piri (chilli sauce), 293
piri-piri curry (hot red chilli curry), 125
piri-piri diabole (Mozambiquan chilli prawns), 168–9
pitta bread, *243*, 257
plantains: Regina's Selfridges banana beans, *178–9*, 202
pollo del molé del Colorado (minced chicken in red molé sauce), 137
pollou (Persian rice), *151*, 241
polo con molé poblano (chicken with chilli and chocolate), 134–5
pomfret: Balinese fish, *154–5*, 176
porco com vinho e alhos (pork with vinegar and garlic), 111
pork: Brazilian roast pork, 108–9
    grilled pork strips with peanut sauce, 62–3, *63*
    ham and pork hot pot, *94–5*, 106
    marinated roast pork, 108
    Peruvian roast pork, *94–5*, 107
    pork and walnut-stuffed chillies, 102–3
    pork vindaloo, 116
    pork with vinegar and garlic, 111
    spicy sausage, 105
potatoes: aloo boti khara kabab, 228
    chilli potatoes, 197
    curried potato and chickpea rice, 244–5
    green herbal potatoes, 185
    hot potatoes, *123*, 205
    Peruvian potatoes, *94–5*, 206
    potatoes in chilli cheese sauce, 208
    stuffed tandoori potatoes, 189
    Venezuelan potatoes, 207
poultry dishes, 130–53
    marinades, 42
prawns: chicken and prawns in coconut shells, *130–1*, 153
    deveining, 169
    Mozambiquan chilli prawns, 168–9
    spicy Thai prawn soup, 90
    see also shrimps
Puchero (ham and pork hot pot), *94–5*, 106

pumpkin: layered fish and pumpkin stew, 160–1
  pumpkin curry, 182
Punjab, 16
puris (deep-fried puff bread), 266
  breakfast puff bread, *270–1, 273*

q'root (savoury yoghurt), 72
quails en croute, duck-stuffed, 144

raitas: chilli, 296
  herbal, 296
  tandoori, 296
red cabbage, spiced, 213
Red Indian fry bread, 258–9
red mullet: grilled garlic fish, *174–5, 174*
rice, 230–53
  African rice, *178–9, 247*
  beans and rice, *230–1, 252*
  Bombay romato rice, *118, 244*
  chilli fried rice, 243
  chillies stuffed with rice, *230–1, 251*
  clove rice, *195, 248*
  coconut chilli rice, 246
  curried potato and chickpea rice, 244–5
  dirty rice, *139, 250*
  Greek fried rice, *242, 243*
  Italian rice, 234–5
  jambalaya, 248–9
  Japanese soup rice, 84–5
  Malaysian fried rice, 240
  paella, *236–7, 238*
  Persian rice, *151, 241*
  plain rice by absorption, 233–4
  plain rice by boiling, 232
  rice and peas, 239
  rice cake, *94–5, 253*
  Spanish saffron rice, 236
rissoles, chicken, *130–1, 133*
roasting chillies and bell peppers, 41–2
rot kohl pikant (spiced red cabbage), 213
runner beans, Levantine, 199

saag dal paneer curry (spinach and lentil curry with Indian cheese), 229
sabzi koresh (vegetable stew), 200
saffron rice, Spanish, 236
sajur tchampur (Indonesian vegetable curry), *154–5, 193*
salad, fish and shrimp, 76
salmon, baked curried, 171
salsas *see* chutneys
saluf bi hilbeh (Yemeni spicy bread), *254–5, 260*
sambal manis (sweet chilli purée). *63, 154–5, 288*
sambal oelek (Indonesian hot chilli sauce), 288
samosas, Gujerati, 66–7
sangritta, *78–9, 284*
sauces: chilli, 293
  Chinese chilli, 289
  Indonesian hot chilli, 288
  Italian chilli, *114, 114*
  Sichuan chilli, 289–90
  sweet chilli, 288
  Thai hot chilli, *127, 289*
  thin chilli, 287–8
sauerkraut chili (chilli pickled cabbage), 212
sausage, spicy, 105
scallop curry, 173
Scoville scale, 29
sea trout, baked curried, 171

seafood and fish, 154–77
  paella, *236–7, 238*
sebzeler plaki (baked vegetables), 210
shabbat Kuwaiti (baked curried salmon or sea trout), 171
Shah Jehan's last stew, *117–19, 118*
shark's fin chilli soup, 92
shashlik kebabs (skewered spicy grilled meat), 110
sheik-el-ma'shi (stuffed courgettes), 198
shichini togarashi (Japanese seven-taste pepper), 47
shikara murgh bharvara ka keema (spicy chicken stuffed with curry mince), 145
shorba sultani (cream of cashew and asparagus soup), *86–7, 87*
shrimps: coconut shrimps, 162
  deveining, 169
  hot shrimp chilli pickle, 294
  shrimps with okra, 168
  see also prawns
Sichuan chilli sauce, 289–90
Sichuan la tang (Sichuan hot and sour soup), 93
Sicilian spicy mince, *114, 115*
sindhi luki masale dar (pumpkin curry), 182
Singapore, 20
singhodas (Gujerati samosas), 66–7
smoked haddock: fish stew, 165
sopa de ajo (garlic soup), 83
sopa de lima (chicken soup with lime), *78–9, 80*
soto ayam (Malaysian chicken soup), 82–3
soups, 78–93
spaghetti: spaghetti alla Siciliana (Sicilian spicy mince), *114, 115*
  spaghetti Western, 99
Spanish saffron rice, 236
spices: baharat, 48
  berbere/baribaray, 293
  blending, 46
  char masala, 48
  Chinese five-spice powder, 46
  Chinese ten-spice powder, 47
  garam masala, 47–8
  grinding, 45
  history, 8–13
  Japanese seven-taste pepper, 47
  mild curry blend, 48–9
  panch phoran, 48
  roasting, 45–6
  storing, 45
spinach: spinach and lentil curry with Indian cheese, 229
  spinach and sweet potato stir-fry, *178–9, 201*
spring onion tassels, 211
spring rolls, Thai, *63, 70–1*
Sri Lanka, 18
stoba (spicy Curaçaoan meat), 124
stock, akhni, 44–5
stomachic mandrum, 293
sweet potatoes: spinach and sweet potato stir-fry, *178–9, 201*
swordfish, skewered, *166–7, 166*

tamago-yaki (Japanese omelette), 224
tamarind purée, 44
tandoori aloo peshwari (stuffed tandoori potatoes), 189
tandoori raita, 296
telur goreng (Javanese omelette), 222

tempura (fish and vegetables in batter), *50–1, 73*
teochew satay (grilled pork strips with peanut sauce), *62–3, 63*
tequila, 283
Thai jungle fowl curry, 148–9
Thai prawn soup, 90
Thai red beef curry, *126, 127*
Thailand, 18–19
thambapu kadala (chickpea curry), 180
tom yam baeng (spicy Thai prawn soup), 90
tomatoes: Bombay tomato rice, *118, 244*
  chilli cold soup, 84
  sun-dried tomatoes, 76
tori-maki (chicken omelette), 225
torshi filfil (pickled vegetables with chilli), 294–5
tortillas, *78–9, 254–5, 262–4*
  fried tortillas with chilli sauce, *58, 214–15*
Trevor Pack's chilli chutney, 295
trout: pickled fish, 77
  spicy marinated grilled trout, 172
tuna: chilli tuna, 158
  tuna in tamarind sauce, 157
turkey: gumbo Creole, *138–9, 139*
  turkey in chilli and chocolate sauce, *22, 135*
Turkish crispy bread, *254–5, 258*
turmeric, 183

United States of America, 24–5

vatapa (coconut shrimps), 162
veal: chillies stuffed with meat, 101
  goulash, 128
  jerk veal, 121
vegetables, 178–213
  baked vegetables, 210
  Indonesian vegetable curry, *154–5, 193*
  pickled vegetables with chilli, 294–5
  red coloured vegetables, *209, 230–1*
  spicy vegetable fritters, *184–5, 191*
  spicy vegetables with apricot, 196
  tempura (fish and vegetables in batter), *50–1, 73*
  vegetable baked pie, *194–5, 195*
  vegetable stew, 200
  see also individual types of vegetable
Venezuelan potatoes, 207
Vietnam, 19
Vietnamese chilli dip, 290
vinaigrette, Pat's spicy, 296
vinegar, red chilli, 286

wei fen (Chinese ten-spice powder), 47
West Indies, 25–6
wine, spicy mulled, 285

yakitori (skewered grilled chicken), 75
Yemeni spicy bread, *254–5, 260*
yoghurt: a cooling chutney, 296
  raitas, 296
  savoury yoghurt, 72
  savoury yoghurt drink, 282
  sweet and sour yoghurt, 281
  sweet yoghurt drink, 282
yu chitang fan chiew (shark's fin chilli soup), 92

Zanzibari chellau (clove rice), *195, 248*